GREAT BUSINESS LEADERS

Jonathan Gifford

Published in 2013 by Marshall Cavendish Business
An imprint of Marshall Cavendish International

1 New Industrial Road
Singapore 536196
genrefsales@sg.marshallcavendish.com
www.marshallcavendish.com/genref

Other Marshall Cavendish offices:
Marshall Cavendish Corporation. 99 White Plains Road, Tarrytown NY 10591-9001, USA • Marshall Cavendish International (Thailand) Co Ltd. 253 Asoke, 12th Flr, Sukhumvit 21 Road, Klongtoey Nua, Wattana, Bangkok 10110, Thailand • Marshall Cavendish (Malaysia) Sdn Bhd, Times Subang, Lot 46, Subang Hi-Tech Industrial Park, Batu Tiga, 40000 Shah Alam, Selangor Darul Ehsan, Malaysia

Marshall Cavendish is a trademark of Times Publishing Limited

ISBN 978-981-4408-09-7

Cover design by Cover Kitchen Co Ltd
Printed and bound by CPI Group (UK) Ltd, Croydon, CR0 4YY

To business men and women around the world

CONTENTS

ACKNOWLEDGEMENTS

I WOULD LIKE TO acknowledge my debt to all of the historians, authors and journalists whose work has made this book possible.

The facts about any leader's business career are reasonably easy to find, since business is carried out in the necessary glare of public scrutiny. What is harder to find, without good journalism and investigative writing, is each leader's real, personal experience: the challenges that they faced; the decisions that they made; the minor triumphs and many setbacks that lie behind any great business success. Also missing would be the leader's tone of voice. Thanks to journalists and other writers, for the great majority of leaders from the modern era, it is possible to find a quotation or comment that helps to bring the person to life.

A special acknowledgement is owed to Justin Lau, the editor of this book, for paring my original manuscript down to a manageable length with his usual flair and skill.

INTRODUCTION

THE CAREER OF ANY great business leader reads like the plot of a novel. Great leaders, by definition, have a vision that is not shared by everyone. There are difficulties and adversities to overcome; they face many obstacles, including self-doubt, but persevere in the hope of achieving their goal.

The earliest leader featured in the book, Cornelius Vanderbilt, was born in 1794. He made a living ferrying people around the waters of New York Bay in a sailing boat. When he saw the first steamboats, Vanderbilt recognised a new opportunity. He went to work for a steamboat operator to learn his trade, sometimes having to hide in a secret compartment of his boat when it was raided by officials of the New York Legislature, who had granted a monopoly of ferry services to another operator. Vanderbilt saved enough money to start his own steamboat ferry service, and finally built an empire that included ocean-going steamships. As Americans flocked to join in California's Gold Rush in the middle of the nineteenth century, Vanderbilt offered a service to take people from the east coast of America to the western Pacific coast, steaming down the eastern seaboard and crossing the Isthmus of Panama via lakes and rivers, crossing the final stage by mule train (the Panama Canal had not yet been built). As the railways began to cross America, Vanderbilt saw a new opportunity, and acquired shares in major east coast rail services, acquiring, with great prescience, the line that served Manhattan itself. At his death, Vanderbilt was one of the richest men in America.

The most recent leader featured here was born in 1984. Mark Zuckerberg, the founder of Facebook, dropped out of university to create the new social networking site. Within a year, the new venture had attracted venture capital of nearly $14 million. A year later, Yahoo offered to buy Facebook for $1 billion. Zuckerberg turned it down. As the CEO of Yahoo at the time said, 'I'd never met anyone who would walk away from a billion dollars. But he [Zuckerberg] said, "It's not about the price. This is my baby, and I want to keep running it, I want to keep growing it."'

Part of the fascination in reading about the careers of the great business leaders over the course of some two centuries is to note the similarities: the personal qualities needed to create a significant business from scratch; the skills that make a great business executive. What is also fascinating – and probably more important – is to see how business leadership is evolving and improving.

The characteristics that define successful leadership today are not the characteristics that would have defined previous generations of business executives, who were, in general, operating in the old 'command and control' model of leadership adopted quite consciously by early twentieth-century business organisations. Modern leaders talk about issues like collaboration; the devolution of decision-making; creating flatter working structures where colleagues may have several leaders and may themselves be leaders in certain circumstances; the need to ensure that colleagues are genuinely excited by their work and by what their company contributes to its community. Successful modern leaders stress the need to create a working environment that encourages lateral thinking and innovation. In the modern business world, efficiency is a given – inefficient businesses will quickly fail in the face of global competition. Innovation, not imitation, is what drives the wheels of progress.

Many great leaders succeed because they grasp the significance of a technological advance that will create new business opportunities. The invention of the semiconductor led inexorably to the microcomputer revolution, but required its own cadre of great leaders to make it a reality. Steve Jobs, Bill Gates, Vinod Khosla, Michael Dell and Andy Grove are featured in this book as examples of these revolutionaries.

The internet – surely the most significant technological revolution of our time – triggered a new business revolution, and has demonstrated how rapidly business change is accelerating. It took some 200 years to move from the age of steam to the age of cars and aeroplanes. It took ten years to move from the commercialisation of the internet in 1995 to the launch of Facebook in 2005.

While many great leaders succeed by grasping a revolution in the making, others create something out of what seems to be nothing. James Dyson decided that the world needed a better vacuum cleaner, when it was not obvious that the world was crying out for one; Romi Haan decided that South Korea (and then the rest of the world) needed a better kind of floor cleaner; Sara Blakely singlehandedly created a new type of underwear ('Shapewear'); Howard Schultz decided that the world needed a new kind of coffeehouse; Tony Hsieh decided that people wanted to buy shoes online. The personal qualities of such great entrepreneurial leaders emerge with great consistency: a burning conviction as to the benefits of their new idea; the strength of mind to continue in the face of criticism and rejection; great powers of perseverance, as they overcome all of the inevitable obstacles in their way; great salesmanship, as they persuade financiers, manufacturers and retailers to back their project or stock their wares.

Finally, there are many leaders who did not found the companies they serve: Alfred Sloan, the great leader of General Motors from the 1920s to the 1950s; Akio Morita of Sony; Indra Nooyi of PepsiCo. This book also celebrates the leaders who have saved great institutions from disaster: Meg Whitman saved Xerox from apparently inevitable bankruptcy by restating the company's mission statement (and by making it her personal mission not to rest until the company was safe); A.G. Lafley pulled Procter & Gamble out of a 'death spiral' by focusing on nimble-footed innovation and inviting outside partnerships to drive that innovation; Zhang Ruimin turned around China's failing refrigerator manufacturer Haier by focusing ruthlessly on quality and inspiring the group to compete with the world's best.

I hope that you will find reading about the world's great business leaders inspiring and exciting. I know I did. It also taught me a great deal more about business and, most importantly, about business success. I hope that it will do the same for you.

RELIANCE INDUSTRIES
Dhirubhai AMBANI
1932–2002

DHIRUBHAI AMBANI WAS STILL a schoolboy when India achieved independence from the British Raj in 1947. Under its first prime minister, Jawaharlal Nehru, India set out to run a planned economy, in which market forces would be controlled by the granting of various licences, quotas and capital controls – a system that was often referred to ironically as the 'Licence Raj.'

When the government offered a scheme incentivising companies to import raw fibre and export finished fabric, Ambani opened a spinning mill in 1966. He soon became a master of the labyrinthine regulations, quick to spot new opportunities created by the system, and adept at working the system in his company's favour. 'Business,' he said, 'is nothing but a web of relationships and obligations.' In creating Reliance Industries, which became the first privately owned Indian company to enter the Fortune Global 500, Ambani transcended the system, showing what could be achieved by Indian industry with entrepreneurialism and drive.

The ideas

Ambani **introduced polyester** to the Indian market in 1966 under the brand Vimal (the name of his nephew). Although he found it hard initially to break into the retail market in competition with cotton fabrics, by the 1980s Vimal was available in 20 company-owned stores, over 1,000 franchise operations and 20,000 retail stores. Indians took to the hard-wearing, stain- and shrink-resistant material for trousers, shirts, saris and household fabrics.

Ambani started his process of **backward integration**, setting up a plant to manufacture his own polyester fibre yarn, as well as licensing technology from U.S. chemicals company DuPont rather than entering into a joint venture – which was the usual business model in India at the time. Reliance became the **lowest-cost producer** of polyester in the world, and Ambani became known as the 'King of Polyester.'

In the 1970s, Reliance pursued backward integration to its ultimate conclusion, producing ethylene – the raw material for all petrochemicals – from ethane, and, in time, moving into **oil and gas exploration** and building its own **refineries**. In 1991, a gas 'cracker' plant was commissioned at the port of Hazira, in Gujarat, which would go on to become the largest facility of its kind in the world.

When the company went public in 1977, millions of middle-class Indians began to **entrust the company with their savings**, creating a new culture of public shareholding. By 2002, one in every four stock market investors in India owned shares in Reliance.

When Ambani died in 2002, according to the IBS Center for Management Research, the Reliance group employed 85,000 people and accounted for three per cent of India's GDP and five per cent of the country's exports. The group contributed five per cent of the government's total revenue and nine per cent of its indirect revenue. 'Often people think opportunity is a matter of luck,' Ambani is on record as saying. 'I believe **opportunities are all around us**. Some seize it. Others stand and let it pass by.'

In practice

- Consider licensing rather than joint ventures to gain technologies but retain control
- Move up the value chain
- Consider vertical integration
- Think big – what's stopping you?

LMVH
Bernard ARNAULT
1949–

BERNARD ARNAULT MADE HIS MONEY in real estate and then built an empire from some of the most glamorous names in French luxury goods, including the iconic house of Dior, the luxury goods and champagne giant LVMH, and renowned brands such as Givenchy, Guerlain, Christian Lacroix and Bulgari. Having outraged the French establishment with his ferocious takeovers of long-established, aristocratic concerns, Arnauld further inflamed opinion by installing bold new designers and introducing modern manufacturing methods to an industry steeped in tradition.

For some, Arnault was seen as a corporate raider dismantling centuries of tradition; for others, he was seen as an entrepreneur invigorating French business. 'He loves the new, he loves to astonish and to be first with something,' the designer Christian Lacroix told *BusinessWeek* in 2001. 'If it means clearing the land to make a new garden, then he'll chop away. And he loves a fight.'

The ideas

After earning a degree in engineering at the École Polytechnique in Paris, Bernard Arnault joined his family's property and construction business. He persuaded his father to shift the company's focus from construction to real estate, with a **well-timed move into developing time-share properties** on the French Riviera. When the French socialist party won power in France in 1981, Arnault France for the USA, building condominiums in Florida. He returned home in 1983, and set up a holding company.

With $15 million of family money and a reported $65 million from investment house Lazard Frères, Arnault set out to **acquire the**

Boussac group, receiving subsidies from the French government in order to do so – some of which had to be repaid subsequently when Arnault offloaded Boussac's unwanted assets, retaining his main interest in the purchase, the house of Dior.

In 1987, Louis Vuitton and Moët-Hennessy merged to form LMVH, with Moët-Hennessy's president Alain Chevalier as chairman and Louis Vuitton's chairman Henri Racamier, who had married into the Vuitton family, as executive vice-president. Much family feuding ensued, with Racamier fearing that the Vuitton family's interest in LMVH would be swamped by the much larger Moët-Hennessy group. Racamier invited Arnault to invest in LMVH in support of the Vuitton family; Arnault used the proceeds of the sale of Boussac's assets to acquire a **24 per cent share in LMVH**. Chevalier responded by inviting Guinness Plc to invest in support of Moët-Hennessy. Guinness sided with Arnault in a takeover; Alain Chevalier resigned and Arnault was elected chairman of the board. Racamier contested the takeover, but Arnault won a series of court challenges, removing Racamier and purging a number of other top Louis Vuitton executives, cementing his **reputation for tough dealing and ruthlessness**.

Arnault continued to build his empire into one of the **world's largest luxury goods groups**, acquiring brands such as Céline, Kenzo, Guerlain, Givenchy, Loewe, Thomas Pink, Fendi and DKNY. When he acquired Givenchy, Arnault had the gall to sack Hubert de Givenchy, the man whose outfits helped to make Audrey Hepburn a style icon. He installed the brash British designer John Galliano at Dior and another British designer, Alexander McQueen, at Givenchy. The American designer Marc Jacobs was brought in to revitalise Louis Vuitton's products, to challenge the likes of Prada and Gucci.

According to *BusinessWeek* magazine, writing in 2011, Vuitton had become the world's best-selling luxury brand 'by far,' with estimated sales of $7.2 billion in that year. Arnault **automated production** at Vuitton, bringing in **management expertise** drawn from industries as diverse as tyre and cellphone manufacture. He rigorously controlled costs, making every possible use of **synergies across the group** – Christian Lacroix's Bazar line is manufactured by Kenzo; a Kenzo perfume is manufactured by Givenchy; Vuitton's first perfume was created by Guerlain – while **spending lavishly on advertising**.

Arnault's great strength, other than his business flair, was to shock, with success, and to **invest in talent**. As he told *Time* magazine in 1997, 'I'm not interested in anything else but the youngest, the brightest and the very, very talented.'

In practice

- Create the foundations for a business empire, then grow organically and by acquisition

- Divide and conquer

- Modernise, automate and control costs

- Invest in brands

- Introduce young talent

- Encourage creativity and disruption

MARY KAY COSMETICS
Mary Kay ASH
1918–2001

MARY KAY ASH STARTED a company in 1963 selling skin-care products at 'home shows' (small-group presentations hosted in customers' own homes), using a team of independent, often part-time and usually female sales representatives.

This was not a new idea; rather, Ash's innovation lay in the motivational methods she used to produce spectacular sales figures from her agents. She set out to 'praise people to success,' believing that positive feedback, rewards and, above all, recognition, could enable the success of her sales agents and of her business. Her motivational rewards were brash and glitzy, involving pink Cadillacs (or, in other countries, pink Mercedes or high-end Toyotas), dream vacations, furs, and diamond-studded gold pins known as 'ladders of success' – all awarded at lavish annual conventions.

Behind all the razzmatazz, however, Ash's management philosophy is startlingly modern: 'make individuals feel important,' 'praise people frequently and in public,' and 'make yourself available to hear what they are trying to say.'

The ideas

In the 1940s, long before the advent and success of Mary Kay Cosmetics, Ash was already acquiring invaluable experience as a direct salesperson, **recruiting her own network** of 150 local sales agents for Stanley Home Products, on whose sales the company paid her a small commission. The company asked her to move to Dallas and set up a new network, but at the cost of losing the commissions from her Houston team, which Ash greatly resented.

She left Stanley in 1953 to start a business venture, but when the venture failed, she returned to Houston to work for another direct sales organisation, where she became **national training director**. Her power base with the national sales team led to tensions within the company. Ash was offered a new and less significant role, leading to her resignation.

After initial thoughts about writing a book of her experiences, Ash, with her husband, decided to market a **beauty product** that she had come across on her travels. The hostess of one of her home shows had been researching a skin product developed by her father, a tanner, who found that the skin of his hands – immersed all day in chemical solutions – looked younger than the skin of his face.

Ash **bought the formula** from the family for $500 and developed a range of products, which she and her husband planned to launch via a direct sales operation, using their life savings of $5,000.

The company's sales agents bought products from the company, cash up front, at a 50 per cent discount on the retail price, and found hostesses willing to bring together a group of friends for a home show, making their 50 per cent mark-up on all sales. If they recruited more sales people, they earned a percentage of those agents' sales.

Because of Ash's personal experience of losing commission from her Houston team at Stanley Home Products, **commission was paid regardless of territory**. This meant that local directors might find themselves training sales people – known as 'adoptees' – from whose sales other directors earned income. Agreeing that this system was generally 'unexplainable to men,' Ash added: 'It works. **Everyone helps everyone else.**'

The company launched on the New York Stock Exchange in 1976. In the 1980s, the company suffered a decline as women began to work full-time, depriving the company of both its pool of part-time sales agents and its audience of female customers who were at home during the day. In 1985, Ash and her son privatised the company again with a **leveraged buy-out**, and led a **recovery in sales**. When Ash died, in 2001, the company had annual sales of over $1 billion and a network of 850,000 sales consultants working in 37 countries around the world.

In practice

- If your career is being blocked, consider starting your own business
- 'Praise people to success'; make them feel important, publicly
- Make yourself available
- Create reward systems that are fundamentally fair – colleagues will understand

BRITANNIA INDUSTRIES
Vinita BALI
1955–

WHEN VINITA BALI TOOK on the role of CEO for food company Britannia Industries – one of India's leading biscuit manufacturers, founded in 1892 in Kolkata – her challenge was described by one director as 'a CEO's nightmare.'

The company had just bought out the shareholding stake of French dairy produce giant Danone. After years of corporate wrangling between the two food groups, Britannia's share of the India biscuit market had fallen from nearly 50 per cent to around one-third; net margins were decreasing. The previous CEO had left in inglorious circumstances and management talent was voting with its feet. When Bali arrived at the office on her first day at 9 a.m., nobody else was at work.

But Bali, whose blue-chip marketing experience – at Tata, Cadbury, Coca-Cola – had earned her two other job offers from prestigious multinationals, chose to take on the Britannia challenge. 'I like to go in and take things apart,' she told *Forbes* magazine. 'There's nothing exciting about doing the doable.'

The ideas

Vinita Bali got to grips with Britannia's ailing business culture in typically no-nonsense fashion, quickly **identifying the company's existing talent as 'great, good or gone.'** Those who found themselves in the third category were swiftly replaced by rising stars from multinationals such as Unilever.

Bali took on a punishing workload, visiting factories around the country and routinely putting in **16-hour days**.

Her overarching goal was to drive profitable growth by **increasing sales and market share** while generating a higher operating margin. She focused on innovation, which she defined as 'anything that is capable of producing new value.' As she told GfK *Market Intelligence Review*, 'Our focus is really on two things. One is to drive **innovation and margin enhancement** through innovative and differentiated products, and the second is to really work on becoming a **lean machine when it comes to cost**.' Bali's commitment to cost-reduction included a programme to reuse previously wasted heat from factories' ovens.

Under Bali's stewardship, Britannia revamped its core products and **introduced new ranges**. A key initiative was the introduction of 'personal consumption' products: packs of four or five biscuits designed to be bought by consumers on the go as an impulse snack.

Bali has also spearheaded a growing focus on the **health and nutritional aspects** of Britannia's products, leading the company to become the first in India to remove all trans fats from its products, introducing healthier products such as a low-calorie multi-grain snacks, and enriching many products with micronutrients in recognition of the fact that, for poorer families, cereal-based biscuits were a cheap source of calories that could also be nutritionally beneficial.

Bali took her concern for the company's contribution to health and nutrition further, distributing micronutrient-enriched biscuits at cost to schools in southern India and founding the Britannia Nutrition Foundation to **champion child nutrition issues**. Bali's views on corporate responsibility are as clear and forthright as her approach to business. She dislikes the notion of 'corporate social responsibility.' As she told *Forbes* magazine in 2012, 'I think it's "corporate responsibility" – I hate the word "social" – which means finding an area of responsibility within your business model. You just have to dig deep enough.'

In practice

- Get the right people on board

- Look for profitable growth

- Focus on innovation and new, differentiated products

- Create a 'lean machine'

- Understand your area of 'corporate responsibility'

AMAZON
Jeff BEZOS
1961–

IN THE EARLY 1990S, while working as a computer analyst with a New York investment house, Jeff Bezos saw that the internet was growing at a rate of 2300 per cent per year, and thought that people would one day buy things over the internet.

The best options seemed to be books and CDs – an online retailer could offer a wider range of products than a bricks-and-mortar store could stock, and they were easy to ship. He decided that book publishers were less formidable competitors than the music industry, where six major labels dominated the industry. When he told his boss then that he wanted to leave and start the new business, his boss said, 'That sounds like a good idea, but it would be an even better idea for someone who didn't already have a good job.' Nevertheless, Bezos, with his wife's support, left his job to follow his dream.

Most early internet start-ups disdained the idea of profit: the plan was to get big fast and turn a profit later; many burned off their investment capital at an alarming rate without being able to show investors a clear route to a return on their money. When the dot-com bubble burst in 2001, Amazon, unlike many, survived. In the last quarter of that year, it turned a profit of $5 million on sales of $1 billion – not a large profit, but a profit nonetheless. Bezos had proved that online retail was a viable proposition.

The ideas

Bezos wrote the program for Amazon – named after the world's largest river – and launched the site in July 1995. The new company's **10–30 per cent discount** on books generated orders from day one. He and a handful or workers ordered the titles from distributors and shipped them out. On day three, Jerry Yang, co-founder of Yahoo, emailed to say that he would like to feature Amazon on their What's Cool page. By the end of the week, the company had over $12,000 in orders; the small team struggled to keep up. By October, the company had its first 100-order day; within a year, it had its first 100-order hour.

Bezos introduced **one-click ordering** (which he patented) and shocked the book trade by allowing customers to **post their own reviews** – even negative reviews.

As Amazon grew on its way to becoming the world's largest online retailer, Bezos introduced other products – CDs, DVDs, music downloads, computer software, video games and, later, electronics – before developing its **full range of retail offerings**, which, according to a Forbes 2012 article, has now passed 20 million items.

Amazon under Bezos is **driven by metrics**: the company uses around 500 measurable goals to monitor its performance, 80 per cent of which are customer-oriented. Bezos focuses on **customer service**, poring over customer complaints and comments and making changes to accommodate them. Some management meetings still use an empty chair to symbolise the customer – 'the most important person in the room.'

Bezos has the classic retail **low-cost, low-margin** mentality. Luxuries and perks at Amazon are few and salaries are relatively low: senior executives are rewarded with restricted stock. Bezos's own salary is around $80,000; his founder's shares are worth around $19 billion.

Bezos is **wedded to competition**, allowing the site to compete, in effect, with itself. The introduction of Amazon Marketplace allowed other retailers and individuals to sell new and used items alongside Amazon's offers, undercutting Amazon's price. When the company bought the online shoe retailer Zappos, Amazon's own shoe site was, and remains, a direct competitor. In 2002, Bezos launched Amazon Web Services, offering other companies the use of what many would consider to be the company's core competitive advantage – its computer software expertise, infrastructure and server capacity.

In 2007, Amazon launched its **first consumer product**, the Kindle e-reader. In 2011 the company launched Kindle Fire, a tablet computer.

It was in 2007 that Amazon started to **deliver on its promise to long-term investors**: sales increased by nearly 40 per cent to almost $15 billion and profits more than doubled to $476 million. Bezos keeps his belief in the importance of the long term. 'We are comfortable planting seeds and waiting for them to grow into trees,' he told *Forbes* magazine in 2010.

Bezos **innovates constantly**. 'We innovate by starting with the customer and working backwards,' Bezos told *Fortune*. He argues that this focus on the customer, rather than on the competition, gives Amazon the edge. 'When they're in the shower in the morning, they're thinking about how they're going to get ahead of one of their top competitors. Here, in the shower we're thinking about how we are going to invent something on behalf of a customer.'

In practice

- Refine and innovate constantly

- Focus on the consumer; listen to feedback

- Encourage competition, even if it means having to work harder

- Think long-term

SPANX
Sara BLAKELY
1971–

SARA BLAKELY IS THE world's youngest self-made woman billionaire. She had an idea for a new kind of underwear that would help to shape women's figures without leaving the dreaded 'visible panty line.' She researched her idea, wrote her own patent application, persuaded a manufacturer to make a prototype, photographed herself for 'before and after' images, got her first distribution with a department store, despatched her own orders and organised her own PR, working evenings and nights while holding down a full-time job as national sales manager of an office supplies company. She used $5,000 of her savings and, when the first sales came in, ran the business on cash.

According to *Forbes* magazine in 2012, Spanx made $4 million in its first year and $10 million in its second year. Blakely never raised any capital for the business and owns 100 per cent; the company is now valued by analysts at $1 billion. 'I didn't know better,' she told *Marketplace* in 2012. 'I have never taken a business course, so I really didn't know even how it was done. I didn't realise that people went out and got tons of venture capital or raised all kinds of money so I thought OK, I've got to do as much of this on my own as I can.'

The ideas

Blakely grew up in Clearwater, Florida, and got a degree in legal communications from Florida State University. She wanted to study to be a legal attorney, but failed the entrance exam, twice. She worked at the nearby Disney World, then took a job at a local office supplies company, selling fax machines by cold-calling local companies. At the age of 25, she was made national sales manager.

At some point, Blakely realised that she needed **an undergarment that didn't exist**. She wore regular pantyhose under trousers, but the feet of the pantyhose looked bad in open toe sandals. She cut the feet of a pair but the ends rolled up her leg. It was Blakely's eureka moment. She spent nights at a library researching hosiery patents. Certain that she had a unique concept, she took out a textbook and **wrote her own patent application**, saving the $3,000 legal fee.

Incorporating her company for $150, she **cold-called manufacturers**, but got turned down. She turned up unannounced at one hosiery mill in North Carolina and was turned away, but her proposal reached the manager. Two weeks later he called to say that his teenage daughters thought she had a good idea. A prototype was made. Blakely **designed her own packaging** on a friend's computer.

Blakely then called department store buyers and eventually got to make a presentation at the Dallas headquarters of luxury department store Neiman Marcus. They liked the product and they liked Sara. With Neiman Marcus on board, other department stores followed. Still working as national sales manager for the office supplies company, Blakely **despatched orders at night** and **wrote PR letters by day** to fashion journalists.

Blakely's big break came from her own efforts: she sent a pair of the figure-trimming underwear to the personal stylist of TV talk show host, Oprah Winfrey. Winfrey featured it as her product of the year on her prime-time *Favourite Things* TV show. Blakely's Spanx products **created a new retail category**: 'Shapewear.'

When Oprah Winfrey's production team had called Blakely, they warned her that her website would get busy. Blakely didn't have a website. She scanned an image of the packaging and put it online. 'I ran a considerable web business for $18 a month,' she told *Forbes* in 2012. The **Oprah Winfrey endorsement** put Spanx on the map. Blakely travelled the country, giving **in-store demos** and appearing on local news stations.

A 2001 article in *Forbes*, describing Blakely as an 'accidental entrepreneur,' helped to land a valuable slot on the **direct sales TV** programme QVC.

After two years running the growing business, Blakely decided to hire a CEO, leaving her to focus on what she felt she was best at: product development and marketing. 'A lot of entrepreneurs end up getting in the way of the growth of their own business,' Blakely told *Marketplace*, 'because it's a totally different skill set to run a business versus be the one who started it. I had to be every department when I started ... I learned very quickly what I liked to do and what I didn't like to do, and what I was good at and what I wasn't good at, so as soon as I could afford to **hire my weaknesses**, I did.'

In practice

- If you have a good idea, make it happen
- Get distribution; create publicity
- It is possible to run a business on cash
- When you can afford it, recruit to your weaknesses
- Keep doing what you do best

BOEING; and related
William BOEING
1881–1956

WILLIAM EDWARD BOEING WAS RUNNING a successful forestry business in the state of Washington when he fell in love with airplanes. He and a local acquaintance, George Westervelt, a lieutenant commander in the U.S. Navy, who had also been smitten with the aviation bug, took their first flights, separately, as passengers in an early biplane in July 1914. They decided that they could make a better plane.

With the First World War about to begin, they felt that the U.S. Navy would be customers. Their first plane was not taken up by the Navy, but their second model was. After the war, Boeing struggled to turn the company into a commercial airline, keeping his factories open by making boats and furniture and underwriting substantial losses. The company won a bid to carry airmail from Chicago to San Francisco, flying over the Rocky Mountains.

In the 1930s, Boeing created a vertically integrated aviation concern, United Aircraft and Transport, including engine, airframe and propeller manufacturers, airlines running transcontinental passenger services, airport companies and a flying school. Boeing, in essence, helped to create the aviation industry.

The ideas

The first B&W (Boeing & Westervelt) aircraft was a wooden two-place seaplane designed as a trainer for the U.S. Navy. Boeing put up $100,000 and incorporated Pacific Aero Products, changing the company's name to the Boeing Airplane Co. a year later. The Navy declined to buy this first B&W model, but the second model **won an order for 50 planes**.

After the war, the business won orders from the military to build versions of existing planes, but struggled to establish itself as a commercial business. Boeing kept the factory open and started work on the company's **own range of fighters**, which were taken up by the military in 1923. In 1920, according to *Business and Commercial Aircraft*, Boeing's company lost $300,000.

In 1927, Boeing won the bid to **carry airmail** from Chicago to San Francisco, and set up Boeing Air Transport. By the end of the 1920s, the company was carrying one quarter of U.S. airmail and an increasing number of passengers, leading to the launch of Boeing's **first passenger aircraft**, the three-engine 12-passenger Model 80 biplane, launched in 1929.

In 1933, the company launched the Model 247, the world's **first modern passenger airliner**. It had to make seven stops between Los Angeles and New York, but, because of its 189 mph cruising speed, still cut seven-and-a-half hours off the journey time of any other plane.

'I've tried to make the men around me feel, as I do,' Boeing said in an interview, 'that we are embarked as pioneers upon a new science and industry in which our problems are so new and unusual that it behooves no one to dismiss any novel ideas with the statement, "it can't be done." Our job is to **keep everlastingly at research and experiment** ... to let no new improvement in flying and flying equipment pass us by.'

By this time, the company was carrying over half of the country's airmail; commercial airmail contracts were investigated by Congress as **potential monopolies**. In 1934, the U.S. government annulled all airmail contracts with private carriers and gave the task to the U.S. Army. When five of the army's relatively inexperienced flyers were killed in the first five weeks of the service during bad winter weather, Roosevelt handed the job back to the commercial sector, but with **new legislation** that prevented carriers from having links to aircraft or engine manufacture. United Aircraft & Transport was broken up;

its airlines became United Airlines, while manufacturing was split between United Aircraft and Boeing Airplane Company.

Boeing resigned his chairmanship, sold his stock and left the aviation business. At one of the congressional hearings investigating commercial airmail contracts, Boeing said, 'I feel that the men that have gone into [aviation] and hazarded what they have and contributed what they have to the development [of the industry] are entitled to remuneration. You must remember that **this aircraft thing is a lifework with me** ... I went through all the hazards – periods when everyone thought I was a fool ... I risked a good, big part of my personal fortune at that time, and I stayed with it.'

In practice

- Build a better product
- Stay with your vision; search for new business
- Seize opportunities; grow and consolidate
- Keep experimenting: 'let no improvement pass you by'

VIRGIN GROUP
Richard BRANSON
1950–

RICHARD BRANSON'S TRANSFORMATION from being a successful music entrepreneur – who had launched a chain of record stores and a record label – to creating a global brand and becoming a multi-billionaire, started with his remarkable decision to start an airline.

Virgin Atlantic, launched in 1984, took timely advantage of the London(Gatwick)–Newark slot made available by the collapse of Laker Airways. Branson limited its potential losses by negotiating a one-year lease of a jumbo jet from Boeing and taking on staff on one-year contracts. Branson's battle with British Airways over the route established him as the consumers' champion, ready to take on established interests, while his slew of high-profile escapades since – including crossing the Atlantic by sea in record time – have cemented Virgin's association with a glamour and daredevil bravery that suit the brand perfectly.

The ideas

At boarding school, at the age of 16, Branson launched a magazine called *Student*, and had the idea of using it to **sell records by mail order** to the music-loving readership. The magazine folded, but the mail order business was a success. Branson formed a mail order music company called Virgin, offering 40 per cent of the new company to his friend Nick Powell, who had worked on *Student*.

When a seven-week strike by postal workers in 1971 put the mail order business out of action, Branson and Powell convinced a shoe store on London's busy Oxford Street to let them **use an upstairs room as a record store**. The Virgin store became the cool place to buy records. The company embarked on an **ambitious expansion plan**, using cash generated by the growing number of stores to open the next new store. By Christmas 1972, Virgin had become one of the UK's largest chains of record stores.

Branson bought a run-down manor house in Oxfordshire and converted it into a recording studio – one that offered musicians the chance to record in a relaxed environment over a period of several days. He then started a **record company**, releasing an album that had been recorded by an unknown artist at the manor, using free studio time. The artist was Mike Oldfield and the record was Tubular Bells, which went on to sell millions worldwide. The revenue was used to take on new artists, often anticipating new trends in popular music. The company's progress was not smooth, however; disaster was often avoided by the sudden success of one of the company's artists. In 1980, with Virgin facing a near £1 million loss, Branson decided to take on two struggling **nightclubs** with interest-free loans provided by the breweries who supplied the clubs. Powell disagreed with the move, and Branson agreed to buy out Powell's 40% share.

It was in 1984 that Branson took the momentous decision to set up a **new airline**, taking advantage of the London Gatwick–Newark New Jersey route freed up by the collapse of Laker Airways, and going into competition with British Airways for the lucrative transatlantic business. Branson estimated that the worst scenario for Virgin Atlantic's one-year trial period was a £2 million loss, which, on current performance, he could afford.

By 1986, Virgin had become one of Britain's **largest private companies**, employing nearly 4,000 people and with sales of £189 million. The company **went public** in that year, with over 100,000 private individuals applying for shares.

Branson, used to making quick decisions with a few key executives, soon found the restrictions of public ownership difficult. After being blocked by the board in his attempt to take over the Thorn EMI group, Branson led a **management buy-out** of the company in 1988. With the company privately owned once more, Branson was back in sole control, albeit saddled with a mountain of debt.

In 1992, in the middle of a bitter battle with British Airways, the company faced the real possibility that Virgin Atlantic would run out of cash and go bust, possibly taking Virgin Music with it. British Airways eventually faced a libel action from Branson and Virgin over denials that they had operated a **campaign of 'dirty tricks' against Virgin Atlantic**, and were forced to pay £500,000 to Branson for the personal libel and £110,000 to Virgin Atlantic. British Airways also picked up the legal bill of some £3 million. Branson gave his £500,000 settlement to Virgin Atlantic staff as a 'BA Bonus.' To solve the company's debt problems once and for all, Branson **sold Virgin Music** to Thorn EMI for £560 million.

Branson runs Virgin Group as a '**branded venture capital conglomerate**,' launching companies and allowing them to develop into independent entities, with his own shareholding varying from case to case. Virgin moved into financial services, a UK train service and even cola and vodka.

Branson's formula has been to '**protect the downside**' – to ensure that no one venture puts the entire group at risk – and to '**enhance the Virgin brand**' with ventures that are consistent with its brand values. 'I give free rein to my own instincts,' he wrote. 'First and foremost, any business proposal has to sound fun. As well as having fun, **I love stirring the pot**. I love giving big companies a run for their money – especially if they're offering expensive, poor-quality products.'

In practice

- Seize any opportunity that you believe in; don't feel limited by your current business area

- Be prepared to let go of parts of the company to guarantee your future

- Ensure no new business can jeopardise the entire group

- Follow your instincts; have fun!

BERKSHIRE HATHAWAY
Warren BUFFETT
1930–

WARREN BUFFETT, the 'Sage of Omaha', whose wealth is currently estimated by Forbes at $53.5 billion – making him the fourth-richest man in the world – lives in the same modest house in Omaha, Nebraska that he bought in 1957 for $31,500. His salary as chief executive has remained at $100,000 p.a. for many years.

Buffett is the opposite of a speculator. He and his company, Berkshire Hathaway, buy or acquire large shareholdings in businesses that they believe have a competitive edge that will allow them to perform well over a period of decades. Consequently, the company has seen an average compounded annual gain over the last 48 years of 19.7 per cent, compared with an equivalent gain of 9.4 per cent from the S&P 500 (Standard & Poor's index of 500 leading U.S. publicly traded companies).

'It's our *job*,' wrote Buffett in his 2012 chairman's letter, 'to increase intrinsic business value at a faster rate than the market gains of the S&P. If we do so, Berkshire's share price, though unpredictable from year to year, will itself outpace the S&P over time.' Otherwise, investors might as well invest in a low-cost S&P Index fund.

The ideas

Accounts of Buffett's early life talk of newspaper rounds, leasing pinball machines to barber shops and investing in farmland. At Columbia Business School, he **studied under investment gurus** Benjamin Graham and David Todd, whose essential investment philosophy was to **see stocks as businesses**, and to look for companies whose business was undervalued by the stock market.

In 1956, he opened his first **investment partnership**, Buffett Associates Ltd, with $105,000 invested by family and friends. Within a few years, Buffett was running five investment partnerships. These were merged to form The Buffett Partnership in 1962, by which time its funds were over $7 million.

One of Buffett's investments was in a textile manufacturing firm, Berkshire Hathaway, which became the **holding company** for Buffett's activities, managing a number of subsidiaries. Buffett acquired a number of insurance businesses which, apart from being profitable investments in themselves, offered the advantage that insurance premiums held against payment of future claims ('the float') can be invested elsewhere. The insurance businesses **generated cash** for new investments; Buffett prefers to buy shares or whole businesses with cash rather than part with equity in Berkshire Hathaway.

Buffett's essential investment philosophy has been to seek companies that are **trading at discounts to their true worth**. He mistrusted the usual measure of company's profitability – **'earnings per share'** – preferring **'return on equity.'** Shareholder equity is defined as a company's assets minus its liabilities – what a company and its shareholders actually own.

Buffett also **thinks long-term**, looking for companies that he believes can continue to succeed for the next 25 years. He declined to invest in the tech sector in what turned into the dot-com bubble, because he didn't think it was possible to know which companies would have a competitive advantage over a reasonable period of time.

The strategy has resulted in a **wide variety of investments**: outside of the company's major interests in insurance, Berkshire Hathaway has investments in clothing, retail, newspapers and building, amongst others. According to *Fortune* magazine,'for all his renown as a stock picker, Buffett has long preferred to have Berkshire grow, not by buying stocks that go up, which is what most people would assume, but by adding businesses.'

Buffett does, however, also **own stocks**: his substantial shareholdings in major corporations include Heinz, American Express, Coca-Cola, IBM, Kraft Foods and Wal-Mart.

Buffett's golden rule is to make money. If an investment loses half its value, the investor is 50 per cent down; but it takes 100 per cent growth to get back to where you started. 'The first rule of investing is **don't lose money**,' says Buffett. 'The second rule is don't forget Rule No. 1.'

In practice

Some tips from Buffett's investment strategies:

- Look for companies whose real earnings performance is undervalued by their market price

- Stick to businesses you understand

- Think long-term; look for enduring competitive advantages

- Stick with your best choices

- When you bet, bet big

- Be patient: don't be in hurry to invest or rattled by short-term market changes

CARNEGIE STEEL
Andrew CARNEGIE
1835–1919

WHEN ANDREW CARNEGIE JOINED the Pennsylvania Railroad in 1853 as a telegraph operator, the company was laying track to connect Pittsburgh with America's eastern seaboard. Soon he became a manager and was given the opportunity to buy shares in companies trading with the railroads. At a time when the infrastructure of modern America was being created, holding shares in the right companies could generate significant income, as generous dividends were paid to shareholders from booming profits. Before he was 30, Carnegie was earning thousands of dollars a year in dividends.

He went on to form a partnership building iron railroad bridges, and then set up the first U.S. steel plant to use the new Bessemer process. In turbulent economic times, Carnegie flourished where others struggled, buying up other steel companies to form Carnegie Steel. A move into open hearth steel manufacture allowed Carnegie to produce the girders that built America's new skyscrapers.

By the late 1890s Carnegie Steel was producing over 25 per cent of America's steel. When John Pierpoint Morgan bought Carnegie Steel in 1901 to create the United States Steel Corporation, Carnegie became the richest man in the world.

The ideas

The American Civil War stimulated the construction of new rail and telegraph links. Carnegie and others formed a **partnership supplying iron bridges** to replace the railways' old timber bridges, acquiring an interest in an iron business that had flourished during the war as a result of government orders. Carnegie also set up a new steel plant outside Pittsburgh using the new **Bessemer process** for producing steel from molten pig iron (he had visited Bessemer's first steel plant in Sheffield on his travels in Europe).

He survived a new economic crisis – the Panic of 1873 – and took the opportunity to **buy up failing steel businesses**. In 1881 Carnegie consolidated his steel and iron businesses into Carnegie Brothers and Co., of which he held over 50 per cent of stock. Another economic downturn gave Carnegie the opportunity to buy more bankrupt steel producers, including Pittsburgh's Homestead Plant.

Carnegie introduced an open hearth system, allowing the manufacture of steel girders and of armour plating for the U.S. Navy. The plant also moved towards continuous production, with **increasing elements of automation**.

Carnegie's company came into increasing conflict with its workforce, as management also sought to **drive down wages** and **increase shift lengths** during periods of recession. In 1892, a strike at the Homestead plant led to violent clashes between locked-out strikers and 300 Pinkerton agents who had been brought in to allow strike-breaking workers into the plant. Seven strikers and three Pinkerton men were killed, and hundreds wounded, making the strike the **bloodiest industrial conflict** in U.S. history. The strike was broken when the Pennsylvania National Guard were sent in.

As the nineteenth century drew to a close, Wall Street banker J.P. Morgan set out to consolidate America's steel industry. Morgan paid $480 million for Carnegie Steel, of which Andrew Carnegie's share was $225 million (over $6 billion at present values). Carnegie **gave most of his wealth to charity**, particularly to educational causes. 'Man must have no idol,' he wrote, 'and the amassing of wealth is one of the worst species of idolatry.'

In practice

- Build a career in a growing industry

- Look for related business opportunities

- Adopt the latest technologies; anticipate likely needs

- Consolidate and grow

CHAROEN POKPHAND (CP) GROUP
Dhanin CHEARAVANONT
1939–

DHANIN CHEARAVANONT TOOK OVER the running of the family's feedstuffs business in 1964 at the age of 25; within four years, the company was Thailand's leading supplier of animal feeds. Chearavanont then moved the company into poultry farming. By dramatically reducing the time taken for chickens to grow to marketable size, he started a revolution in food productivity that effectively helped turn the country's small farmers into large and efficient agribusinesses. The leap in productivity helped Thailand become Asia's first net exporter of food; it also gave many Thai farmers a middle-class income. 'Asia's farmers are poor [only] because they lack access to capital, modern know-how and markets,' Chearavanont told *Forbes* magazine in 2011. Today the CP Group is a multinational conglomerate with annual revenues of over $30 billion.

The ideas

Dhanin Chearavanont's 'revolution' started when he forged a strategic alliance with leading U.S. poultry breeder Arbor Acres, who had bred a fast-growing broiler chicken (chickens grown for their meat). Chearavanont employed nutritionists to help develop a **scientifically formulated feed**, and began to supply Thai farmers with Arbor Acres chicks, the special feed, automated chicken houses and the other supplies that they would need to set up as poultry farmers, further undertaking to buy back the grown broilers at a guaranteed price. The chickens grew to a marketable size in six to seven weeks, compared with three to four months for a typical farmyard chicken.

In 1985, Chearavanont began to research shrimp farming, developing a **special shrimp feed**. Thai farmers converted rice paddies into shrimp farms, bought the shrimp larvae and special feed from CP and sold the grown shrimps back to the company to be frozen and exported to Japan, the U.S. and China.

At the same time, the company opened its own Chester's **grilled chicken restaurants** and Five Star take-away stands, its own branded **processed foods**, and a chain of CP Mart **fresh food stores**.

Chearavanont cultivated a **special relationship with China**. CP became the first multinational to take advantage of Deng Xiaoping's market liberalisations by winning 'Foreign Investor Certificate No. 001' in 1979 to open a feedmill and poultry farm in Shenzhen, operating as

Chia Tai Co Ltd. The company was China's biggest foreign investor for many years and began to derive more than half of its agribusiness profit from China.

CP made huge investments in modern **large-scale, high-tech farming operations** in China, producing millions of broiler chickens, eggs and pigs per annum far more efficiently and productively than China's traditional small farmers. CP's new state-of-the-art egg-producing farm in Pinggu District, east of Beijing, is 70 per cent owned by a cooperative of local farmers, with CP and local government owning 15 per cent each. CP gains a **guaranteed source of supply** at stable prices, close to Beijing, with the logistical benefits of dealing with one large supplier.

Chearavanont weathered the storm of the **Asian financial crisis** of 1997. The banks called in $400 million of loans, forcing the company to sell assets such as brewing and motorcycle operations in China. 'I was prepared to use any means to ensure our survival,' Chearavanont told *Time* magazine in 2004. 'It felt bad, but I always believed we'd get it back tomorrow.' One of Chearavanont's sons described his father's stoic approach to the crisis: 'All through the financial crisis **I never heard him sigh**. He just put his hand over the bullethole to stop the blood and kept marching.' The group went on to pay down its debts.

In the 1990s, the company **diversified into petrochemicals and telecoms**. Today, CP Group interests stretch from food to telecoms, plastics, IT and finance. Chearavanont proclaims his **'Three Benefits' philosophy**: wherever CP Group operates, its activities must benefit the country and its society as well as the company itself.

In practice

- Create wealth by helping other people to create wealth
- Build networks rather than giant companies
- Deliver mutual benefits: 'the country, the people and profits'

TREND MICRO
Eva CHEN
1959–

EVA CHEN IS THE CEO of Trend Micro, one of the world's leading online data security firms, which she co-founded in 1988 with her sister Jenny, and Jenny's husband, Steve Chang.

It was a role she had to be persuaded to take. When Chang stepped down as CEO in 2005 to concentrate on his role as chairman, he nominated Chen to replace him. But Chen saw herself as primarily an inventor, with her more outgoing sister and brother-in-law taking the lead.

Having finally accepted the post, however, Chen set out on a risky new strategy to move the company, which had established itself as a supplier of online security services to the corporate sector, into the highly competitive consumer retail sector. She argued that this was essential if the company was to become a well-known name and a global brand. Chang eventually gave his support, as he told *Forbes* magazine in 2007, with the comforting words, 'Make sure you don't screw up.'

The ideas

Eva Chen was born in Taichung, Taiwan's third-biggest city. Her grandfather was a politician who started a bank, which her father, a philosophy graduate, inherited. Chen followed in her father's footsteps by studying philosophy at National Chengchi University in Taipei. 'I think that philosophy is a base that trains you how to think,' she told the *New York Times*.

After a spell running Trend Micro's **Taiwan office** (while moonlighting as a sports writer), Chen moved to the U.S. in 1995, becoming the company's **chief technology officer** a year later.

In 1997, Chen developed an **early malware scanner** called HouseCall, to detect and remove viruses, worms, Trojan horses and other malware. In 2001, the Nimda worm infected computers around the world, crashing Trend's own network. The company was able to offer its clients tools to repair the damage done, but it had no mechanism to prevent such attacks.

Chen came up with **the idea for a piece of hardware** sitting between servers and protected devices that would scan data packets and compare them with real-time information about current malware threats. She and a team of chosen engineers worked round the clock at her home, with the engineers sleeping in shifts in the spare rooms, to develop a prototype. There was resistance to the solution, since it was a piece of hardware and the company's expertise was in software, but it worked, and entered the company's product roster.

Chen pursued her idea of taking on U.S. **consumer online security** market leaders Symantec and McAfee by targeting Best Buy, the leading U.S. electronics leader, **undercutting her rivals on price** and working with Best Buy to include the features and meet the standards that would make Trend Micro products a recommended buy. Trend Micro began to gain market share.

Chen's strategy of **establishing a consumer brand** began to pay off as she struck deals to ship Trend Micro security software with Dell computers and Sony PlayStations. She set herself a new goal, positioning the company as a leading provider of security solutions for the growing trend in **cloud computing**.

Chen finally accepted the role of CEO when she realised that she would otherwise spend her life wondering if she would have been successful. She found an **additional talent in herself**: 'I've changed from an individual inventor to a kind of inventor that can put people together and make them innovate,' she told *Forbes* in 2009. 'And that's been really fun.'

In practice

- Study widely; explore many avenues

- Consider supporting yourself in the early days of a start-up, before taking on a full-time role

- Don't get used to being 'in the back room'; consider your own leadership talents

- Be bold: compete with major brands

- Develop new goals; keep adapting

HYUNDAI
CHUNG Ju-Yung
1915–2001

CHUNG JU-YUNG GREW UP in Kangwon Province, in what is now North Korea, during the Japanese occupation of Korea. His family were poor rice farmers. Chung made several attempts to run away from home to escape the life of rural drudgery, but was tracked down by his father and brought back to the farm. On one occasion, Chung sold one of his father's cows to raise the money for the train fare to Seoul, only to be found again and taken back to the farm.

In 1933, he made it to Seoul once more, and this time he began a career that would end with the creation of South Korea's largest business, the Hyundai empire. Chung's creation of a modern industrial giant was an integral part of the transformation of South Korea from one of the world's poorest economies to one of the world's largest, led by key entrepreneurs supported by the South Korean government.

The ideas

On Chung's successful arrival in Seoul in 1933, he joined and became a valued employee in a rice business. But when Japan invaded China in 1937 and requisitioned rice for the war effort, the Korean rice trade collapsed. Chung then started a **successful auto-repair business**, but it was taken over by the Japanese colonial government. The war, and Japan's occupation of Korea, finally ended in 1945. Korea was divided into two territories, with the Soviet Union having control of territories north of the 38th Parallel, in what was intended to be a temporary solution.

Chung set up a small **construction business** in Seoul, the Hyundai Civil Works Company (Hyundai means 'modernity' in Korean), in the hope that the newly independent South Korea would embark on construction projects. Chung got work from the provisional government and, with the help of his English-speaking younger brother, from the U.S. Army. When North Korean troops invaded the south in June 1950, capturing Seoul and triggering the Korean War, Chung and his brother fled to the southern port of Bhusan. When Seoul was retaken by U.N. forces in September, Chung moved back and re-established his connections with the army.

After the Armistice Agreement in 1953, reconstruction work by both the U.S. military and the South Korean government began in earnest. Hyundai completed the Gyeongbu Expressway in 1970 – an **incredible piece of road engineering**, traversing the length of the mountainous country from Seoul to Bhusan – and the hydroelectric Soyang Dam in 1973.

South Korea was by then controlled by President Park Chung-hee. Park instigated the remarkable, **state-led transformation of Korea** from one of the poorest countries in the world into an industrial giant, providing targeted state funding and harnessing the energies of entrepreneurs like Chung.

Chung launched Hyundai Motors in the seaside town of Ulsan in 1967, manufacturing Fords. In 1976, the company launched the Hyundai Pony, the **first Korean passenger car**. By 1984 Hyundai was exporting its cars to Canada, and by 1986 to the U.S., where the new Excel range was ranked by *Forbes* as 'Tenth Best Product' in the U.S. for its **quality and affordability**.

In 1972, Chung won a contract from a Hong Kong shipping magnate to **build a supertanker**, despite the fact that he had not yet built a shipyard. Ship and yard were constructed simultaneously in Ulsan. Koreans who, like Chung, had been raised in rural poverty, watched the growing factories and shipyard with awe and hope.

Chung was a **famously hard worker** and an **exacting boss**, rising at 3 a.m. and demanding 15-hour days from his family (Chung's eight sons achieved high positions in the company as, over time, did numerous nephews) and from his workers. He **rallied his workers** by telling them that they would soon own TVs and refrigerators and maybe even a car.

Through the 1970s and 1980s, the company grew to be the world's leading shipbuilder and a significant force in automobiles and new technologies, such as semiconductors; and by the 1990s, Hyundai was one of the **largest business entities in the world**.

In practice

- Explore every business opportunity
- Anticipate likely needs
- Make your business known to major contractors
- Nothing is impossible: take on major new challenges
- Compete globally
- Help to create wealth

GENERAL ELECTRIC COMPANY
Charles A. COFFIN
1844–1926

IN THE LATE NINETEENTH CENTURY, electricity was still a new discovery, its possible uses barely explored. When Charles A. Coffin, one of the founders, along with Thomas Edison, of the General Electric Company, died in 1926, *Time* magazine ran an obituary describing Coffin as the man who 'sold new uses for electricity.'

The telegraph and the telephone were establishing themselves, and electric lighting was an exciting new innovation, but industrial uses of electricity were rare. Coffin brought power-generating equipment to local industries and, by implication, to local communities. These communities began to develop into the cities of modern America.

Coffin not only played a huge role in the electrification of America, he also helped to create the modern corporation by pioneering the systems of modern management. As business writer Jim Collins wrote: 'Coffin oversaw ... the idea of systematic management development. While Edison was essentially a genius with a thousand helpers, Coffin created a system of genius that did not depend on him. Like the founders of the U.S., he created the ideology and mechanisms that made his institution one of the world's most enduring and widely emulated.'

The ideas

Charles Coffin joined his uncle's shoe factory in Lynn, Massachusetts, at the age of 18 and spent 20 years learning the trade before opening his own factory in the same town. He established an effective sales team whose success drove higher manufacturing volumes and allowed him to achieve **economies of scale**. In 1883, a group of local investors asked Coffin to manage a struggling start-up run by two early electrical entrepreneurs, Elihu Thompson and Edwin J. Houston. The 40-year-old Coffin accepted the challenge.

The Thomson-Houston Electric Company sold power equipment to individual companies. Coffin's grasp of **economies of scale** led him to offer local power plants serving whole communities, accepting part payment in cash with the balance in **loans backed by securities in participating companies**. By 1892, the company had equipped 870 local power plants. In comparison, the company's key rival, Thomas Edison's Edison General Electric, had equipped 375.

In 1889, Charles Brush of Brush Electric Light Corporation accused Thomson-Houston of a patent infringement. To avoid a legal battle, Coffin offered to buy Brush at $40 per share. Brush suggested $75 per share, an asking price of $3 million, and Coffin accepted the next day. **Consolidation**, Coffin decided, was the only way to prevent the industry from an unending series of patent disputes. In the next few years, he bought out seven other competitors.

In 1892, he himself faced a buy-out from Edison General Electric, backed by financier J.P. Morgan. Due diligence revealed that Thomson-Houston was the more profitable company, generating twice the return on capital. The **merger** went ahead, creating the General Electric Company (GE), but with Thomson-Houston as the senior partner and Coffin as CEO. Coffin created a major **strategic alliance** with Westinghouse Electric Corporation, involving various cross licences, creating an effective duopoly of the electrical industry.

Coffin's major contribution to the development of the modern corporation was his understanding that the corporation is not an empire to be controlled, but an entity full of potential to be developed. He invested in a **research and development facility** in the face of opposition from directors who believed that investors' capital should only be used to purchase the essential means of production. In 1896, GE used the discovery of X-rays by scientist Wilhelm Roentgen to develop the world's first X-ray images. The company developed the world's largest electric locomotives and transformers, and installed the world's largest steam turbine at its Chicago power-generating plant, using one-tenth of the space of previous units at one-third of the cost.

In 1912, Coffin handed over the presidency and took on the role of chairman, retiring in 1922. His obituary in *Time* magazine said that the impact of Coffin's GE on the developing United States was such that, 'in less than half his own lifetime [Coffin] helped considerably to **change the character of civilisation**.'

In practice

- Look for economies of scale

- Accept new challenges

- To drive growth, build partnerships

- To avoid patent conflicts, consider consolidation and strategic partnerships

- Invest in innovation

- Focus on developing, not controlling, the company

HABITAT; and others
Terence CONRAN
1931–

BRITAIN IN THE YEARS immediately following the Second World War was a bleak and rather exhausted place. The nation had put up with the austerities of wartime; it had obeyed the government's exhortations to make do and mend clothing to avoid importing cotton; food rationing had imposed a frugal diet; most household furniture was old-fashioned and worn-out – new furniture in wartime had been restricted to newlyweds and families that had been bombed out of their houses, and was made to designs approved by the government's aptly named Utility Furniture Scheme.

As the economy began to improve, so the country began to undergo a dramatic transformation. Terence Conran played a large part in this transformation of the nation's lifestyle when he opened the first Habitat store for furniture and household goods in 1964, introducing a unique blend of modernism and continental sensuality that would change the interior of British houses in a way that is still obvious today.

The ideas

In 1950, Terence Conran left his textile-design course at London's Central School of Art to work with an architecture firm on a project for the 1951 Festival of Britain – a hugely influential exhibition that was being staged to promote Britain's contribution to science, technology, design, architecture and the arts. 'At the start of the fifties we still had rationing and there was still a terrible austerity hanging over the country,' recalled Conran. 'The Festival of Britain was a beacon of hope ... It also started people thinking in a different way – **not just about their needs, but about their wants**.'

Conran thus set out on his lifelong mission to supply what people might want. 'People can only buy what they're offered,' he said, 'so their taste is made by what they're offered.' In 1952, he formed Conran & Co, **making furniture** in a basement in Notting Hill and selling it from a showroom in London's elegant Piccadilly Arcade.

He and others set up The Soup Kitchen in 1953, serving mugs of homemade soup with French baguettes in a smart, modern interior with tiled floors and the second Italian Gaggia espresso machine in London. In 1954 he sold his shares in The Soup Kitchen and opened his own soup and coffee restaurant on the Kings Road, Chelsea, near the first shop of fashion designer Mary Quant. Conran designed Quant's second shop via his newly opened Conran Design Group, the first consultancy in Britain to offer a **multi-discipline design service**.

Sales of his furniture line through Britain's old-fashioned furniture retail outlets were disappointing. Conran decided to **open his own store**. Habitat offered modern furniture with clean lines made from tubular steel and leather, assemble-it-yourself modular storage systems, beds made from pale Scandinavian pine, huge spherical Japanese paper lampshades, brightly coloured coffee pots from the bistros of France, fabrics from North Africa. Above all, Habitat products were affordable. There were small, impulse purchases, creating 'that irresistible feeling of plenty you find on market stalls.' Glamorous stars of the 1960s shopped at Habitat, and the rest of London soon followed. In 1977, 'Conran's' opened in New York, by which time there were 32 Habitat stores in the UK, France and Belgium.

In 1981, Habitat launched on the **London Stock Exchange**; Conran used the capital to build a **retail empire**. He bought the mother-and-baby retail group Mothercare, and then merged with the established high street department store British Home Stores, creating the Storehouse retail group. The group came to employ tens of thousands of people and had a turnover of around £1.5 billion.

Conran's venture into large publicly owned companies was not entirely successful, as is often the case with entrepreneurs whose **vision and personal contribution defines their business**. Conran eventually lost financial control of the company, stepping down as CEO in 1988 and as chairman in 1990. Along the way, it was generally agreed that Habitat had lost its soul; in the mid-1980s, the chain was known by the unkind nickname of 'Shabitat.'

In 1996, Conran went through an acrimonious divorce from his wife of 33 years, Caroline. He recovered to **open a string of restaurants** – large and small, grand and everyday – becoming one of Britain's leading restaurateurs. He bought back control of Conran Shops, opening a hugely successful store in Japan.

His design consultancy, Conran & Partners, continued the tradition of the Conran Design Group, offering a range of **design services** from graphic, product and interior design to architecture and urban renewal projects. As *Fast Company* magazine wrote in an editorial acknowledging Conran's contribution to design, 'Conran's guiding principle was simple: create **intelligently designed products** for as large an audience as possible at a price just about anyone could afford.'

In practice

- Pursue your talents and passions

- Use your vision to offer people things that they might want but are not yet aware of

- If there is no outlet for your wares, create one

- Stick to what you know and love – running a large public empire may not be what you do best

DELL
Michael DELL
1965–

MICHAEL DELL WAS BORN ten years after Steve Jobs and Bill Gates – not quite old enough to be part of the first wave of the computer revolution, but one of the first generation to grow up with computer technology as part of everyday life.

At university, where he was supposed to be studying medicine, Dell upgraded computers in his room and sold them to local businesses. He was so successful that he dropped out of university and set up a business with $1,000 in capital, selling upgraded computers and components. Soon PCs Unlimited began to make its own computers from off-the-shelf components. Dell sold his products direct, cutting out the middleman, and was thus able to offer lower prices than the major brands.

Dell Computers went public in 1988, with a market capitalisation of $80 million, making Dell a multimillionaire at the age of 23. By 1992, Dell Computers featured in *Fortune* magazine's list of the top 500 U.S. companies, making Michael Dell the youngest-ever CEO of a Fortune 500 company.

The ideas

In 1985, PCs Unlimited, the company Dell set up on dropping out of university, manufactured its first own-brand computer, the Dell Turbo PC. Customers were able to order a **custom-made machine** by selecting from various advertised options. By the end of the first full year of trading, revenues were over $70 million. Computers were **assembled and dispatched within 36 hours**. This business model became a cornerstone of the company's success, allowing it to carry very **low inventories**, while **dealing direct with the consumer** gave Dell a competitive edge on price.

Dell set up **telephone-based technical support** and customer service teams to reassure customers about buying direct, rather than from a retail outlet.

The company forged **close relations with its suppliers**, demanding keen prices and 'just in time' delivery. As the company's headquarters at Austin, Texas, grew, suppliers set up facilities close to the factory to service the growing giant. The company quickly **expanded internationally**, opening manufacturing facilities in Ireland in 1986, and subsequently in Malaysia, China and Brazil.

In 1992, the company made its products available through **retail**

outlets such as Best Buy, PC World, Business Depot and others, fuelling further growth. But this dramatic expansion nearly derailed the enterprise, leading to a shortage of cash and, in 1993, the company's first operating loss.

Dell recognised that he needed more **management talent**. He hired top executives from Motorola and from management consultants Bain & Company, and poached engineers from Apple to solve a design problem with Dell notebooks that had contributed to the crisis. The company **pulled out of retail**, which had contributed growth but not profits, and focused on Dell's original concept of selling direct. Profits recovered in 1994, and five years of explosive growth followed, with sales growing at nearly 50 per cent every year.

In 2001, Dell overtook Compaq as the **best-selling computer brand** in the world. The merged HP-Compaq brand took back the number one slot in 2002, but Dell was to regain the position for the period 2003–2006.

Michael Dell handed over the role of CEO to Mike Rollins in 2004, staying on as chairman. In 2007, Dell returned as CEO amid concerns that the company was faltering, as old competitor HP-Compaq held its number one position in computer sales and introduced a new range of TVs, cameras and handheld computers, forcing Dell to lower prices to compete. Dell was blamed for having **relied on an innovative business model and logistical skills** rather than on innovative products.

In response, Dell introduced a new, dramatic range of computers and focused increasingly on **servers and storage**. New web forums were launched to deal more effectively with customer complaints and **harness useful customer ideas**. There was also a significant development of the company's consultancy services.

Most dramatically, Dell is moving back into retail outlets. 'The direct model has been a revolution,' *Forbes* magazine reported Dell as telling his staff, 'but it's not a religion.'

In practice

- If a business idea is making money, pursue it

- Follow the logic of your business plan to its conclusion: carry even less inventory, get faster delivery times, turn around orders more quickly

- Not all growth is good growth

- Make sure management talent keeps pace with your business

- Keep innovating; diversify

THE WALT DISNEY CO
Walt DISNEY
1901–1966

WALTER ELIAS 'WALT' DISNEY needed a new character. As an early pioneer in the art of animation, he had achieved some success with a series of short films called the *Alice Comedies* – which featured a mixture of live action and animation – and a series of cartoons called *Oswald the Lucky Rabbit*. But Disney had ill-advisedly signed the rights to the Oswald character over to Universal Pictures, and his distributor cut the Disney Studio out of the second series. Disney lost his main source of income and all but one of his illustrators.

What Disney did have were some sketches of a mouse that he had kept as a pet at an earlier studio. His loyal colleague Ubbe Iwerks turned these into a new character called Mickey Mouse. The first two Mickey Mouse shorts were silent, like all of Disney's films to date, and they failed to find a distributor.

Then Disney struck a deal with film executive Pat Powers, who offered Disney a distribution deal for a new Mickey Mouse cartoon, with sound, made using Powers's own Cinephone system. Disney himself provided the voice of Mickey Mouse and much of the character's personality. The new short, *Steamboat Willy* (1928), was a sensation; by the 1930s, Mickey Mouse was a household name.

The ideas

Returning from service with the Red Cross in the First World War, the artistically inclined Walt Disney found work in an art studio, creating advertisements for newspapers and magazines, and to be shown as 'still' advertisements in the new movie theatres. There he met a cartoonist called Ubbe Iwerks; the two young men tried but failed to establish themselves as Iwerks-Disney Commercial Artists, and then found employment with the Kansas City Film Ad Company. In 1922, Disney and a colleague left the advertising company to form Laugh-O-Gram Films, making **short cartoons that were shown in theatres** around Kansas City. Disney hired more illustrators, including his friend Iwerks, but the company later went bankrupt and was closed down.

Disney and Iwerks eventually achieved lasting success with Mickey Mouse. By 1932, the Mickey Mouse Club – a **fan club** to promote Mickey and other Disney products – had more members than the Boy Scouts and Girl Scouts of America.

Disney introduced a new, music-based Mickey Mouse series called *Silly Symphonies*. He began to **streamline production**, using lower-paid assistants to do some of the more routine illustration work. He produced his **first colour cartoon** (*Flowers and Trees*) in 1932, using Technicolor. His studio developed a multiplane camera capable of filming up to seven layers of artwork moving past the camera, creating an illusion of depth.

Disney raised a loan from the Bank of America to undertake what was widely derided as **'Disney's Folly'** – a feature-length animated

Technicolor film. *Snow White and the Seven Dwarves* was released in 1937, and against all expectations, took $4.2 million in the U.S. and Canada alone.

With the proceeds, Disney was able to **build a new studio** in Burbank, California. He then went on to make what are now regarded as classic animated feature films: *Pinocchio* (1940), *Fantasia* (1940), *Dumbo* (1941), *Bambi* (1942).

As TV established itself, Disney teamed up with Coca-Cola to make a special programme, *An Hour in Wonderland*, for the NBC television network. In 1954, the studio launched a TV series, *Disneyland*, with the ABC network, which went on, under various names, to become the **longest-running weekly primetime series** on American television.

One of the conditions of Disney's deal with ABC was an investment in his latest project, Disneyland, which opened in Anaheim, California, in 1955. The **theme park** came to deliver one-third of the company's revenues.

In practice

- If you are involved in new technology, become a pioneer
- Expect failures and set-backs; be prepared to walk away from bad deals
- Follow your vision: ignore sceptics
- Keep up to date: adapt your technology to new business models
- Fully explore your brand promise (Disney sells 'fantasy,' not 'cartoon films')

GREE ELECTRIC APPLIANCES
DONG Mingzhu
1954–

In 1990, there was one air-conditioner for every 300 urban householders in China. By 2009, there was an average of one per household. And because the typical domestic air-conditioner cools only one room, the number is set to rise further, to an average of two or three per household.

When Dong Mingzhu started work at Gree Electric Appliances as a salesperson, it was a small state-owned factory. Retailers were in the habit of paying for their goods only after they had sold them. Dong insisted on payment up front, and came to the attention of the company's chairman; she was made sales director in 1994, when accounts receivable stood at $6 million. Dong implemented her payment policy, in the face of stiff opposition from a sales team who believed they would lose sales. But with retailers now having an incentive to sell the goods that they had bought, real sales – as opposed to paper sales – grew by 135 per cent in 1995. At the end of the year there were no accounts receivable.

Dong went on to become CEO, developing Gree into a high-tech manufacturer and the largest supplier of residential air-conditioning units in the world. Dong's steely business approach has given her a formidable reputation. 'I never give up,' she told *Forbes Asia*. 'I am willing to accept responsibility and meet a challenge. And I never compromise.'

The ideas

The early death of her husband left Dong, then 35 years old, with a three-year-old son to support. She found work as a sales executive for an air-conditioning manufacturer in the city of Zhuhai, one of China's original Special Economic Zones, created in the 1980s.

Dong's sales territory was the poor rural province of Anhui. She found that one of the retailers had bought goods worth $73,000 but not paid for them. Most sales people didn't buck the system; Dong was made of sterner stuff. 'As an employee, I needed to **put the corporate benefits before my own personal gains**,' she told *Forbes Asia*. When she **asked retailers for payment**, she got a lecture about her inexperience in the wholesale-retail relationship. She discovered that the air-conditioners were not even on display, but were still in storage.

Dong began to work her territory, setting out the **new terms of business of payment**. She won her first piece of business, worth $35,000 – with payment in advance. Two years after starting with the company, Dong's sales from her poor northern territory were worth $2.8 million, one-tenth of total sales for the year.

When Dong started work with the company, it was a State-Owned Enterprise (SOE). Chairman Zhu Jianghong restructured a number of local SOEs, renamed the new entity Gree Electric Appliances, and launched on the Shenzhen stockmarket in 1996. According to a China analyst quoted in *Businessweek*, Gree is 64 per cent owned by the state and 36 per cent owned by shareholders, including management.

In 2001, Dong was made CEO. Having initially bought in technology from Japan, Gree found that the very latest technology was not being made available to them. They created their own. Dong focused on **innovative technology, quality and reliability**, offering **six years' free service to customers**. 'When you make promises, you need to follow through,' Dong told the *New York Times* in 2011. 'You must offer good service. And quality. And then trust follows naturally.'

The company has a **state-of-the-art research facility** at its Zhuhai headquarters, testing products in extremes of temperature and simulated weather conditions.

Gree is now the **biggest seller of residential air-conditioners** in the world, with manufacturing plants in Brazil, Pakistan and Vietnam. The company manufactures for leading brands like GE, Panasonic and Whirlpool, but plans to offer products on a global basis under the Gree brand. 'Our way isn't to use advertising but to use the product,' said Dong. 'Our brand will build itself up as consumers purchase our product.'

Dong has never expected any **special treatment for being female** either. 'What kind of victory is it where you are given privileges, or where you play to your gender?'

In practice

- Take responsibility for your actions as an employee: do what is right for the company

- Bring people with you; lead the way

- Focus on quality; develop proprietary technology

- Deliver quality and reliability; consumer trust will follow

DYSON

James DYSON
1947–

JAMES DYSON DECIDED THAT the world needed a better vacuum cleaner at a time when most people would have felt that the world was adequately supplied with vacuum cleaners that were reasonably well-fitted to the task in hand.

And not only did he decide that his new kind of vacuum cleaner would be better than anyone else's and that there was, indeed, a market for his new vacuum cleaners, he spent nearly five years developing his new machine, famously producing 5,126 prototypes before achieving success at the 5,127th attempt. He and his wife lived off her earnings as an art teacher, grew their own vegetables and ran up debt. 'I wanted to give up almost every day,' Dyson told *Forbes* magazine. 'But one of the things I did when I was young was long-distance running ... In long-distance running, you go through a pain barrier. The same thing happens in research and development projects, or in starting any business. There's a terrible moment when failure is staring you in the face. And actually if you persevere a bit longer you'll start to climb out of it.'

In 2011, Dyson, the company, achieved £1 billion in sales for the first time. The company is still 100 per cent owned by James Dyson.

The ideas

The idea for a new kind of vacuum cleaner came to Dyson from a visit to a sawmill, where a cyclonic separator was used to take sawdust out of the air. Dyson thought that **the technology could be used on a smaller scale** to power a vacuum cleaner, separating out dust without needing to filter air through paper bags, which clog over time, leading to loss of suction and cleaning power.

The disposable paper bag had been a revolution in its own day; when Dyson tried to **license his prototype** to manufacturers in both the UK and the U.S., they were reluctant to get involved in manufacturing a product that would damage the lucrative market in disposable bags. Dyson finally **found a manufacturer in Japan**, and worked with them on the final development of a machine that was released in 1986 as the G-Force, in bright pink, retailing at the equivalent of $2,000. Ownership of a G-Force vacuum cleaner became a status symbol for upmarket Japanese households. In 1991, the cleaner won the International Design Fair prize for **best innovation**.

Dyson licensed his vacuum cleaner to a U.S. manufacturer, but described the experience as 'a disaster.' He decided to **go into**

manufacturing for himself. He re-mortgaged the family home, set up a factory and research centre in Wiltshire, England, and began manufacturing vacuum cleaners under his own 'Dyson' brand.

Advertising the new premium-price machines on television with the copy line, 'Say goodbye to the bag,' Dyson's new machines became the UK's fastest-selling vacuum cleaners ever; with the introduction of new variants of the original machine, Dyson went on to capture a leading 38 per cent of the UK vacuum cleaner market by 2002.

As the company grew, Dyson brought in **outside talent to take over the running of the business**. 'I didn't enjoy being CEO that much,' Dyson told *Inc* magazine. 'At an operational level, that becomes an enormous job, too big for me. I've never really been a businessman. I wanted to carry on the design and engineering myself. That's what I love doing.'

Dyson faced a constant battle to **protect his patents**. In the early days, the cost of renewing his patents nearly bankrupted him. Later, he took the U.S. company, Hoover, to court over a patent infringement when it introduced its own cyclonic cleaner – and won.

In 2002, Dyson created a foundation to **support education in design and engineering**. Dyson himself, with his team of research engineers, is still inventing. Dyson introduced other products based on air technology: a bladeless air fan, and a fast-working, energy-efficient hand dryer. He ventured into uncharted regions with a revolutionary new washing machine, but lost money. He allowed his managers to stop production. 'It wasn't my decision, and emotionally, I wasn't ready for it,' said Dyson. 'The products, they're like children.' Dyson has been clever to let other managers influence his business decisions.

Like any entrepreneur, Dyson is a risk-taker. 'I liked **living on the edge**,' he told *Inc*. 'All those years that my house was in hock to the bank ... I liked the danger, the idea that everything depended on getting that next product right in every way.'

In practice

- Follow your idea; become obsessed; persevere

- Licensing is an option; for full control, manufacture yourself

- Bring in management talent to run the business if this is not your forte

- Protect your intellectual property

EDISON GENERAL ELECTRIC COMPANY
Thomas EDISON
1847–1931

THE ELECTRIC LIGHT BULB has become the defining symbol of invention – an image of a bulb above someone's head translates universally as 'I've just had a brilliant idea!' or simply 'I've got it!'

Thomas Edison didn't invent the electric light bulb, but he was the one who developed a long-lasting and commercially practical light bulb. He also developed the phonograph (capable of recording and playing back sounds), the carbon microphone (a key component of early telephony), the motion picture camera (the 'Kinetograph'), and the electro-magnetic railway.

Early in his career, having made money from his invention of the first Quadruplex telegraph signal, Edison set up what can be regarded as the world's first R&D centre at Menlo Park, New Jersey. Menlo Park produced some 400 patented inventions, notably in the fields of sound recording and transmission and in electric lighting. Edison's personal inventiveness and his creation of an environment that enabled others to be equally inventive helped to find commercially viable uses for the new wonder of electricity.

The ideas

Thomas Edison was the **world's most prolific inventor** until very recently; his record of over 1,000 U.S. patents was only surpassed in 2005 by the Japanese inventor, Shunpei Yamazaki, whose own record was overtaken in 2008 by the Australian inventor, Kia Silverbrook.

Edison was also a great business leader: he harnessed the developing technique of **mass production** to bring his inventions to market.

Edison's famous Menlo Park research and development centre was the first of its kind. Edison played a pivotal role in the transition from 'invention' to 'innovation': he filled Menlo Park with **every material known to man** and with the brightest inventors and technicians from around the world, effectively creating an 'invention factory.'

His team of innovators worked whatever hours they pleased, pursuing whichever train of thought they deemed most fruitful. Everyone worked in one open space, **encouraging collaboration and the cross-fertilisation of ideas**. The best ideas were then honed and refined into commercial propositions. This recipe for successful innovation is being rediscovered today by many of the world's leading corporations.

Edison founded the Edison Electric Light Company in 1878, with the backing of the Vanderbilt family and J.P Morgan, amongst others. In 1880, he **patented a system for electricity generation**, set up the Edison Illuminating Company, built a generator on Pearl Street, Manhattan, and provided power to 59 households in Lower Manhattan.

Edison **fought a PR battle** – known to history as the 'Current Wars' – to try to establish his DC (direct current) supply of electricity as the standard, in competition with the AC (alternating current) supply favoured in America by George Westinghouse of Westinghouse Electric. One of Edison's tactics in this PR war was to illustrate the greater dangers of AC: his technicians electrocuted cats, dogs, horses, and even a rogue circus elephant that had killed its keeper.

In 1890, Edison **consolidated several businesses** into the Edison General Electric Company. In 1892 this company merged with the Thomson-Houston Company to form General Electric, which became one of the world's largest companies.

In practice

- Look for commercially useful applications for new technologies

- Empower teams to pursue their own ideas, working in close collaboration with others

- Make things happen: turn ideas into businesses

FORD MOTOR CO
Henry FORD
1863–1947

HENRY FORD, IN THE EARLIEST DAYS of motorised transport, set out to build a motorcar that was affordable for middle-class Americans. He focused on efficiencies in the manufacturing process and adopted the assembly line method of manufacturing, but also recognised the need to retain a motivated and skilled workforce. Ford's 'high wage, low cost' manufacturing model moved his own workforce into the middle class, allowing Ford workers to buy the cars that they had built.

Ford created the template for modern manufacturing and helped to create the consumer society, but his autocratic and paternalistic instincts led to the loss of talented colleagues and, for a time, to violent clashes with his workforce. Ford's worst fault was that he stopped innovating, refusing to acknowledge that the iconic Model T could be improved on.

The ideas

Ford grew up on his father's farm near Dearborn, Michigan, but was drawn more to mechanical devices than to farming; as a young man he left to work in a machine shop in nearby Detroit. Having seen both steam-powered road vehicles and a stationary German-made 'Otto' internal combustion engine being used in a soda-bottling plant, Ford began to develop his own **rudimentary petrol-driven automobile**: the Quadricycle.

Investors backed Ford to found the Detroit Automobile Company, with Ford as **chief engineer**, but the new company made only 20 vehicles and was dissolved, losing the investors $86,000. The company was reorganised, with new investment, creating the Henry Ford Company. Ford resigned from this company also after falling out with his backer; the company later became the Cadillac Automobile Company, which was in time acquired by General Motors.

Ford had some success in **creating racing cars** that won headline-grabbing races, and found a new partner to form Ford & Malcomson Ltd, which was reincorporated in 1903 as the Ford Motor Company and began production of the Model A, a two-seater passenger car.

In 1906, Henry Ford and small band of trusted engineers began work on the design of a **revolutionary new model** in a secure area of the company's Piquette Plant in Detroit: the Model T. The new robust and reliable car went on sale in 1905 at a price of $825, and demand outstripped supply.

At the time, cars were still made individually, using non-standard components that needed adapting. The team began to develop an **assembly line** method of production – starting with cars pulled by rope past lines of workers and ending with a prototype of the modern assembly line, with standardised parts delivered to specialised workers on conveyor belts. **Assembly time was cut from 12 hours to 1 hour**. In 1913, the price of the car was reduced to $550 and in 1915 to $440.

To retain skilled workers (and in the hope of preventing unionisation), Ford **doubled his workers' pay** to $5 a day and moved, in time, to a **five-day week**. Ford argued that increased leisure kept workers 'so fresh and keen that they are able to put their minds as well as their hands into their work' and that increased leisure time also increased demand for consumer goods – including motor cars. In 1914, a Ford worker could **buy a Ford car for only four months' wages**.

In 1919, Ford, who by then owned 59 per cent of Ford Motor Company, bought out the minority shareholders. For a time, Ford slipped into paternalism, sending investigators from Ford's 'Social Department' to monitor workers' private behaviour. Later, Ford's adamantly **anti-union stance** led to violent clashes between workers and Ford security staff and police. In 1941, an all-out strike forced Ford to agree to a secret ballot, in which 95 per cent of workers voted to allow union membership.

Ford propagated virulently anti-Semitic views and became **increasingly conservative** in his business views and **intolerant of disagreement**; talented individuals resigned or were fired, often moving on to successful careers with direct competitors. For a time, the man who created the world-changing Model T refused to admit that it needed a replacement. Ford's 50 per cent share of the car market in 1923 fell to 36 per cent by 1926.

Nevertheless, Ford has earned his place in history as one of the great businessmen of all time. The first automobiles were playthings for rich people – quite literally 'horseless carriages'. By making cars affordable to the middle classes, and by rewarding his skilled workers with wages that brought them into the middle classes, Ford began to **create the consumer society**.

In practice

- Keep innovating
- Persevere with new ventures; *expect* several failures

- Use pioneering manufacturing techniques to offer high quality products in large volumes at low costs

- To drive a consumer society, create products that your own workforce can afford to buy

MICROSOFT
Bill GATES
1955–

WILLIAM HENRY GATES III was one of the first generation of children to grow up in a world where the power of mainframe computers was being made available to people outside scientific institutions and big businesses. When 'microcomputers' appeared, Gates was among the first to see their potential – albeit reckoning in the early days that they would be used mainly in the home, rather than in the office.

Gates and his school friend Paul Allen co-founded Micro-Soft, and established themselves as the experts in computer language for these microcomputers – writing the programs that enabled the machines to do something useful for the ordinary person. When IBM entered the personal computer market, it chose Microsoft to deliver the software for their machines. The IBM personal computer was a huge success; other manufacturers were able to copy IBM's non-proprietary model and launch their own 'IBM clones' using Microsoft software. Gates's intense, focused and ruthless business drive ensured that Microsoft became a dominant force in personal computing software.

The ideas

At the exclusive Lakeside preparatory school he attended, Bill Gates had his first taste of computers – a teletype terminal giving access to computer time on a mainframe computer. He learned the BASIC

programming language, which had been recently developed to allow people without a scientific background to program computers. He also became friendly with another computer addict, an older student called Paul Allen.

In 1975, Gates was studying at Harvard when a small company called MITS launched what was to become the first commercially successful microcomputer, the Altair 8800. Gates called MITS, and said that he and Allen had a BASIC program that would run on the Altair, though in fact they had not – nobody had yet adapted BASIC to microcomputers. When the owner of MITS, Ed Roberts, said that he would be interested, the two men **worked frantically to create a program**. Because they didn't own an Altair microcomputer, Allen had to simulate the workings of its Intel 8080 chip on the mainframe computer that they had access to, while Gates had to write the BASIC program to fit onto the machine's tiny four kilobytes of memory. Allen then flew to MITS's small shop in Albuquerque, New Mexico, and ran the new program though the Altair's tape reader. On the teletype that the machine was connected to, he typed in *Print 2+2* and the Altair printed *4*. Allen ran an early computer game called Lunar Landing through the machine. It worked. What was to become Microsoft BASIC was a functioning microcomputer language.

Gates and Allen started Micro-Soft and **licensed their software** to MITS. As the new microcomputers gained in popularity, Microsoft BASIC became the established software. The company also developed other computer languages for use on microcomputers – they supplied the software for a new microcomputer from Tandy, which sold over 10,000 units in its first month.

'We set the standard' became Microsoft's motto and Gates was the company's **main salesman**. The company employed the publisher of a Japanese computer magazine, who had contacted them from Japan, to be their agent there. The agent helped to persuade NEC to **launch a personal computer in Japan** using Microsoft software. Other Japanese computer manufacturers followed suit.

The 'Microkids' at Microsoft **worked as intensively** as Gates himse.
One early programmer is recorded as saying, 'We'd often be there 24
hours a day, trying to meet a deadline ... We noticed the long hours,
but it wasn't a burden. **It was fun.**'

The deal to supply software for IBM's new personal computer and the
emergence of 'IBM clones' from manufacturers such as Columbia and
Compaq made Microsoft software the **industry standard**, ensuring
compatibility for a range of software applications. Gates struck
licensing deals with manufacturers, and was later accused by the
U.S. Justice Department of using the company's **increasing leverage**
to strike deals that effectively penalised computer manufacturers for
using other operating systems.

Microsoft launched its own **spreadsheet and word-processing
applications**, Excel and Word, and in 1985 introduced the first version
of a new, graphical-interface **operating system**, Windows.

In 1986, the company went public, making Gates a multimillionaire.
Paul Allen, who had left the company in 1983 after contracting (but
recovering from) cancer, was also a very wealthy man. An economist
quoted in the *New York Times* estimated that the rise in Microsoft's
share price had created 10,000 millionaires by the year 2000 from
the 'Microkids' who had been rewarded with stock options. The
continuing growth of Microsoft over the coming decades would make
Bill Gates the **world's richest man**.

In practice

- Look for world-changing opportunities: 'catch the wave'

- Keep control of your product; protect your licence terms

- Set the standard; establish a dominant position

- Diversify; establish your brand throughout your business area

BM; and others
Louis GERSTNER
1942–

WHEN LOUIS GERSTNER was offered the CEO role at the troubled computer giant, IBM, he hesitated. The head of IBM's recruiting committee said to him, 'You owe it to America to take this job,' adding that, if necessary, President Bill Clinton would put in the call to persuade him to accept.

The favoured rescue plan was to break IBM up into a number of smaller, independent businesses. But Gerstner believed that the company's unified structure potentially allowed it to offer a unique level of customer service. His programme of reform put user-based solutions, customer service and a commitment to quality at the heart of IBM, as he sought to re-establish a leadership position for the company. Gerstner realised that changing the established IBM culture – cushioned, secure, bureaucratic, risk-averse – was the key to re-creating the company: 'I came to see, in my time at IBM, that culture isn't just one aspect of the game – it *is* the game.'

The ideas

Founded in 1911, IBM developed a near-monopoly in the supply of mainframe computers and became one of the most important companies in America. But it also became an **unwieldy bureaucracy**, with a large number of virtually independent units and much duplication of services. And because it had outsourced the development of the operating system for its ground-breaking PC to Microsoft and bought the microprocessor from Intel, the IBM PC was easy to reverse-engineer and copy. Companies like Compaq developed 'IBM clones' and achieved quick success. By 1989, IBM's revenues had shrunk to £3 billion, and in 1992 the company posted the U.S.'s biggest corporate loss to date: $8.1 billion.

Taking the reins at the embattled company, Gerstner told a press conference that 'the last thing IBM needs right now is a vision.' There was much muttering in the press about a new leader apparently lacking a vision, but Gerstner stressed the 'right now' element of that sentence. His first job was **classic McKinsey restructuring**. Gerstner cut the shareholders' annual dividend; sold the corporate HQ in New York, the fleet of airplanes and the fine-art collection; reduced the workforce by over 100,000 worldwide; and shed considerable parts of the business to focus on high-margin areas.

One of Gerstner's most radical decisions was to **slash the price of mainframe computers** while committing $1 billion to investment in new technology to deliver more powerful mainframes at lower cost. Mainframe sales began to increase dramatically from 1994 onwards, and the new technology helped regain profitability.

Gerstner terminated the long-running project to create an operating system to compete with Microsoft Windows. He saw this as 'yesterday's war.' 'Desktop leadership might have been nice to have,' he wrote, 'but it was **no longer strategically vital**. The decision to drop OS/2 nevertheless caused 'immense emotional distress' amongst IBMers.

Gerstner pursued a commitment to customer needs, creating an Integrated Services Unit to supply all of a customer's IT needs, **even if it meant recommending non-IBM products**. The new division came to deliver 50 per cent of IBM revenues. This was the vision that Gerstner had kept concealed at the beginning of his rescue mission. IBM would stay as one company to offer a **unique depth of customer service**, and it would put customers first: 'Everything at IBM would begin with listening to our customers and delivering the performance they expected.'

To this end, Gerstner asked the top 50 members of the senior management team to **visit at least five major clients**, and for each of their direct reports to do the same. For very visit, he asked for a short report. He read these reports and took action when necessary. Staff began to see that he was serious about keeping customers happy.

In practice

- Restructure; cut costs; focus on high-margin areas

- Drive sales; discount temporarily, if necessary; invest for the future

- Make tough decisions: let unproductive projects go

- Set a new long-term vision

- Change the culture

RENAULT-NISSAN; and others
Carlos GHOSN
1954–

As a result of his actions to reduce Renault's overheads in the late 1990s, Carlos Ghosn had become known in the French media as '*Le Cost-cutter.*' This was an approach that he would hone to perfection when he was made chief operating officer of Renault's new partner, Nissan in 1999.

When Ghosn took control at Nissan, the company had lost money for eight of the previous nine years, and had accumulated debts in excess of $20 billion. Ghosn promised to resign if the company did not make a profit at the end of his first year in office. When he set out to change the entrenched cultural values at Nissan, Ghosn was fluent in French, English, Arabic and Portuguese – but not yet in Japanese. As he said in an interview with *BusinessWeek* in 2011, 'You know what really helped me? I didn't understand what they were saying about me in Japan.'

The ideas

At Renault, Carlos Ghosn had presided over an unpopular but essential round of **cost-cutting**, closing factories, laying off staff and ending relationships with uncompetitive suppliers.

When he was charged with the same task at Nissan, Ghosn found that his colleagues **knew that change was essential, but were emotionally resistant**. Nissan was a classic example of Japan's *keiretsu* system: groups of companies locked together by cross-shareholdings, a system that arose after WWII – when Japan was obliged to remove restrictions on foreign investment – as a way of protecting Japanese companies against foreign takeovers. Relationships between companies and their suppliers would be mutually supportive, but not necessarily efficient. Senior executives in satellite companies were likely to be ex-executives of the mother company. Change, especially in Japan's complex context of social obligation, was almost impossible.

'I had to **close down plants** in a country where the plant is a sacred place,' Ghosn told *BusinessWeek*. 'I had to **reduce head count** in a culture that expects lifetime employment. I had to **challenge seniority**, when everything was based on the oldest guy getting the job. Every single thing that was needed for Nissan went against their values. It was a **complete clash with the culture**.'

Ghosn closed five factories at a cost of 21,000 jobs. He introduced **new compensation systems based on merit** rather than seniority, and a new stock option plan for high-performing executives. He sold off the company's prestigious aerospace unit, part of Japan's national space programme.

He slashed the number of *keiretsu* companies linked to Nissan from 1,400 to four, raising cash from the sale of unwanted cross-shareholdings and maintaining relationships only with the **most competitive suppliers**. Along the way, Ghosn acquired a new nickname: 'Keiretsu Killer.'

He hired top car designer Shiro Nakamura from Isuzu, and charged him with **injecting new excitement** into the Nissan range; under the previous regime, design had been driven by the engineering team, leading to cars that a *Time* magazine journalist described as 'hot under the bonnet but tepid in the showroom.'

When Ghosn joined Nissan in 1999, the company recorded a loss of $6.1 billion. In the 2000 fiscal year, Ghosn had achieved his brave promise of **moving the company into profit** in one year, achieving earnings of $2.7 billion.

Nissan reintroduced the Z-car, an iconic sports car range first launched in 1969. Ghosn invested $1 billion in a plant in Mississippi, USA, to manufacture Nissan's successful range of pick-up trucks for the U.S. market.

In a blog entitled 'Partnership and Alliances,' Ghosn talks of the need to respect and build on different cultural identities: 'The most successful and enduring partnerships are those created with a **respect for identity** as the constant guiding principle. I am convinced this is the principle driver of our success and durability in the Renault-Nissan Alliance.'

In practice

- Think the unthinkable and challenge preconceptions

- Do what is right for the business, regardless of established practice and sentiment

- Establish meritocracy and results-based rewards

- Allow design and innovation to drive production

- See multicultural teams as a benefit; base partnerships on respect for cultural identities

GILLETTE SAFETY RAZOR COMPANY
King C. GILLETTE
1855–1932

KING C. GILLETTE CHANGED the world by introducing one of the first consumer items that was designed to be thrown away: the disposable razor blade.

Before Gillette, food and drink were almost the only things that people 'consumed.' Almost everything else was maintained and mended; tools and implements – like a straight razor made from hollow-ground cast steel, for example – were expected to last a lifetime or more. In time, Gillette had his big idea. What if a thin, sharp blade could be manufactured in large quantities and, as Gillette later wrote, 'made cheap enough to do away with honing and stropping and permit the user to replace dull blades by new ones'?

Manufacturing the blades was said to be impossible; Gillette found an inventor who believed that it could be done. The company was launched, and sold 51 razors and 168 blades in its first year, by mail order. Gillette pushed for retail distribution and consumer advertising and saw sales begin to take off. Gillette's face appeared on every packet of blades, making him an international icon.

The ideas

As a young man, King C. Gillette, a travelling salesman and aspiring inventor, worked for William Painter, the man who invented the Crown Cork – a cork-lined bottle top. Painter's advice to Gillette was simple: try to think of a product, which 'once used is thrown away, and **the customer keeps coming back for more**.'

In 1895, when Gillette had his idea for disposable razor blades, he was told it could not be done. Then he met a chemist called William Nickerson who had manufactured light bulbs by a process that Thomas Edison had rejected as impossible. Nickerson took on the challenge, and with $5,000 in seed capital from backers, the American Safety Razor Co was launched in 1901, with Gillette as president.

Gillette razors and blades were launched to the public by **mail order** in 1903, selling few in the first year but, encouragingly, selling 90,000 razors and 10,000 packets of blades in 1904. Gillette quickly moved from mail order to **retail distribution**, sought to prevent retailers from discounting, and began to **advertise heavily**, investing 25 cents per razor in advertising, increasing this to 50 cents in 1905.

By 1915, the company was selling nearly half a million razors and 70 million blades in North America and Europe. Neither the razors nor the blades were, at first, cheap. According to *Investors Business Daily*, razors initially cost $5 (around $130 today, adjusted for inflation) and blades cost $1 for a pack of 12. The price of a pack of blades would stay the same until 1924 – though by then each pack contained only 10 blades.

During the First World War, the company sold razors and blades to the **U.S. military** for soldiers serving in Europe. By the end of the war, American GIs had used 3.5 million Gillette razors and 32 million blades. They returned home with the **Gillette shaving habit firmly in place**.

In 1921, with his patent about to expire, Gillette introduced a new, improved model, sold the original model at a discount and introduced an intermediary version – giving the company **three price points** at which to compete.

Gillette also began what a later CEO called '**the give-away years**,' when razors where given away with various other consumer products to drive sales of blades; the tactic worked in the short term but, according to *Fortune Small Business*, 'came home to roost' in the 1930s.

A competitor introduced a new blade design, which Gillette copied. After **patent infringement suits** on both sides, the companies merged.

Weeks before the stock market crash of 1929, the 75-year-old Gillette, whose health was failing, sought to sell shares in the company to clear his debts. He was dissuaded by the board, who were worried that sales of shares by the founder would drive the share price down. The effect, given what was about to happen, would have been negligible: the historic crash wiped out the value of Gillette's shareholding.

In practice

- Be innovative; look for new ideas

- Create products that can become part of people's everyday lives

- Launch at premium price; establish the brand

- Develop and improve the product

- Consider merging with competitors to avoid patent disputes

W.L. GORE & ASSOCIATES
Bill GORE
1912–1986

WHILE WORKING FOR THE chemicals giant DuPont, Wilbert Lee 'Bill' Gore was struck by two things. First, 'communication really happens in the carpool' – people only communicate properly with each other when they are outside the corporate structure. And secondly, 'task forces work' – when companies have a crisis, they form cross-disciplinary task forces and throw away the rule book in search of a solution; this produces good results. So why don't organisations operate like that all of the time? Bill Gore took those two perceptions and built a new kind company, one with a very unusual organisational structure designed to encourage innovation, which would be the lifeblood of his new enterprise.

The ideas

At DuPont, Gore worked in research on the fluoropolymer, polytetrafluoroethylene (PFTE), best known in its DuPont branded form: Teflon. After 16 years with the company, Gore left with a licence to **explore the further possibilities of the molecule**, and co-founded W.L. Gore & Associates with his wife Genevieve, working out of the basement of their home in Newark, Delaware, on a process to insulate parallel electrical wires.

Their son, Robert, suggested a solution while he was still at university, leading to the company's **first patent** for a multi-wire ribbon cable. An order from the Denver Water Company for seven-and-a-half miles of cable got the new start-up off the ground.

From the very beginning, Gore and his wife organised their company in an unconventional way, aiming to create an atmosphere in which employees would feel free to **explore their own ideas**.

Gore's founding principles were Fairness, Freedom, Commitment and Consultation. **Fairness** rules every associate's dealings with every other associate, supplier and customer. **Freedom** confirms every associate's right (and obligation) to explore every avenue that may contribute to the success of the organisation, and acknowledges that there will be failures along the way. **Commitment** is a key concept: associates choose which projects they want to work on; everyone is called on to deliver only what they have signed up to, and is encouraged to join multiple projects. Success is rewarded by groups of 20–30 associates who assess their peers' contributions. If associates fail to live up to their commitments, their contribution is marked down. **Consultation** means that every associate is obliged to consult with colleagues if their project has outcomes that could potentially damage the company 'below the waterline.'

The effects of the implementation of these fundamental principles are far-reaching. The company has a CEO, and there are leaders for key support functions, such as Human Resources and IT; other leaders must emerge by **establishing a followership**. New recruits are assigned a sponsor, who guides them though the process. As people find their feet, they may have their own idea for a new project; if so, it is up to them to persuade colleagues to join the project. People have **multiple leaders** and may themselves be a leader in some contexts.

Associates are encouraged to use **'dabble time,'** spending about ten per cent of their time working on some pet initiative – though they must also fulfil their core commitments.

As the company grew, Gore built new, **low-rise workplaces** to accommodate about 200 people – with researchers, engineers, sales people and machinists all working in the same buildings – believing that teams of around 200 were the largest groupings that were still able to **interact naturally** and informally.

It was Robert, Bill's son, who made one of the company's most significant discoveries: expanded PTFE, a material that is about 70 per cent air, but resistant to water, and now better known by its brand name, **Gore-Tex**. The company's innovative approach has led to an astonishing list of applications for the material, from waterproof fabrics that still breathe to dental floss, guitar strings, industrial sealants and cardiovascular patches.

In practice

- Make innovation a core objective
- Give people a choice of projects, but insist on commitment thereafter
- Encourage 'dabble time'
- Fairness, Freedom, Commitment and Consultation
- Assess results using groups of peers
- Encourage people to start their own projects and find followers
- Keep teams small and multi-discipline to allow interaction

THE WASHINGTON POST GROUP
Katharine GRAHAM
1917–2001

WHEN KATHARINE GRAHAM'S HUSBAND died in 1963, she took over a media business that had started with the acquisition by her father of the bankrupt *Washington Post* newspaper. Her father later handed control of the business not to Graham, but to her husband. Graham thought that it was natural that the business should be run by a man. 'Curiously,' she wrote, 'I not only concurred but was in complete agreement with the idea.' After her husband's death, Graham reassured the board of directors that the group would stay under family ownership, with a view to passing on control to her sons. After a month of mourning, Graham decided to take on the presidency of the company herself, despite feeling inadequate to the task.

At the time, the group consisted of *The Washington Post*, *Newsweek* magazine and two television stations. When Graham stepped down as chairman of the company in 1993, revenues had grown by a factor of 20 and the company had acquired a number of other media organisations and launched on the New York Stock Exchange. Graham was the first woman to lead a Fortune 500 company, and under her leadership, *The Washington Post* became one of the most respected and influential newspapers in the United States.

The ideas

Katharine Graham's father, Eugene Meyer, had bought the bankrupt *Washington Post* in 1933 and spent millions restoring it to health. In 1946, he left to take up a position with the World Bank, and handed over the reins to his son-in-law Philip Graham. He transferred 3,500 voting shares to Philip and 1,500 to Katharine. Katharine ran the family home and paid for their living costs from her trust fund while her husband paid off the debt he had incurred to buy his shareholding.

It became increasingly obvious, however, that Graham's husband was suffering from what would now be diagnosed as bipolar disorder. His behaviour grew erratic, with alternating periods of brilliant activity and bouts of depression and heavy drinking. In 1963 he killed himself.

It was a friend who gave Graham the courage to take on the running of the media group, telling her, 'You've just been pushed down so far you don't **recognise what you can do**.' Graham struggled in the early days, conscious of her inexperience and often finding herself the only woman at meetings. She unsettled *Newsweek* magazine with a series of hirings and firings.

Two years later, she made a **spectacularly successful appointment** at *The Washington Post*, hiring Ben Bradlee as editor. Graham and Bradlee began to forge the perfect working relationship, with Graham giving the editorial team a **high degree of autonomy** while retaining a firm grasp of the paper's overall direction.

In 1971, *The New York Times* received a restraining order to prevent it from publishing further government documents, known as the Pentagon Papers, covering key decisions made by the U.S. government during the Vietnam War. *The Washington Post* obtained a copy of the papers. It was for Graham to decide whether they should publish; her lawyers felt that to publish could jeopardise the future of the whole group. 'Frightened and tense,' wrote Graham, 'I took a big gulp and said, Go ahead ... **Let's publish**.' The two newspapers faced the Supreme Court together and won the right to publish.

In 1972, the paper began a series of articles investigating a possible conspiracy behind a break-in at the U.S. Democratic Party's headquarters in the Watergate building in Washington. Evidence suggested that the governing Republican Party were behind the break-in, but the *Post* was exposed and vulnerable in its **lone pursuit of the story**. In 1973, tape recordings showed that President Richard Nixon had ordered a cover-up of his party's involvement in the break-in. The following year, Nixon resigned. *The Washington Post* was awarded the **1973 Pulitzer Prize for public service**.

Over the years, Graham, initially shy, lacking in self confidence and uncertain of her abilities, became the friend and confidant of presidents and ministers of state, and was considered to be **one of the most influential women** in the U.S. In 1998 she won the Pulitzer Prize for her autobiography, *Personal History*.

In practice

- Believe that you have the capabilities to do the job

- Appoint talented people; give them autonomy

- Make key decisions yourself

- Stand by morally correct decisions

ARCADIA
Philip GREEN
1952–

PHILIP GREEN WAS A high school drop-out who went on to make a fortune through a series of shrewd, privately funded purchases of under-performing retail chains, which he had the uncanny knack of turning into profit.

Green had only one role as chairman and chief executive of a public company. He resigned when the financial markets became uneasy after two directors left the company and Green failed to deliver his profit forecast. Since then, Green's business has been privately funded. 'It means I can spend 100 per cent of my energy and focus on my business without distraction,' Green told *European Business Forum* in 2006. 'I don't have to please anyone else.'

Being private also means that Green reaps most of the rewards for his efforts. In 2005 he announced a shareholders' dividend for his Arcadia retail empire of £1.3 billion. Since Green's family owned 92 per cent of the shares, Green's dividend was worth £1.2 billion.

The ideas

After leaving his first job selling shoes to retailers and travelling in Europe, USA and the Far East, Green's first business venture, funded by a £20,000 loan, was to import jeans from the Far East and sell them to UK retailers. After a time, Green thought that he should set up in retail for himself. 'I got bored with trying to supply retailers and thought: why not have a go yourself?' he told *European Business Forum*. 'I also saw having my own shop as a chance for me to use my **vision and creativity**.'

Green bought a batch of designer-label clothing at a knock-down price from a struggling upmarket retailer, opened a store in London's high-status Mayfair and sold the clothes at a discount. He established a business selling respected designers' **outdated stock at half-price**.

At the age of 33, he bought the Jean Jeanie denim chain for £65,000, and sold it a year later for £3 million. In 1987, he took over the publicly listed Amber Day company, and oversaw a period of **soaring share prices**, but resigned after the departure of two directors sent share prices falling, and the company failed to meet its profit forecast.

In 1995, Green teamed up with sports shoe billionaire Tom Hunter to acquire Olympus Sports to add to Hunter's existing Sports Division chain. The asking price for Olympus was £1, plus the assumption of £30 million in debt. When Hunter sold the merged retailers to another sports chain, Green reportedly made £73 million.

His **eye for a good deal** persuaded private investors to back Green's £538 million acquisition of the UK's Sears chain (which is unrelated to the U.S. Sears Roebuck & Co); the group was broken up and its assets sold for £729 million, making Green £150 million in six months.

When Green acquired the struggling BHS chain (previously British Home Stores) from Storehouse group for £200 million, the chairman of Storehouse said, 'Green had a **crystal-clear vision and strategy**. He had the guts to do the deal, to make it work when nobody else thought he could.'

In 2002, Green privately acquired the publicly quoted Arcadia fashion retail chain, using £10 million of his own money and £800 million from the banks. 'Everyone thought we'd overpaid,' Green told *Fortune* magazine, 'but I managed to turn ten million into £1.3 billion.'

In practice

The following ideas are drawn from an interview with Green in the Spring 2006 issue of *European Business Forum:*

- Give people the freedom to operate; reward them for short-term and long-term success; have the respect and trust of staff

- Be efficient on every level; execute with speed; keep it simple, don't complicate things; remove bureaucracy from the workplace

- Don't over-promise and under-deliver; better to under-promise and over-deliver

- The is a fundamental and important difference between deciding not to win and losing; know when to walk away

INTEL
Andrew GROVE
1936–

ANDREW GROVE'S BEST-SELLING BOOK is called *Only the Paranoid Survive*. His early life, growing up as a Jew in Budapest, Hungary, during the Second World War, was a series of life-or-death stratagems aimed at surviving first the Nazis and then, after the war, the Soviet regime.

When the Hungarian uprising against the Soviet regime of 1956 was put down by the Red Army, the 20-year-old Grove and a friend fled by train to Austria, crossing the border via an unguarded route used by local smugglers. Grove was delivered safely to the United States by the International Rescue Committee, and started a remarkable career, defined by his piercing intelligence and determination to succeed on his own merit.

As Intel's president and CEO, Grove made a series of calculated risks to steer the company through the treacherous waters of the technology revolution, radically changing the company's direction at key moments.

The ideas

When Andrew Grove became president of Intel in 1979, the company's main product was memory chips. It faced increasingly stiff competition from Japanese manufacturers, but merely agonised about courses of action until profits began to plummet. Grove then turned to CEO Gordon Moore and asked, 'If we got kicked out and the board brought in a new CEO, what do you think he would do?' To which Moore replied, 'He would **get us out of memories**.' 'I stared at him, numb,' wrote Grove, 'then said, "Why shouldn't you and I **walk out the door, come back, and do it ourselves?**"'

Intel switched from being a producer of memory products to being a **producer of microprocessors**. The company had invented the microprocessor in 1971 (Texas Instruments is credited with the simultaneous invention), in partnership with Japanese electronic calculator company Busicom. Microprocessors had been a small part of Intel's business, but in the early 1980s they were at the heart of the new personal computers. Intel **shed some 8,000 jobs** and posted a loss of $180 million, but Grove had made the right call: he was about to make another, arguably more far-reaching, decision.

At the time, computer manufacturers insisted that microprocessor manufacturers like Intel license their technology to other chip manufacturers. This guaranteed computer manufacturers, such as IBM, a choice of suppliers at competitive prices, but ate into Intel's profits. With the introduction of the Intel 80386 chip in 1985, Grove knew that the company had an industry-beating product, and his focus on manufacturing quality control meant that Intel could guarantee its reliability. Intel announced that it would **no longer license its technology**. IBM was unhappy. Compaq, the first manufacturer of 'IBM clone' personal computers, had used the Intel 80286; it took up the better 80386 ahead of IBM. Grove took part in negotiations to persuade IBM to accept the new deal; a compromise allowed IBM to manufacture its own 386 chips.

Grove became CEO in 1987. In the 1990s, he took Intel's new direction to its logical conclusion and launched the consumer-focused **'Intel Inside' marketing drive**. Intel moved from being an anonymous supplier of obscure computer technology to being a brand.

Grove had been a **famously demanding manager** in the early days of Intel, but having bawled out a valued manager to the point where the manager 'had been so hurt that no apology could get through to him,' Grove recognised that he was in danger of damaging his **open relationship with the team**. 'You cannot cut off one person's head one day and balance it out by being nice to the next person,' wrote Grove in an article for *Business Strategy Review*.

His renewed **dedication to openness** paid off. In the 1990s, two engineers confronted Grove about his decision to use a new, more elegant architecture to replace Intel's fundamental technology. As Grove told Harvard historian Richard S. Tedlow, 'We had established our technology as the industry standard. This franchise was worth millions, billions. We ... I ... almost walked away from it because the elegance of a new product seduced me into taking my eye off the market.'

In practice

- In times of crisis, think what a new CEO from outside the business would do

- Risk major contracts to establish the right terms of business

- Establish a brand

- 'Success breeds complacency; complacency breeds failure; only the paranoid survive'

- Be demanding, but don't 'cut peoples' heads off'; stay open to debate and persuasion

HAAN CORPORATION
Romi HAAN
1965–

THE ROLES OF MEN AND WOMEN in South Korea have traditionally been quite strictly defined, and business has been dominated by large, family-run conglomerates with a distinctly patriarchal flavour.

When Romi Haan tried to launch her innovative new cleaning product in 1999, male merchandise buyers failed to see the sales potential, and male bankers and venture capitalists struggled with the idea of a woman entrepreneur. Some assumed that her business proposition was merely a ruse to raise money for her husband, whose business they assumed must be in difficulties.

As the development of her product took longer and cost more than budgeted for, both Haan's parents and her husband's parents mortgaged their properties to fund the effort – proving that even the most traditional of families can be supportive of a young woman's dreams.

The ideas

The idea that propelled Haan to international fame as an entrepreneur and businesswoman derived from her **dislike of housework**. Korean families traditionally sit, eat and sleep on the scrupulously clean floor of one central room; the job of keeping the floor clean falls to the housewife. It occurred to Haan that the use of steam – increasingly common in hand-held devices for cleaning clothes – could make floor-cleaning not only easier but also more hygienic, destroying bacteria, viruses and house mites without the need for chemicals. In a nation that is almost obsessive about cleanliness, Haan felt that she was on to a winner.

The basic concept was simple: a kind of mop with a built-in steamer. Haan hoped that she could develop the prototype for about $40,000. She and her husband mortgaged their house and started a company in 1999, but creating a working prototype took longer and cost far more than they had expected. Haan got a **business development loan** from the government, but still needed to ask both her husband's and her own parents to mortgage their own houses – an act of great faith in Haan's vision and in her abilities.

Even with a working prototype, however, male buyers for retail outlets couldn't see the appeal of the new product. Housewives already had vacuum cleaners, mops and buckets – who needed a new cleaning device?

Haan got her products into a **discount mart** and began **selling online**. Word of the product began to spread and in 2004 she was approached by South Korea's TV shopping channel, GS Home Shopping. Sales of the second model of the cleaner took off.

Revenue in 2004 was $15 million; by 2005 it was $85 million and Haan was able to pay off the mortgages on her family's homes. In 2006, Haan opened a **manufacturing plant in China** and then started a **business in the USA**, selling the HAAN Steam Cleaner via home-shopping ads on TV and online.

The company has diversified into carpet and garment cleaners, beauty products and a range of magnesium, ceramic-coated cooking pans. 'Our mantra is to develop and market products that **improve the end user's quality of life**,' Haan told *Response* magazine on being nominated for a direct marketing award. 'In order for a HAAN product to come to market, it must provide a **solution to a real problem**. That solution must be better than any other solution available on the market.'

There is another secret to her success: as she told the innovation networking site Idea Connection, 'The environment changes so quickly. To survive you have to be **innovative** every day. So we have a motto: "Change every day."'

In practice

- Pursue your idea; expect setbacks

- Use all of your own financial resources

- If traditional outlets will not stock your products, try other routes to market

- Offer better solutions to real problems

- 'Change every day'

ICI
John HARVEY-JONES
1924–2008

SIR JOHN HARVEY-JONES turned around Britain's giant chemicals manufacturer ICI in the late 1980s. He argued that leaders should set objectives and strategic direction, and then leave it up to the team to find the best way of achieving these. He also believed that it is easier to create organisational structures that de-motivate people than it is to create structures that 'switch people on,' and that many large organisations become more concerned with creating the perfect bureaucracy, with all of the political infighting that inevitably results, than they are with facing the organisation's real challenges in the outside world. His course of action was to oversee 'a bonfire of our control systems.'

The ideas

John Harvey-Jones joined the navy as a midshipman at the age of 16. In the winter of 1946, he was sent to supervise the dismantling of the dockyard of the German port of Wilhelmshaven, which was to be shipped back to Russia as part of war reparations. The German workforce, though glad to have paid employment, were understandably unenthusiastic.

Harvey-Jones, who spoke both Russian and German, found that the workers were able to achieve progress **only when he and his supervising team were physically present**; the moment they left the scene, things fell apart. The experience left an abiding impression. Harvey-Jones saw that in any organisation that was too big to allow personal, face-to-face communication between the leader and the rest of the organisation, the leader has to find some way to **transfer his or her belief and commitment** to others. 'Making it happen,' he wrote, 'means involving the hearts and minds of those who have to execute and deliver.'

In 1956, Harvey-Jones joined ICI as a junior manager; he worked his way up, and in 1982, at the age of 58, he became chairman of the board of directors.

Harvey-Jones believed firmly that teams of people should have the **freedom to find their own solutions** to the challenges that face them, making mistakes and learning from them as they go along. Business leaders, he argued, have a delusion that they can legislate against mistakes.

'A business mistake is made, and it is assumed that the mistake would have been avoided if somebody at a higher position in the organisation had known about it, or had intervened.

'A power that had been delegated is removed, usually in quite a small way, by an instruction that in such and such a case the matter is to be referred upwards. Of course exactly that case never occurs, or if it does it occurs in such a way that it is not recognised as being a repeat run of the previous bitter experience.

'You therefore get an increasing **tangle of bureaucratic instructions** which seek to legislate for an endless series of unlikely events which have occurred at some time in the organisation's past.'

Harvey-Jones's aim was to reduce the tangle of bureaucracy, so that people throughout the organisation felt a **personal responsibility** for, and commitment to, the achievement of the agreed objectives.

As chairman of ICI, he set about **restructuring the massive company**, closing down or selling off loss-making divisions or those that he felt did not fit with ICI's core business. In less than three years, having laid off a third of the workforce and reorganised the chemicals giant from top to bottom, Harvey-Jones had turned ICI's bottom-line from a loss into a £1 billion profit and doubled ICI's share price. He was awarded a knighthood and voted Britain's Industrialist of the Year for three years in a row.

In practice

- Teams will only deliver if they feel a personal commitment to the task and derive personal satisfaction from its completion

- 'Involve the hearts and minds of those who have to execute and deliver'

- Decide what your core business is; let everything else go

- Give teams the freedom to find their own ways to achieve objectives within the overall strategy

- Carry out a 'bonfire of control systems'; strip out bureaucracy and allow people to take ownership of solutions

HEWLETT-PACKARD
Bill HEWLETT *1913–2001*
David PACKARD *1912–1996*

THERE ARE OTHER EXAMPLES where a famous leader has a partner who deserves to share in their glory – Steve Jobs *and* Steve Wozniak, Bill Gates *and* Paul Allen, for example – but it is impossible to separate Bill Hewlett and David Packard. The two men started their company in a garage in California, creating the modern archetype for creative entrepreneurialism: small numbers of people exploring innovative ideas free from the constraints of an established corporate structure. The objectives that they set for the way in which they felt that their growing business should function – 'The HP Way' – still stand as a model of enlightened corporate behaviour.

The ideas

Bill Hewlett and David Packard both graduated from Stanford University in 1935 with degrees in electrical engineering. Hewlett then went on to get his master's from MIT, while Packard went to work with General Electric.

In 1938, he and Packard set up a partnership **working in the garage** of the house in Palo Alto, California, that Hewlett shared with Packard and Packard's wife, Lucile. The garage would take its place in history as the birthplace of Silicon Valley.

The partnership's first product was an audio oscillator designed to test sound equipment. Their **first customer was The Walt Disney Company**. By 1940, the company had employees and had leased a small building, also in Palo Alto, as their workshop and office.

By 1957, the company employed more than 1,200 people. Hewlett and Packard held an off-site meeting of senior managers; they wanted to maintain the **small-company atmosphere**, and to agree a set of common objectives. They felt that if the senior managers agreed with the overall objectives and with how the company should be organised, then 'we could **turn them loose** and they would move in a common direction.'

The objectives that emerged became known as 'The HP Way':

- To make a profit (as the best measure of the company's contribution to society) consistent with the other objectives

- To strive for continual improvement in quality, usefulness and value of the products offered to consumers

- To concentrate on fields where the company can make a contribution

- To emphasise the need for growth as a measure of strength and a requirement for survival

- To provide employment opportunities that include the opportunity to share in the company's success; to provide job security based on performance; to provide personal satisfaction from a sense of accomplishment in work

- To maintain an organisational environment that fosters individual motivation, initiative and creativity, and a wide latitude of freedom in working towards established objectives and goals

- To meet the obligation of good citizenship, making a contribution to the community and to the institutions that generate the environment in which we operate.

Several real-life examples demonstrate that Hewlett and Packard were committed to these objectives in practice, not merely in principle. When Hewlett went into the plant one weekend and needed a microscope, he found that the storeroom was locked. He broke off the padlock and left a note instructing that the storeroom should never be locked again. If employees wanted to work outside of normal hours, perhaps to work on a new idea, then they should be **trusted with access** to tools and equipment.

When Packard instructed that a project for a new display monitor should be scrapped, the engineer who had developed the product, who was convinced that it represented what customers wanted, persuaded his immediate manager to rush the monitor into production. Packard later rewarded the engineer with an award for '**extraordinary contempt and defiance** beyond the normal call of engineering duty.' The fact that both the engineer and his manager felt that this defiance would not be career-threatening demonstrates the extent to which the objectives of 'The HP Way' had become part of the fabric of the company – in this case, 'a wide latitude of freedom in working towards established objectives and goals.'

In practice

- Keep the small-company spirit; establish common goals and 'turn people loose'

- Allow colleagues freedom of action in pursuit of agreed objectives

- Foster initiative and creativity

- Stand by your principles; trust colleagues and reward brave initiative

- Ensure ideas and good practice can easily flow through the company

- 'Make a contribution' to your field and to the community

HONDA MOTOR COMPANY
Soichiro HONDA
1906–1991

SOICHIRO HONDA HAD A lifelong love affair with motor vehicles. His first job on leaving school at age 15 was as an apprentice car mechanic at the Art Sokai auto repair shop. But when he found that his main duty was to look after the shop owner's baby, he went back home to Hamamatsu, disheartened.

After the devastating 1923 Tokyo earthquake, when several of the workshop's mechanics were forced to leave work to rebuild their family homes, Honda was called back. He spent six years working as mechanic, and then returned to Hamamatsu to open his own branch of the auto shop, which later became his own business. In 1937, he and an acquaintance started a piston-ring manufacturing company, running the auto repair business by day and working on developing piston-rings by night.

He enrolled at technical college, but found it hard to interest himself in anything that didn't involve the internal combustion engine. He was warned by the principal that he would not receive his diploma if he refused to sit the examinations. 'I am not impressed by diplomas. They don't do the work,' Honda is reported as saying. 'The principal called me in and said I should leave. I told him that I didn't want a diploma – it had less value than a cinema ticket. A ticket at least guaranteed you would get in. A diploma guaranteed nothing.'

The ideas

In the aftermath of the Second World War, Honda had fitted generator engines from military radio transmitters to bicycles to provide people with a basic form of transport in desperate times; the new small, two-stroke A-type engine was the first Honda-designed product. In 1948, he formed the Honda Motor Company, and by the following year, the company was producing **its own motorcycle**, the 'Dream' D-Type.

Honda went into partnership with businessman Takeo Fujisawa, who joined as managing director, invested capital and supplied the marketing and sales skills to complement Honda's engineering expertise. He urged Honda to create a **killer product**: a two-wheeler for everyman. The machine's engine, wiring and hosing would be concealed behind casing – as with the new motor scooters made popular by Lambretta and others – but it would have larger wheels and simpler technology to cope with rougher roads and poor maintenance facilities.

Soichiro began work developing the Super Cub, a 50cc 'moped' or 'step-through' with plastic fairings that went on to become the **biggest-selling motor vehicle in history**. It was decided at the outset that 30,000 Super Cubs could be sold every month on a global basis

– more than Japan's entire monthly market for two-wheelers.

The company invested in the **world's largest motorcycle plant** at Suzuka, capable of producing 30,000 bikes per month, or 50,000 with a double shift. It was seen as a reckless investment at the time, with the American market for motorcycles thought to be 'saturated' at less than 5,000 sales per month.

Honda opened its first U.S. dealership in Los Angeles in 1959. With the help of a **brilliant advertising campaign** ('You meet the nicest people on a Honda'), the company began to achieve its vision of a vehicle that could appeal as much to the middle classes of urban California as to the rural communities of developing nations. By 1964, Honda was the world's largest manufacturer of motorcycles.

Honda went on to develop **a range of successful products**, including electricity generators, outboard motorboat engines and lawnmowers. In the face of opposition from Japan's powerful Ministry of Trade and Industry, who wanted Honda to stick with motorcycle manufacture, Honda launched a mini pickup truck, a low-priced sports car and various mini-cars.

In the late 1970s, Honda set out to become **truly multinational**, opening manufacturing plants in the U.S., partly to avoid the possibility of stricter U.S. import regulations, but also because Honda could not hope to compete with Toyota and Nissan in Japan. Honda was soon selling one-half of their cars in the U.S., compared with Toyota's and Nissan's one-third.

Honda retired as president in 1973, but stayed on as a director and later as 'Supreme Advisor.' Late in his life he visited the newest test track that had been built in Nevada, U.S., by the company that he had founded, and was driven round the track at high speed in the high-performance Honda NSX sports car, the most advanced car that the company had produced to date. At the end of the day, Honda didn't want to leave the test track, telling his staff: '**I love it here.**'

In practice

- Follow your interests and passions

- Learn what you need to know; knowledge is more important than qualifications

- Study the competition; take up their best ideas and improve them

- Look for a 'killer product'; be ambitious in terms of scale

- Keep innovating; think globally

 LINKEXCHANGE; ZAPPOS
Tony HSIEH
1973–

TONY HSIEH WAS A co-founder of LinkExchange, which in the early days of the internet offered websites the opportunity to promote themselves by means of banner advertisements to other members of the network. After selling the company to Microsoft in 1998 for $265 million, Hsieh started his own venture capital firm, Venture Frogs, with another Harvard friend and LinkExchange veteran, Alfred Lin. The firm funded start-ups such as Ask Jeeves, OpenTable, and online shoe retailer Zappos. In 2000, Hsieh joined Zappos as CEO and steered the company to an eventual purchase by Amazon, in 2009, for $1.2 billion.

At Zappos, Hsieh created a corporate culture of 'fun and a little weirdness.' As he said in an interview for Harvard University's website, 'Our belief is that if we get the culture right, most of the other stuff, like delivering great customer service or building a long-term enduring brand, will happen naturally on its own.'

The ideas

Hsieh had a particular vision for Zappos. As he told Inc.com in 2006, he decided the company was **'a service company who just happened to sell shoes.'** Hsieh's logic was clear: nothing was more influential than **word-of-mouth** recommendation; if customers had exceptional experiences dealing with Zappos, and talked about it with their friends, this was more valuable than expensive advertising.

Hsieh followed his logic with several radical investment decisions. The Zappos warehouse started to **operate 24/7** to allow faster shipping. Customers were offered 365 days to return unwanted items, with **free shipping** both ways.

Hsieh invested in **making his call-centre staff happy**. Calls were not time-restricted. Staff were fully empowered to do whatever they felt was needed to make a customer happy.

There was a **nap room** because Hsieh believed that a short sleep made people more effective; managers were encouraged to spend time out of the office with their teams, because Hsieh believed that **teams that became friends** were more productive. Hsieh worked in a cubicle alongside everyone else. Co-workers were encouraged to decorate their cubicles to express their individuality, and were offered **free food and drink**, and even free dry cleaning.

When the dot-com bubble burst in 2000, Hsieh had to lay off half of the staff. Although by 2002 sales reached $32 million, the company was still losing money. At one point, Hsieh **sold his San Francisco apartment** to pay for a new warehouse. He managed to raise more venture capital. By 2007, revenues reached $840 million and the company finally turned a profit, but the 2008 credit crunch hit hard. The board pressured Hsieh to drop his **'social experiments'** in favour of profitability.

Amazon had offered to buy Zappos in 2005, but Hsieh had refused, believing that the company would be absorbed and lose its identity. In

2009, Hsieh visited Jeff Bezos at Amazon to see if Hsieh could buy out his venture capital investors but keep the company's distinctive culture. He presented his theories on 'happiness.' Hsieh argued that Amazon also tried to **do what was best for customers**, even at the expense of short-term financial performance. 'Zappos has the same goal,' he argued. 'We just have a different philosophy about how to do it.'

Amazon agreed to buy Zappos for $1.2 billion, and to **guarantee the company's independence**. 'Amazon is not trying to change our culture, and we're not trying to change Amazon's culture,' Hsieh told *Marketplace*. 'But at the same time, both of us have a lot to learn from each other.'

In practice

Tony Hsieh's ten core values for Zappos:

- Deliver wow through service

- Embrace and drive change

- Create fun and a little weirdness

- Be adventurous, creative, and open-minded

- Pursue growth and learning

- Build open and honest relationships with communication

- Build a positive team and family spirit

- Do more with less

- Be passionate and determined

- Be humble

FORD; CHRYSLER
Lee IACOCCA
1924–

LEE IACOCCA IS SOMETIMES called the Father of the Ford Mustang. When the racy sports-car-style Mustang was launched in 1965, it appeared on the covers of both *Time* and *Newsweek* magazines. Originally forecast to sell no more than 100,000 in its first year, it sold nearly 500,000 in year one and 1,000,000 in the first 24 months – the fastest sale of one million models in history.

Iacocca was made president of Ford in 1970, and managed to walk the fine line between achieving results and not upsetting the autocratic Henry Ford II, grandson of Henry Ford – at least until 1978, when Ford fired Iacocca without any particular reason, saying, after the event, 'Sometimes you just don't like somebody.'

Iacocca was quickly taken up by Chrysler. The company had been hit hard in the 1970s by two spikes in oil prices, contributing to a slowing U.S. economy, higher inflation and rising interest rates. The higher cost of finance slowed car purchases; consumers were also turning to more energy-efficient European cars. As sales fell, credit-rating agencies downgraded Chrysler's debt, increasing the cost of its borrowing. With the company's working capital shrinking rapidly, it was in danger of violating its credit agreements. Iacocca's turnaround of Chrysler is the stuff of legend.

The ideas

As a trainee at the Ford River Rouge plant, Iacocca learned the business of making motor cars, but decided that the engineering was not what interested him most; he asked to be **transferred to sales**. In the 1950s, soon after the first finance deals were introduced for car purchase, Iacocca introduced a plan called '56 for 56' – the chance to buy a 1956 Ford for a 20 per cent deposit and monthly payments of $56 over three years. The scheme was adopted by Ford nationwide.

By 1960, at the age of 36, Iacocca was head of the Ford Division of the world's second largest car manufacturer (after General Motors). After the **successful launch of the Mustang**, Henry Ford II and Lee Iacocca went their separate ways.

As president of Chrysler, Iacocca found that the company had thousands of unsold cars sitting in secure car parks, costing the company money. He organised a **low-price 'Tent Sale'** in Minneapolis-St Paul. The event worked so well that it was rolled out to major cities across America under the slogan, 'Let's do a deal.'

Iacocca renegotiated the company's contracts with rental firms Hertz and Avis, encouraging them to add more Chryslers to their fleets. He offered buyers **cash incentives to test-drive a Chrysler**, with enhanced guarantees and a promise of reliability.

Iacocca brought in **management talent**, introduced a programme of layoffs, and is said to have talked to over 100 banks, as well as many private investors, in his **search for capital**.

In the end, his only resort was to **approach the U.S. government**. Iacocca presented in Washington to both the House of Representatives and the Senate, arguing that the failure of Chrysler would cost the American government $2.7 billion in unemployment compensation and other payments to employees laid-off at Chrysler and in the company's network of dealerships and suppliers. A government guarantee of the company's loans would cost the American taxpayer nothing. In the face of arguments that the government guarantee was a reward of failure that was unfair to Chrysler's competitors, Iacocca was able to point out that government had guaranteed loans for similarly troubled players in the railroad (Penn Central Railroad in 1971) and aerospace industries (Lockheed Corporation, also in 1971). He argued that Chrysler was the biggest builder of U.S. and NATO military tanks, and a significant supplier of other military vehicles. Iacocca got his government guarantee for $1.5 billion of private loans.

Between 1979 and 1982, Iacocca closed 20 of Chrysler's 60 plants, reduced staffing levels from 130,000 to 74,000 and negotiated pay cuts with unions, reducing his own salary to a token $1 per annum (Iacocca was also rewarded with stock options that were to prove highly valuable). Iacocca became a **symbol of Chrysler's struggle to survive**, and started to appear in the company's advertisements, offering a personal backing of the company's commitment to deliver quality and good value.

Iacocca's programme turned Chrysler around from a $1.1 billion loss in 1979 to an $800 million profit in 1983. In that year he wrote a cheque for $813,487,500 to **clear the outstanding debt** guaranteed by the U.S. government.

In practice

* When times are hard, get out and sell

* In a crisis, lobby any institution that can help

* If you are asking for cut-backs, make sacrifices yourself

* If you become the public face of your brand, make the most of it

MSI; CELTEL
Mohamed 'Mo' IBRAHIM
1946–

BORN IN SUDAN and educated in Egypt and the UK, Mohamed Ibrahim became an expert in the use of radio frequencies when cellular mobile telephony was in its infancy. He joined the UK's Cellnet mobile telecoms provider (now O2) as technical director, but was frustrated by the company's lack of progress, and left to set up his own consultancy. The company, MSI, grew to become the largest independent technical group in Europe, with 800 employees and subsidiaries around the world.

At MSI, Ibrahim acquired licences for cellular operations in Africa. Everyone advised him that Africa would be a 'money pit.' The bursting of the dot-com bubble in 2001 made funding difficult and Africa's lack of infrastructure posed physical and technical challenges. Ibrahim nevertheless created the Celtel network – Africa's first borderless network. 'I am proud of what we achieved in Africa,' Ibrahim told *African Business*. 'We were there first, against all advice and we made it work ... We have created 4,000–5,000 jobs, real, quality jobs ... A huge industry has grown up around us in retailing, servicing, etc. I sincerely believe we have helped to develop the continent.'

The ideas

To Mo Ibrahim, developing a cellular network in Africa seemed an obvious choice. 'I noticed – we noticed – that there was a big scramble for licences everywhere, and countries had started to charge large sums of money to operate,' he told the *Observer*. 'The one place on earth where licences were available for free was Africa. **Nobody wanted to go in.**'

Once in, however, Ibrahim's venture faced major obstacles with transport ('We used everything we could get hold of: **helicopters, mules, camels,**' Ibrahim told *African Business*) and with reliable electricity supplies, having to rely on generators that needed to be fuelled every morning. They also faced petty bureaucracy and corruption, but the company made it clear from the outset that they would not make any illegal payments.

The company **did not lack for talent**. 'There were marvellous, very competent African professionals working in the West,' Ibrahim told

African Business. 'It had been impossible for them to return to Africa because there was nothing there for their talents.'

As the Celtel network grew, the number of mobile phones in Africa grew from 7.5 million in 1999 to 76.8 million in 2004, according to the *Observer* – an average annual increase of 58 per cent. A small **support industry** sprang up, including small kiosks selling airtime and recharging phone batteries.

When Ibrahim sold his Celtel network to the Kuwaiti telecoms company MTC for $3.4 billion, Celtel had 24 million subscribers in 14 African countries. Ibrahim's share was £363 million. Celtel employees shared $500 million; 100 become millionaires.

'Telephony was virtually dead before we came in,' Ibrahim told *African Business*. 'Now people can communicate very easily ... The effects of this communications explosion are still gathering momentum and you can see it in the banking systems, in production and distribution, in export and imports. Now Africa is beginning to do serious business because it can communicate.'

In practice

- If you have a better vision of how a new industry could develop, set up on your own

- Encourage colleagues to become shareholders

- See the potential of new opportunities, not the problems

- Offer a home for talent

- Do not get involved in bribery

- Make a contribution; change people's lives

APPLE INC
Steve JOBS
1955–2011

STEVE JOBS AND HIS partner Steve Wozniak started making Apple computers in the garage of Jobs's parents in 1976. In 2012, a year after Job's death from pancreatic cancer, the company that they founded became the world's most valuable traded company, with a market valuation of $623 billion.

It was not a straightforward journey. Jobs was ousted from the company he had created for being a divisive manager and unrealistic leader who put vision before corporate realism. He went on to found the hugely successful computer animation company Pixar, then returned to Apple to lead the company through a period of remarkable creativity and growth, launching a series of iconic products.

'I was worth about over a million dollars when I was 23,' said Jobs, 'and over ten million dollars when I was 24, and over a hundred million dollars when I was 25. And it wasn't that important, because I never did it for the money.'

The ideas

The Apple II was launched in April 1977. Unlike the Apple I, a basic DIY kit aimed a hobbyists, the Apple II was **a real consumer product** with moulded plastic casing, an integral keyboard and a display monitor. The 1979 launch of the world's first spreadsheet application, VisiCalc, written specifically for the Apple II, made the personal computer a potential business tool. Sales took off, and IBM began to wonder if they had misjudged the personal computer market, leading to the rapid launch of the IBM PC.

Mike Scott from National Semiconductor came in to Apple as CEO in 1977 to provide the professional management that Jobs and Wozniak were felt to lack. Scott and Jobs fought incessantly over strategy and implementation. In many ways Jobs was a **disruptive influence** in the company he had founded, though he was also an inspiring, if demanding and often unreasonable, leader.

A visit to a research facility run by Xerox gave Jobs a glimpse of the **first computer Graphical User Interface (GUI)** – a more intuitive way of controlling a computer using a menu, icons and a pointing device, rather than instructions typed on the keyboard. The first Apple computer to feature a GUI was the Apple Lisa, but the project ran out of control, loading the machine with features that would lead to a far higher selling price than had been intended.

Apple went public in 1980, generating more capital than any stock market launch since Ford Motor Company in 1956. Jobs, Wozniak, the company's early investors and many employees became instant millionaires.

Steve Jobs was a very wealthy young man and chairman of the board of Apple, but was becoming a **loose cannon**. A developer called Jef Raskin had come up with the concept of an inexpensive computer that would deliver the easy-to-use benefits of the GUI: the Macintosh. Jobs argued against the Macintosh, believing that it would take resources away from his Lisa project. When he saw that the Macintosh would become the more successful project, he switched his attention to the Macintosh, driving Raskin out, and began to run the project as a private empire, creating divisions and tensions within the company. The **Macintosh launched in 1984**, but achieved disappointing sales at first.

Jobs continued to wrangle with the company's CEO, now John Sculley, hired in from PepsiCo, and attempted to engineer a **boardroom coup** against him. The board backed Sculley against Jobs, who was stripped of all managerial responsibilities. Some months later, Jobs resigned.

In 1986, Jobs bought the computer animation division of George Lucas, to create **Pixar**. Always more at home with hardware than with software, Jobs set out to sell Pixar computers to be used for image manipulation and storage, and set up sales offices around America. But the computer was prohibitively expensive for most customers and the software was so specialised that few organisations were prepared to train staff to use it.

John Lassiter, an ex-Disney animator, had been employed by Lucasfilm and was kept on by Pixar to produce short films to demonstrate the power of Pixar's animation software. After one of these won an Oscar for Best Animation Short Film, Disney commissioned Lassiter and Pixar to make what was to become the hugely successful *Toy Story*. Pixar went on to produce a series of equally successful computer-animated films; Disney bought Pixar in 2006 in an all-stock transaction that valued Pixar at $7.4 billion. The deal made Steve Jobs the **biggest private shareholder in the Walt Disney Company** – but by this time Steve Jobs had returned to Apple and become CEO of the company that he and Wozniak had created.

After leaving Apple, Jobs had also launched a new company called NeXT. The company's workstations, aimed primarily at the higher education market, were not successful, but its NeXTSTEP operating system represented a real advance. In 1996, Apple **bought NeXT to acquire its operating system**, to replace the outdated Mac OS. Steve Jobs was given a post as 'special adviser' but was soon to become the company's CEO – a title that he had never previously held.

Jobs went on to slash Apple's bloated roster of products and then, working closely with the company's designer, Jonathan Ives, to introduce a dazzling list of **innovative products**: the iMac, the iPod, iTunes (making Apple, almost as an afterthought, the world's biggest music retailer), the iPhone, the iPad.

In its January 2010 issue *The Harvard Business Review* named Steve Jobs as the **top-performing CEO in the world**, having taken over as CEO in 1997 when Apple was in 'dire shape' and led the company so successfully that its market value had increased by $150 billion by September 2009.

In practice

- Inspire people with your vision, but stay in touch with reality

- Do not allow 'mini empires' to form within the organisation

- Enable creative people to do what they do best

- Remember what really matters (after Apple, Jobs became distracted by hardware, when the magic was in the software)

- Stretch people's horizons

SOUTHWEST AIRLINES
Herb KELLEHER
1931–

HERB KELLEHER WAS THE legal counsel for a small aircraft charter business in Texas when the owner set out his idea for a new low-cost airline operating between the state's three key cities. Over drinks in a bar, the owner sketched out his vision for Southwest Airlines' first destinations on a paper napkin. Kelleher was convinced. He put in $10,000 of his own money and set about raising venture capital. He was to spend the next five years fighting legal actions brought by competitive airlines.

A party-loving, gregarious man, Kelleher later accepted the role of chairman, and then of president and CEO; he did so, he said, because he loved the company and the people who worked for it. For Kelleher, the people came first. 'The business of business is people, people, and people!' he said. 'Of course, you have to be interested in and like people; otherwise, why would they be interested in or like you or follow you?'

The ideas

After Southwest Airlines' legal fight for survival, its competitors started a fierce price war, and Southwest sold one of its four planes rather than having to lay off any of its 70 employees. By 1973, Southwest was turning a profit. Kelleher **never laid off any staff**, even during severe downturns in the industry, but Southwest stayed in profit for every year of Kelleher's leadership – the only major U.S. airline to do so.

The airline's business plan – which has since been copied by budget airlines around the world – was based on **short flights** and a **rapid turnaround of planes** on the ground, leading to more flights per day. Costs were tightly controlled; seats were allocated on a first-come first-served basis. The airline dispensed with meals, offering only drinks and peanuts (which were offered free of charge, because Kelleher thought that taking payment was more bother than it was worth). The aim, wrote Kelleher, was 'to provide **more service for less money rather than less service for less money.**'

In his early years as chairman, as he told *Fortune* magazine in 2001, 'I sort of served a **three-year apprenticeship**. That was a very enjoyable period for me. You'd go over to maintenance and talk over how the planes were running. You'd talk to the flight attendants and get involved in such discussions as what their uniforms ought to be.'

Kelleher's business philosophy was unusual, but simple. As he wrote in a 1998 article quoted in the *Journal of Leadership Studies*, 'Years ago, business gurus used to apply the business school conundrum to me: "Who comes first? Your shareholders, your employees, or your customers?" I said, "Well, that's easy," but my response was heresy at that time. I said **employees come first** and if employees are treated right, they treat the outside world right, the outside world uses the company's product again, and that makes the shareholders happy.'

Kelleher put **decision-making as close to the customer as possible**: if regular customers arrived as a flight was about to leave, it was the local team's decision whether to hold up the flight to take them on.

Kelleher's outgoing personality and sense of humour began to rub off; Southwest became known for its **zany attitude**. Flight attendants sang safety instructions and told jokes. Any opportunity for a celebration was seized on. Employees were encouraged to **spend a day in somebody else's role**, to experience work from their perspective. Kelleher himself would join the baggage-handlers in moving luggage or the flight attendants in handing out drinks and nuts.

During Kelleher's time as CEO, from 1978 to 2001, Southwest grew from a $270 million company with 2,100 employees and 14 U.S. destinations to a $5.7 billion company with 30,000 employees and 57 U.S. destinations.

In practice

- Fight vested interests that try to stop you from trading
- Put employees first; have a genuine interest in their well-being
- Let your personality impact on the organisation
- Get decision-making close to the customer
- Talk to colleagues; understand how they experience their roles
- Get people to swap roles

SUN MICROSYSTEMS
Vinod KHOSLA
1955–

WHEN HE WAS 14, Vinod Khosla read an article about the start-up in California of the semiconductor chip manufacturer, Intel, and was inspired. 'The entrepreneurship bug grabbed me very early in life,'

Khosla said in a Stanford University lecture in April 2002. 'I just was enamoured by the idea of having to start your own company and I have pursued that dream since and never regretted it.' Khosla went on to become a co-founder of Sun Microsystems and the company's first CEO and chairman, before starting a new career as a venture capitalist.

The idea

Towards the end of his studies at Stanford, Vinod Khosla wrote to 400 small, recently started electronics companies, but got no job offers. Then he heard about a new start-up called Daisy Systems, developing software to help engineers design circuit boards, **called them up and got himself a job**.

Computer-aided design (CAD) needed powerful workstations to run on. A few companies were manufacturing workstations, but these would not run Daisy's software; the company built its own hardware. Khosla personally delivered the first machine. 'A day after they got this complete tool set, which they paid a lot of money for, they wanted to start changing it and adding programs to it,' Khosla told Harvard Business School in 1989. 'That basically told me that there really was **a market for a general-purpose machine.**'

Khosla left Daisy to pursue the idea. He was introduced to another Stanford student, Andy Bechtolsheim, who was developing CAD tools, and had come to the same conclusion as Khosla. He had invested $25,000 of his own money building a prototype workstation and was licensing his technology to companies for $10,000. He offered Khosla a licence. As Khosla told Harvard, 'I said to him, "I want the **goose that laid the golden egg**, and I don't want the golden egg."' Khosla persuaded Bechtolsheim that they could start a successful company.

The two men wrote a business plan and talked to a venture capital group that Khosla had met through Daisy Systems. They were offered $300,000. With **seed capital in place**, Khosla persuaded

Scott McNealy, a friend from his MBA class, to leave his job as director of operations for a small high-tech firm and join Sun to oversee manufacturing. When it was decided to use a Unix operating system being developed at Berkeley University, Khosla approached Bill Joy, the post-graduate student who had been largely responsible for developing Berkeley Unix, and convinced him that Sun was the vehicle which could turn his ideas into commercial reality.

The company set out to **compete with major players** like IBM and Digital Equipment Corporation. 'We had big dreams,' Khosla told Harvard. 'I remember seeing this motto: "Success comes to those that dare to dream dreams and are foolish enough to try and make them come true." You have to try doing something extraordinary, because unless you try something extraordinary, you won't ever do anything extraordinary.' Sun pitched its products to universities and quickly made sales.

Khosla **tightly controlled the company's costs**; Sun turned a profit in its first quarter and stayed profitable for the 1982 fiscal year. Khosla moved on to pitch to original-equipment manufacturers. Further venture capital was put in place. The company went public in 1986, survived the bursting of the dot-com bubble, and was acquired by Oracle in 2010 for $7.4 billion.

Khosla had served as CEO and chairman of Sun from 1982 to 1984, when he left to become a venture capitalist. In 1986, he joined the firm of Kleiner Perkins Caufield & Byers. In his 2002 Stanford lecture, Khosla said, 'Entrepreneurs are generally, I believe, far less successful when they try and make money. They're much more successful when they have **a mission to change the world**.'

In practice

- Be single-minded and persistent in pursuit of your goals
- Build the right team – get the best talent on board
- Set achievable short-term goals and then develop

- Control costs

- Set out to achieve something extraordinary

 PHILIPS
Gerard KLEISTERLEE
1946–

PHILIPS AND CO. WAS FOUNDED IN 1891 as a family company manufacturing carbon filament lamps, and soon became a leading manufacturer of radios and, later, of televisions. Philips developed a number of innovative consumer devices that became part of the fabric of modern life: the rotary electric shaver, the compact audio cassette, the home video cassette recorder; the compact disc (in partnership with Sony). By the 1990s, however, Philips had become a sprawling giant heading for financial disaster.

Gerard Kleisterlee had worked in various divisions of the company before becoming managing director of Philips Display Components worldwide and then president of Philips Taiwan, subsequently running Philips's activities in China. In 2001, he became president and CEO. He undertook to bring together the company's fragmented divisions to create 'One Philips,' introducing a new vision and a new focus on consumers' experiences of the company's products and of the Philips brand. Kleisterlee set about creating a more agile, entrepreneurial mindset within the organisation to help the company become 'the leading company in health and well-being.'

The ideas

On becoming president, Kleisterlee's first aim was to simplify Philips; to create an understandable, overarching vision for the company that would **give purpose and meaning** to all its activities. His core perceptions were that Philips was still driven by the manufacturing process – marketing what it made, as opposed to focusing on what consumers wanted – and that it had developed a serious case of silo mentality. 'We had become an armada of independent companies that all acted independently,' he told *Fast Company* magazine in 2002.

Kleisterlee replaced the company's previous slogan of 'We make things better' with 'Sense and Simplicity' and asked the company's entire 125,000 workforce worldwide to contribute to **'Simplicity Days'** – stopping work for the day to think of ways in which the company could simplify and improve its operations.

Kleisterlee's other key mantra was 'One Philips.' Kleisterlee **reduced the company's previous six divisions to three**: consumer technology, lighting and healthcare. He took the major decision to move out of the manufacture of semiconductors, using the proceeds to acquire new lighting and healthcare companies.

The consumer technology division was struggling, contributing one-third of Philips's sales, but no profit. Kleisterlee issued an ultimatum to the division to make money in the key U.S. market, or be shut down. His insistence on **cross-boundary communication and collaboration** led to the development in record time of the first consumer DVD player to use the rewritable DVD+RW standard. The new generation of machines captured 60 per cent of the U.S. DVD recorder market.

'Our solutions today may contain a lot of complex technology, but the user experiences them as something simple and easy to operate,' Kleisterlee told *The Focus* magazine, adding that the move 'downstream' to **focusing on consumers' experience** of the products, as opposed to the technical aspects of the products themselves, was creating 'a different buzz' around the company. 'If you don't just sell cool gadgets, but introduce things that enable people to live a healthier and more fulfilled life, that in itself boosts motivation.'

Kleisterlee wants his teams to have assignments that they feel excited about, projects 'with which they can **form an emotional bond**, so that they will invest everything they've got in their work, and will do so voluntarily, not because they have a contract.'

He worked to create a new atmosphere of innovation within the company, **encouraging executives to take risks**. As he told the *European Business Forum*, 'The only thing I always say is: Don't make the same mistake twice, because then you have obviously not learned.'

In practice

- Simplify complex organisations into a few meaningful divisions

- Insist on cross-boundary communication and collaboration

- Focus on consumers' perceptions of how products improve their lives

- Spell out the company's real purpose

- Create an emotional bond between colleagues and their work

- Encourage risk-taking via larger numbers of smaller initiatives

NIKE
Phil KNIGHT
1938–

A KEEN RUNNER, Philip Hanson 'Phil' Knight competed for the University of Oregon's track and field team in the late 1950s. His coach was Bill Bowerman; famously demanding and inspirational, Bowerman constantly experimented with different training techniques and fitness regimes. Convinced that a lighter sports shoe would improve athletes' performance, he hand-crafted shoes for his runners to try out.

Bowerman made a lasting impression on Knight. 'Maybe next to my parents I've been more influenced by him than by any other human being,' Knight told *Fortune* magazine in 2005. 'He really did get in your mind that you could be the best in the world.'

After graduating, Knight started to import running shoes from Japan to America, and Bowerman joined his former student in the enterprise, contributing his ideas about shoe design. The company that they founded became Nike, one of the world's biggest brands.

The ideas

In the early 1960s, the best sports shoes available were expensive German imports like Adidas. Knight, while travelling in Japan, discovered a high-quality, low-cost running shoe called Tiger, made by the Onitsuka Company (now ASICS). Knight got an appointment with Kihachiro Onitsuka, the company's founder and owner, and Knight's fictitious 'Blue Ribbon Sports Company' was appointed as the **U.S. agent for Tiger shoes**. Knight sent a pair of Tiger shoes to Bowerman, hoping that he would spread the word. Bowerman offered to join Knight in the venture, and Blue Ribbon Sports was incorporated in January 1964, placing its first order for a shipment of Tiger shoes.

Knight, who was working for an accounting firm in Portland, Oregon, drove to track events around the region, selling Tiger running shoes **out of the back of his automobile**. Sales went well. A store was opened in Santa Monica, California. Bowerman's book, *Jogging*, was published in 1966, and running began to become a popular activity. By the end of the decade, the company had opened more stores. In 1971, following disputes with Onitsuka, Knight and Bowerman set up on their own.

Bowerman had an idea that the family waffle-maker might make a good pattern for a shoe sole, providing good grip while reducing weight. He poured rubber solution into the waffle-maker (ruining it) and made the prototype of the Nike 'Waffle' shoe. In 1972, the shoe was seen being **worn by athletes** at the U.S. Olympic trials in Eugene, Oregon. Aspiring athletes and everyday joggers all began to follow suit.

Operations expanded into Canada, and then into Australia. A manufacturing plant was opened in New Hampshire. Revenue reached $14 million in 1976 and doubled the following year. New **manufacturing plants** were opened in Taiwan and South Korea, and sales operations were opened in Asia and South America. By the end of the 1970s, Nike commanded nearly **half of the U.S. market** for sports shoes. Nike went public in 1980.

In 1983, Knight decided to take a break and handed over the presidency of the company. His timing was bad. With sales of running shoes slowing down and consumers increasingly wearing Nike trainers for everyday use, Nike launched a range of **casual shoes**. At the same time, aerobics became a popular fitness regime and UK manufacturer Reebok established themselves with a range of aerobics shoes. Nike had missed the aerobics movement; its casual shoe range failed.

In 1984, Knight took back the president's role, and set about **reinventing the company**. The company had focused on producing products for top athletes and assumed that the rest of the market would follow these leaders. Knight began to turn to turn the company from being **product-led** to being **market-led**. Along the way, he identified the core of the Nike brand. As he told *Harvard Business Review* in 1992, 'We wanted Nike to be the world's best sports and fitness company and the Nike brand to **represent sports and fitness activities**. Once you say that, you have focus, and you can automatically rule out certain options ... you don't do casual shoes under that brand.'

Knight began to focus on **creating an emotional tie** with the consumer. 'Our advertising tries to link consumers to the Nike brand through the emotions of sports and fitness ... competition, determination, achievement, fun, and even the spiritual rewards of participating in those activities.' The company continued its policy of using **sporting heroes** to represent the brand. Nike's fortunes revived with its tie-in with Michael Jordan, the basketball star, and the Air Jordan range. 'Emotions are always hard to explain, but there's something inspirational about watching athletes push the limits of performance. You can't explain much in 60 seconds, but when you show Michael Jordan, you don't have to.'

In practice

- A product that appeals to the elite in any field will appeal to aspiring others

- Understand your brand's core values

- Find the emotional link between your brand's values and the consumer

- Focus on products that fit the core values

- Communicate with symbols and ambassadors

LG CORPORATION (LUCKY-GOLDSTAR)
KOO In-hwoi
1907–1969

KOO IN-HWOI CO-FOUNDED the two companies that were to become Lucky-Goldstar and which have since been rebranded as LG Corporation, one of the world's leading electronics, chemicals and telecoms companies.

Like the leaders of South Korea's other *chaebol* (family-run conglomerates), Koo succeeded in establishing an entrepreneurial business in Korea after the end of the Second World War (which also saw the end of the period of colonisation of Korea by Japan), putting his companies in a position to work with the South Korean government to lead the country's dramatic industrialisation in the 1960s and beyond. The Korean word *chaebol* is derived from the words *chae* (wealth or property) and *pol* (clan or faction). It describes what became the typical structure of the companies that led South Korea's economic development – groups of companies linked by cross-shareholdings and run largely by extended families. The structure served South Korea well at the time, helping the nation to transform itself from a small, agricultural economy into a global industrial powerhouse in the course of a few decades.

The government of President Park Chung-hee, who seized power in 1961 in a military coup, benefited from grants and soft loans from Japan, in reparation for its 1910–45 colonial occupation of Korea, and from foreign aid from the United States following the Korean War. South Korea became one of the four 'Asian Tiger' economies (South Korea, Taiwan, Singapore and Hong Kong) that achieved rapid industrialisation and consistently impressive growth rates from the 1960s to the 1990s.

The ideas

Koo In-hwoi and his partner, Huh Man-jung, started a trading company call Lak-hui Chemical Industrial Corp in 1947. Their main product was a popular face cream. Problems with the caps for containers led Koo to manufacture his own caps, and later containers, followed by a range of other moulded plastic items, which he also began to export, becoming Korea's **first plastics manufacturer**, and generating valuable foreign earnings. The company also launched Korea's first cream-style toothpaste, which became one of the best-known 'Lucky' brands.

In 1958, inspired by the export success of Japanese consumer goods companies such as Matsushita and Mitsubishi, Koo took the radical step of **diversifying into electronics** with a new enterprise, Goldstar Co Ltd. The company's first product was a simple electric fan; it went on to manufacture Korea's first domestically produced radios, telephones, refrigerators and, in 1965, a black-and-white TV set.

Koo's strategy was to **supply the domestic market** with goods that it had previously been necessary to import, and then to **refine and develop** these products to the point where they could compete on the world stage and be exported. By the late 1960s, Goldstar was supplying U.S. retailers Sears and J.C. Penny with television sets that the American companies sold under their own brand name, becoming the first Korean company to achieve significant levels of exports of electronic goods.

The other half of the company, Lucky Chemicals, entered into a number of **joint-venture partnerships** with foreign companies, generating new revenue streams while acquiring hands-on experience of the latest technologies. It partnered with Continental Carbon to form Lucky Continental Carbon, the largest Korean producer of carbon black, a key ingredient in the production of rubber, and with Caltex Petroleum to create Korea's first privately owned, and largest, oil refinery. The refinery reduced Korea's dependence on expensive imports of oil products and allowed foreign exports – another example of the **virtuous circle** created by the country's rapid industrialisation.

The relationship between the favoured *chaebol* and President Park's government was, by definition, close and cosy. One of the directors of Koo's companies was a minister in Park's government. The most significant benefits were access to **cheap finance** and a **favourable tax environment**; the company was also able to persuade the government of the need for highly qualified engineers: government funds were made available to allow Korean students to study at leading universities around the world in a far-sighted recognition of the need for a **highly qualified workforce**.

Koo established a Lucky-Goldstar foundation to **promote science and technology** and to encourage talented individuals. Koo died in 1969 and the chairmanship passed to his eldest son, Koo Cha-kyung. A year later, President Park, patron of the *chaebol*, was assassinated, and their uniquely close relationship with government was at an end. Koo's son undertook a radical reorganisation of the company to create one parent company, Lucky-Goldstar, with a growing number of subsidiaries, laying the foundations for the development of the modern company.

In practice

- Create businesses to supply consumer needs and wants

- Think globally

- Form joint ventures to acquire experience of the latest technologies and to drive major projects

- Promote education, talent and technology

 LG CORPORATION
KOO Bon-moo
1947–

Koo Bon-moo, grandson of LG's founder, Koo In-hwoi, became the company's third chairman, taking over from his father, Koo Cha-kyung. He led the company to global leadership in a wide range of consumer goods, from chemicals and household products to TVs, mobile devices, washing machines and refrigerators. His commitment to 'wow technologies' and his determination that the group should stay focused on creating customer value kept the company at the industry's leading edge.

Koo also led the radical restructuring of LG Corp into an American-style holding company for the group's many divisions, making the group more financially transparent and encouraging outside investment.

The ideas

Lucky Chemicals and Goldstar Electronics had been brought together to form Lucky-Goldstar. The company's consumer division focused on production of colour televisions and set up a **research centre** to explore new technologies for televisions, VCRs, personal computers and semiconductors. In the second half of the 1980s, the company suffered many setbacks. South Korea's workforce demanded a higher share of the country's increasing prosperity; wage settlements after a series of costly strikes resulted in an average eight per cent increase in the price of Lucky-Goldstar products. Limited access to overseas funding forced the company to fuel its growth with short-term loans from domestic financiers, creating a heavy debt load.

Koo Bon-moo's father turned to management consultancy McKinsey & Co for advice and took radical action to turn around the company's declining profitability (net profits fell by over 100 per cent between 1988 and 1990). In recognition of the fact that the company's traditional family-run structure was failing to cope with modern market conditions, he **devolved power to frontline managers** and created three executive committees to handle strategy, budgeting and human resources.

Koo took over as chairman in 1995, on his father's retirement, and picked up the banner of modernisation. He **stripped out seven layers of management**, rebranded Lucky-Goldstar as LG and bought a controlling share in Zenith Electronics Corporation, the last domestically owned television producer in the United States – gaining access to Zenith's flat-tension screen technology, an increased share of the U.S. market and exposure for LG executives to American management techniques.

The Asian economic crisis of 1997–98 led to South Korea accepting an International Monetary Fund bail-out with tough conditions attached. South Korean companies were obliged to **reduce their high levels of debt and improve overall efficiencies**, selling off unproductive divisions. Companies also came under government pressure to consolidate businesses that were duplicated by other South Korean companies: LG sold off its semiconductor business to Hyundai.

By 2003, Koo had completed a **radical restructuring** of the group to create LG Corporation, which is described as an 'American-style' holding company for its businesses. The founding families retain sufficient shareholdings to retain control of the corporation, but the complex cross-shareholdings of various parts of the business by family members have been removed. The new structure is intended to justify LG's description of itself as 'the first major Korean corporation to introduce a holding company structure with **advanced corporate governance**.'

Koo's chairmanship has seen the group's sales increase fourfold and its market capitalisation increase tenfold, according to the *Korea Times*. The company is investing in technology for the next generation of smartphones and is spearheading the development of organic light emitting diode technology for televisions and monitor displays. Koo has also promised to recruit more board members from research and development, and that a proportion of **royalties from the licensing of patents will be paid to the researchers** responsible for developing those patents.

As of 2012, all board members will be assessed on measures that assess the concrete results of their decisions. Koo stresses the need to establish a corporate culture 'where every one of our members concentrates on creating customer value ... to build a **wall of ability** that our competitors cannot easily climb over.'

In practice

- Strip out layers of management

- If necessary, acquire advanced technology, market share and management expertise

- Create modern corporate structures with advanced corporate governance

- Reward innovation

- Seek 'wow technologies'

- Focus on customer value

- Build 'a wall of ability' to protect competitive advantage

MCDONALD'S
Ray KROC
1902–1984

RAYMOND 'RAY' KROC, who created the McDonald's restaurant chain, has been described as the Henry Ford of the service industry. He took what he saw as the core elements of an affordable restaurant meal – quality, service, cleanliness, and value – and devised a system that would replicate the experience for diners in any McDonald's restaurant, anywhere in the world.

His original business model, however, would have been doomed to failure – the franchise fee that he set was too low to fund a profitable business – were it not for the venture having attracted other talented people, one of whom came up with a winning formula. In a similar way, though Kroc was single-minded in standardising the McDonald's experience across every franchise, individual franchisees were able to contribute their own entrepreneurial flair: it was franchisees who would invent the Big Mac, the Filet-O-Fish and the Ronald McDonald character.

The ideas

When the First World War came to an end, Ray Kroc became a travelling salesman for the Lily Tulip Cup Company, selling paper cups to the catering trade. Over the next 20 years, Kroc rose to become the company's Midwest sales manager. One of his clients manufactured a machine that could make five milkshakes at the same time; Kroc negotiated the **exclusive marketing rights** and spent the next 17 years selling machines across America.

By the 1950s, Kroc's Main Street drugstore soda fountain clients were beginning to shut up shop as Americans moved to the suburbs, and Kroc himself was approaching middle age. One of his clients, a drive-in restaurant called McDonald's in San Bernardino, California, had bought eight of his machines. Kroc wanted to know what kind of restaurant needed to be able to make 40 milkshakes at a time. He found a **slick, industrial operation** offering a stripped-down, nine-item menu of hamburgers, fries, milkshakes and fruit pies. There was no seating – customers drove to the restaurant, got out of their cars to buy their meal and went back to their cars to eat their meals. An efficient production-line kitchen meant customers could be served in one minute. 'Visions of McDonald's restaurants dotting crossroads all over the country paraded through my brain,' said Kroc.

McDonald's was owned and run by two brothers, Dick and Mac McDonald. They had already franchised two restaurants, but had seen little return. They were not particularly interested in the work involved in attempting to set up a **nationwide franchise operation.** Kroc persuaded them to let him become their agent, selling franchises for a fee of $950 and a licensing fee of 1.9 per cent of revenues, of which 0.5 per cent would go to the MacDonald brothers.

In 1955, Kroc opened his first showcase McDonald's in Des Plaines, Illinois. By 1958, he had sold 34 franchises; the following year, he sold a further 68.

In 1961, he got the McDonald brothers to sell their interest in the company for $1 million each, tax paid – a total sum of $2.7 million. Kroc **mortgaged the company** to raise the money from investment funds. He had given away equity in the company to raise earlier loans and to reward early head-office employees in lieu of pay-rises.

Kroc, who was fanatical about **standardising products and customer experiences** in every McDonald's, then discovered that his buy-out did not include the brothers' original McDonald's restaurant, which was renamed The Big M. It was the last straw in an increasingly fractious relationship. He opened a new McDonald's just round the block and put the original restaurant out of business.

Unfortunately, Kroc had got his sums wrong. His 1.4 per cent fee of revenues barely generated a profit for head office. Fortunately, other people believed in Kroc's vision of the potential for McDonald's. Finance executive Harry J. Sonneborn had left a well-paid position with the Tastee-Freez franchise chain in 1956 to work for Kroc for only $100 per week. Sonneborn devised a scheme to **build real-estate into the MacDonald's franchise package**: the company would buy or lease land, and sell this on to franchisees at a healthy mark-up. Franchisees entered a 20-year lease, and paid a minimum fee or a percentage of sales, whichever was greater. Profits from the real estate element of the franchises began to generate healthy profits.

By 1963 the one billionth McDonald's hamburger had been sold – a figure displayed on the front of every outlet. McDonald's went public in 1965, making Kroc a multimillionaire. He began to spend an unprecedented **one per cent of sales on national advertising**. By 1972, there were 2,200 McDonald's in America, with $1 billion turnover. Kroc also embarked on a programme of international expansion. He died in 1984. In 2012, the company served 68 million customers per day in 199 countries.

Kroc credited his early success to his efforts to **treat individual franchisees as partners**, not simply a source of income. 'My belief was that I had to help the individual operator succeed in every way I could. His success would ensure my success.'

In practice

- If you see something exceptional, explore it further

- A great idea that works in one place will work in other places

- Do your sums carefully!

- Bring talented people on board

- Adopt successful new ideas

PROCTER & GAMBLE
A.G. LAFLEY
1947–

In June 2000, Alan George Lafley was head of the global beauty care division of Procter & Gamble, based in San Francisco, when he got a call from the chairman, telling him to take the company jet and fly overnight to headquarters in Cincinnati, Ohio. First thing next morning it was announced that Lafley was taking over as CEO, after the disastrous 17-month reign of Lafley's combative predecessor had led the company into what some commentators called a 'death spiral.'

'The biggest decision we made was to move to an open innovation platform,' Lafley told an Ernst & Young Strategic Growth Forum in 2010. 'The problem at P&G in 2000 was not that we weren't inventive. The problem with us was that we weren't turning that invention into innovation that ... created value for customers or a better experience for customers.'

By the time Lafley retired in 2009, the company had grown from having ten billion-dollar brands to 24 billion-dollar brands; total sales had doubled, and profits had quadrupled.

The ideas

A.G. Lafley joined P&G on obtaining his MBA from Harvard Business School. He worked his way up the company, working on major brands such as Tide and Cheer, before becoming president of laundry and cleaning products. He served as president of P&G Far East, building the company's business in China and revitalising its cosmetics business in Japan, then as president of both global beauty care and of P&G USA – the role from which he was promoted to CEO. Lafley had a reputation for being approachable, and **a good listener**.

His predecessor in the CEO's role, Durk Jager, had tried to shake the company out of what he saw as a 'job for life' mentality and had implemented what *Time* magazine described in 2002 as 'an overly aggressive, ill-timed restructuring programme' that left many of the company's 110,000 employees 'in new jobs, disoriented and distracted.' There had also been a number of unsuccessful new product launches.

Lafley decided that many of the existing management team did not have the right mindset to make the necessary changes 'as a collaborative team.' Over half of P&Gs top 30 executives were **replaced from within the company**. Lafley **rationalised P&G's product range** to focus on the core areas of household products, baby care and, increasingly, health and beauty and male grooming. P&G acquired Clairol's hair-care business for $5 billion in 2001 – the company's biggest acquisition to date.

In 2005, the company made the huge $57 billion acquisition of Gillette, making P&G the **world's biggest household goods manufacturer**, pushing rival Unilever into second place. 'We didn't buy Gillette because we wanted their male shaving business,' Lafley told *Smart Business* magazine in 2011. 'We bought Gillette because we thought Gillette would be a fabulous platform for male personal care innovation for the next 50 or 100 years. **Innovation drove everything.**'

P&G had traditionally developed all of its own new products; Lafley looked outside. 'We reached out to **universities and research laboratories** and tried to get the word out to individual entrepreneurs. One of the things we did was we ran these **big innovation fairs**.'

P&G tapped into its network of past employees and launched a website inviting new ideas from the world at large. The open innovation strategy has resulted in **over 2,000 agreements with innovation partners**, and, according to *BusinessWeek*, more than half of all products brought to market in 2008 included at least one component from an outside partner.

Lafley pushed for simpler prototype products to be tested on a faster time scale, arguing that consumers were smart enough to get the general idea. 'You're going to fail and you're going to fail multiple times,' he told *Smart Business*. '**I always encouraged fast failure and I preferred cheap failure.**'

In practice

- Encourage a collaborative mindset
- Rationalise to core product areas
- Make strategic acquisitions
- Invite outside contributions to drive innovation; improve existing products and processes as well looking for new innovative products
- Failures are inevitable: speed up trial and error; reduce the cost of failures

ESTÉE LAUDER
Estée LAUDER
1906–2004

ESTÉE LAUDER WAS BORN Josephine Esther Mentzer in the Queens borough of New York City. Her uncle John Schotz had founded a small laboratory producing a range of health and beauty products. Lauder developed a fascination for the process of manufacturing skin creams and beauty aids, and discovered a natural talent for marketing.

It took Lauder several decades of hard graft to develop a significant cosmetics company. Its first significant breakthrough came in 1953, with the launch of a strongly scented product called Youth Dew, which could be used as a perfume or bath oil. Lauder positioned the product as an affordable indulgence at a time when perfumes were seen as luxury purchases or expensive gifts. She honed her promotional skills in the early years of her business, when advertising was unaffordable, and pioneered the use of free samples offered in-store, via direct mail or charity giveaways, and as 'gift with purchase.'

The ideas

Lauder's parents were Hungarian immigrants to New York City. Her father is reported to have been 'prosperous' in Hungary, but not quite as aristocratic as he was later implied to be. He worked in New York as a tailor, and then ran a hardware store.

Lauder's mother's brother, John Schotz, a chemist, arrived in New York from Hungary in 1900 and set up a makeshift laboratory in the family stables (in the days when the horse was still the main form of transport), producing **beauty aids** such as *Six-in-One Cold Cream* and *Dr Schotz Viennese Cream*, as well as less glamorous products such as suppositories, a poultry-lice killer and an embalming fluid. Lauder acquired a fascination both for beauty creams and for the process of manufacture. She dreamed of becoming a scientist and sold Schotz's products to friends and acquaintances.

In 1930, she married Joseph Lauder; they had a son in 1933. Lauder continued to work on **making and selling new products**: 'I cooked for my family and during every possible spare moment cooked up little pots of creams for faces.' The couple divorced in 1939, but were to remarry three years later.

Lauder became a lifelong friend of Arnold van Ameringen, one of the founders of International Flavors and Fragrances. According to the *New York Times*, Ameringen helped Lauder's fledgling company with financial aid and, possibly, with the formula for fragrances, though there was no formal link between the two companies. When she and Joseph remarried, Joseph took on the management of the venture's finances, while Lauder **focused on marketing**.

They sold their products via concessions in beauty salons in New York and the surrounding area, and in 1948 made a major breakthrough when Lauder persuaded the prestigious Manhattan department store Saks of Fifth Avenue to give them counter space. Lauder deployed her own considerable **personal sales skills** – applying creams to potential customers, **giving away samples** and **offering 'makeovers'** – and trained store staff in her methods. Other department stores around the United States began to stock Lauder's products.

The launch of Youth Dew in 1953 boosted earnings 'from a sales volume of no more than $400 a week to around $5,000,' according to Lauder's *New York Times* obituary. By 1958, the company's annual sales were round $800,000.

In 1967, Lauder led the radical move into **male skin-care** and grooming with the launch of the Aramis range. In 1968, the **allergy-tested** Clinique range was introduced.

Lauder's company was privately owned until 1995, when its initial public offering valued the company at $5 billion. In the year before her death, her company employed over 20,000 people in 130 countries around the world and had an estimated value of $10 billion. 'The pursuit of beauty is honourable' said Lauder and, perhaps most memorably, 'Time is not on your side, but I am.'

In practice

- Develop new products and market them; explore every route to market

- Use sales promotion: free sampling, gifts with purchase, demonstrations

- Develop a 'luxury' item at an affordable price

- Continue to innovate and create new markets

SAMSUNG
LEE Byung-chull
1910–1987

THE LIFE AND CAREER of Lee Byung-chull reflects the history of modern Korea. Lee was born in 1910, the year in which Korea was annexed by the Empire of Japan. He built a successful business in Korea under Japanese rule, moving his businesses to Korea's capital, Seoul, when colonial rule ended with the defeat of Japan at the end of the Second World War. He and his business survived the Korean War (1950–1953), which ended with the country divided into South and North Korea. South Korea was established as a democracy but, after a period of political instability, underwent a period of military government following a coup by General Park Chung-hee.

Lee, who was in Japan at the time of the coup, was under suspicion of corrupt dealings with the previous administration, but returned to Seoul and struck a deal to work with the military government, using his corporation, Samsung, to help with the goal of transforming Korea into an industrial nation. Lee went on to make Samsung a major multinational corporation, with interests ranging from ship building to electronics. With the success of *chaebol* (family-run conglomerates) like Samsung, Korea transformed itself from one of the nation's poorest countries to one of the richest in one generation, returning to full democracy after free presidential elections in 1987.

The ideas

Lee came from a wealthy land-owning family. When his father died, Lee used his inheritance to start his first business venture in rice milling, and then moved into transportation and real estate. The Samsung Trading Company was established in 1938, and acquired the licence to move into brewing. The company moved into import-export and, in 1947, moved its headquarters to Seoul, quickly becoming the country's **leading trading company**. After the Korean War, Lee moved into manufacturing, starting with sugar and textiles.

In 1953, Korea's Gross National Product per head of population was a mere $67 – the lowest in the world. '**The necessities of people's lives must be home-produced**,' said Lee. 'This will build domestic industries, provide a stable supply of inexpensive goods, and offer more jobs to people as well as contribute to the nation's technological development and expansion of industrial activities.'

Lee set out a **clear vision** of the contribution that corporations could, and should, make to the nation – perhaps because of his experience of Japanese rule, during which both capital and investment opportunities had been controlled by the colonial power. 'Companies make investments with the most reasonable combination of various production factors. In the process, they pay the price to the provider of material resources, ... wages to the provider of labour, interest or dividends to the provider of capital, tax to the nation for providing social stability and an investment environment, and use the remaining net profits [for] expansion of production.'

With **strategic investment from the government**, Samsung moved into almost every industry. Korea has few natural resources; the goal was to turn Korea into a factory producing goods for the Korean people and for the world. Lee stressed that his company's main resource was the **talent of its employees**.

In the course of the next three decades until Lee's death in 1987, Samsung moved into agrochemicals, paper, electronics, light engineering, heavy industries, ship building, semiconductors, chemicals, petrochemicals, hotels, retail and finance. Lee espoused three key business principles: **economic contribution to the nation, priority to human resources, and pursuit of rationality** (the need to address business decisions with logic and reason).

Lee invested heavily in **recruitment and training**. He put in place a structure that encouraged business units and even individual workers to take ownership of their business objectives and the means by which those objectives would be attained.

He later set out the four core principles that define the 'Samsung Spirit': **creation**, or entrepreneurship and innovation; **morality** – 'most important is the spirit of honesty'; **ambition** – the pursuit of perfection; and **coexistence** – the mutual prosperity of business, workforce, stakeholders and nation.

In practice

- 'Supply inexpensive goods, offer jobs to the people and contribute to the nation's technological development'

- 'A company is its people'

- Encourage colleagues to take ownership of objectives and means

- 'Creation, morality, ambition, coexistence'

BAIDU
Robin LI
1968–

Robin Li Yanhong left China to study in the USA in 1991. After earning his master's degree at the University of Buffalo, Li worked at IDD Information Services, a division of Dow Jones and Company, where he had a eureka moment. It occurred to him that a good measure of the usefulness of any piece of information was the number of times that the information was cited in other sources. In the language of the then rapidly growing Internet, this meant that the usefulness of a particular website could be gauged by the number of other sites linking in to it. In 1996, Li developed an algorithm based on hyperlinks that was used to develop a search engine for IDD called RankDex. Li also patented his 'link analysis' programme.

In a classic example of synchronicity, two PhD Students called Larry Page and Sergey Brin at Stanford University were working on the same concept. They were to cite RankDex as an example of qualitative search engine technology in their patent application for Google PageRank. Only a few years later, the search engine founded by Li, Baidu, would be fighting for dominance in China with Larry Page and Sergey Brin's Google.

The ideas

Robin Li was an **early evangelist** for the significance of search technologies; he felt that IDD had not grasped the full potential of his invention. 'The moment I created this thing I was very excited,' Li told the *New York Times* in 2006. 'I told my boss and pushed him, but he wasn't very excited.' Li paid for his own booth at a Silicon Valley computer conference to **demonstrate his search technology**. He was recruited by the new search engine operator Infoseek, who were the first search engine company to sell online advertising on a 'cost per thousand impressions' basis, and the first to develop behavioural targeting.

In 1998, Li's wife, Melissa, introduced her husband to a colleague of hers, Eric Xu. Xu was making a documentary about innovative American companies, and had arranged to interview Jerry Yang, the Taiwanese founder of Yahoo. Another interviewee for Xu's film was the Silicon Valley venture capitalist Bob King. Li was invited to sit in on the interviews. Xu says that both he and Li were **inspired by Yang's achievements**.

A return visit to China convinced Li that the internet was beginning to take hold in the country; he persuaded Xu that they should start a search company for the Chinese market. They approached Bob King with their business plan, and King and his partners put up $1.2 million of seed capital. Li and Xu returned to Beijing, renting one hotel room between them, and laboured on the development for the new search engine for a year, putting in **15-hour days** at a nearby office. Before the year was out, they had made sufficient progress to win a further $10 million of backing from two other U.S. venture capital firms.

The new company's first model was to **license their search index** to two of China's leading portal websites, following the model of Yahoo, whose search facility was initially supplied by a search company called Inktomi and would later be powered by Google, until 2004.

Li had been watching the development of the California-based internet company called Overture, who were using an **electronic bidding system** to control the price that advertisers paid to have their ads appear in conjunction with chosen key search words. Despite reservations from some of the original investors on the company's board, Li decided that search engines did not have to operate 'behind the scenes' making money from licensing. He launched baidu.com in September 2001.

The **'pay per click' model** was as big a success in China as it would be for Google in the U.S., who launched their own Adwords advertising programme in 2000. As internet use in China began to take off, traffic to the site and advertising revenues rocketed. Baidu became profitable in 2004, and in 2005 the company went public on NASDAQ. Shares were offered at $27 and closed on the first day of trading at $122, briefly valuing the company at $4 billion and making Li's shares worth $900 million. The company's late-2012 market valuation was around $35 billion and Li is listed by Forbes as **China's second-richest man**, with a wealth of some $8 billion.

Li fought off Google's attempt to challenge Baidu's supremacy in China, but sees no reason to limit the company's ambitions to China alone. 'I hope in ten years, Baidu will become a household name in 50 per cent of the world,' Li told *BusinessWeek* in 2010. 'Sooner or later you will see a China-based company that really has a global impact and I think Baidu has a chance to become one of those companies. We should be able to **compete on a global basis**.'

In practice

- If you believe you have made a breakthrough discovery, have faith in yourself

- Sell your idea to whoever will listen

- Be prepared for a spell of very hard graft

- Try to establish your brand in the public eye, not behind the scenes

- Don't be daunted by major competitors

- Think globally

HUTCHISON WHAMPOA
LI Ka-shing
1928–

ASIA'S RICHEST MAN, Li Ka-shing, built Hutchison Whampoa into a major investment holding company, with interests in ports, property, energy, retail and telecoms. Li has been referred to as 'superman' because of his knack of buying and selling assets advantageously: Hutchison Whampoa made profits of more than $15 billion in 2001 when it sold its interests in the Orange mobile network in Europe to Mannesman; in 2007 Hutchison Telecoms sold its controlling share in India mobile operator Hutchison-Essar to Vodaphone, realising a profit of around $9 billion.

Via his investment company, Horizon, Li became a major investor in high technology. He is a fan of what he sees as 'disruptive technologies': he was an early investor in Facebook and in Skype, in the days when Skype was losing money and before it was bought by eBay for $2.5 billion. He invested in the artificial intelligence and voice recognition system Siri before it was bought by Apple, and is a backer of digital music service Spotify. 'Making a business from these investments is secondary,' Li told *Forbes* magazine. 'It is more important that we are learning so much.'

The ideas

Li Ka-shing grew up in Chaozhou, in China's Guangdong Province, not far from Hong Kong. While Li was still at elementary school, Japan invaded China. Chaozhou was bombed; the family fled to Hong Kong, then a British colony (though Hong Kong was occupied by the Japanese from 1941 until Japan's defeat at the end of WWII). Li's father, a primary school headmaster, had fallen ill with tuberculosis and the family could not afford to send Li to school; at the age of 12,

Li started work at a factory making plastic watch straps. Two years later, he went to work for a plastics trading company.

Three years after the move to Hong Kong, his father died. 'The most terrible experience during my childhood,' Li told *Forbes*. 'The **burden of poverty** and this bitter taste of helplessness and isolation sort of branded on my heart forever the questions that still drive me. Is it possible to **reshape one's destiny?** Is it possible to minimise challenges through lessening complexities? And is it possible to enhance chances for success through meticulous planning?'

Li set about trying to control his own destiny. In 1950, having saved and borrowed $8,700, he started his own plastics company. He read in a trade journal that plastic flowers were very popular in Italy, and retooled his factory to manufacture them, preparing diligently for a visit from a large overseas purchaser. Li got the contract. He went on to become the **largest manufacturer of plastic flowers** in Asia.

By 1958, unable to renew the lease on his factory, Li bought and **developed his own site**. During the 1967 riots brought on by Mao Zedong's Cultural Revolution in mainland China, Li **bought up property** in Hong Kong at rock-bottom prices, making a killing when the market recovered.

By 1979, Li's Cheung Kong (Yangtze River) company was able to buy a controlling share in Hutchison Whampoa, which had been created in 1977 from the merger of Hutchison International trading company and the Hong Kong and Whampoa Dock, both founded in the nineteenth century by the British merchant, John Hutchison.

Li turned Hutchison Whampoa into an investment holding company. If his investments lose money, Li covers this personally; if they are successful, he **hands the shares to his philanthropic foundation**, which Li describes as his 'third son' – Li has two sons, Victor, who is generally seen as Li's heir apparent, and Richard, who runs his own investment company. In 2006, Li pledged to give one-third of his fortune to the foundation, which has an especial interest in education.

Li told the *Wall Street Journal* in an interview about his philanthropic interests that, following the death of his father, 'I realised that when you are less fortunate how much support you need. So when I started my own business in 1950, I tried to spend money to **help the poor**.'

Li's business advice to his sons was straightforward: always **leave something on the table** for the other side of a deal, because you want them to come back for deals in the future, and – in an echo of the young Li's determination to 'enhance chances for success through meticulous planning' – that the secret of success lies in **careful planning**, **brilliant execution** and a clear **analysis of the downside risk**. 'For a young entrepreneur today,' Li told *Forbes*, 'hard work is more important than opportunities. If you don't work hard, opportunities will slip away.'

In practice

- Plan for the future; seize opportunities
- Prepare meticulously, execute brilliantly, and always analyse the downside
- Leave something on the table for the other side
- Explore disruptive technologies
- 'If you don't work hard, opportunities will slip away'

LENOVO GROUP
LIU Chuanzhi
1944–

LIU CHUANZHI IS THE co-founder of Lenovo Group Ltd, currently the world's second largest manufacturer of personal computers after Hewlett-Packard.

Liu studied radar systems and gained an introduction to computing at the Xi'an Military Electronic Engineering Institute, graduating in 1966. He went to work for the Chinese Academy of Science, but was sent to work on state farms during the Cultural Revolution for political re-education along with many other 'intellectuals.' He returned to computer-related research at the Academy, and, when the market reforms of the 1980s began to take effect, was given a government loan to start a business bringing electronics products to the Chinese market. The tiny business, originally named Legend, went on to become the leading manufacturer of personal computers in China and Asia, outselling any overseas brand.

In 2005, the company acquired IBM's personal computer division – the first-ever takeover of an American company by a Chinese company.

The ideas

Although the new electronics company was a state-owned enterprise, Liu structured it **as if it were a private company**, giving him the ability to raise capital, choose his own employees and set wage rates and bonuses. 'The country's leaders called for the conversion of research and development results into **products that could be marketed**,' Liu told *McKinsey Quarterly*. 'I was excited about doing this type of work, but most people didn't understand it. Chinese people put scientific work on a pedestal, while commercial activities were looked down upon.'

Liu and his team of researchers built a formidable business despite their lack of experience – largely, at Liu's own admission, by **trial and error**. At first, the company imported and distributed foreign-manufactured electronics goods, especially computers and peripherals. When the company decided to manufacture its own computers, it was forced to relocate to Hong Kong because the

Chinese government would not grant it the necessary manufacturing licence for the mainland.

Once it proved its capabilities in Hong Kong, the company was granted a licence to manufacture in mainland China in 1990. In the same year, China reduced import tariffs and Legend found itself **competing with the global brands** that it had studied and, in some cases, emulated: 'Our earliest and best teacher was Hewlett-Packard,' Liu told *The Economist* in 2001. 'It was as HP's distributor that we learned ... how to organise sales channels and how to market.'

In 1994, Legend went public on the Hong Kong exchange. When the company moved into international markets, it was renamed Lenovo.

Lenovo's 2005 acquisition of IBM's personal computer division made the company the third-biggest PC manufacturer in the world, but **merging the management cultures** of the two companies proved difficult. Lenovo's share price fell; then came the collapse of Lehman Brothers in September 2008 and the start of the financial crisis. Lenovo's share price dropped from $22.50 in October 2007 to $5.50 in December 2008; the company recorded a loss of almost $97 million in its third quarter.

Liu had stepped down as chairman in 2005, but resumed the role after the financial crisis, guiding the company to recovery. He found the company's previous decision-making process to be less collective than the Chinese model and that there was a culture of over-promising on targets and failing to deliver. Lenovo's company motto is now **'We do what we say and we own what we do.'**

Liu talks of 'The Lenovo Way' in what seems a clear echo of Hewlett-Packard's 'The HP Way.' The company's new top leadership team represent what Liu calls **'a blending of talent from East and West.'** 'The key or essential part of our core values is to put people first,' said Liu in an interview with knowledge@wharton. 'We need to make sure our employees love this company. And when we are successful, we need to **give back to our employees** with incentives and rewards.'

In practice

- If an opportunity exists, acquire the necessary skills, knowledge and talent

- Study the competition; adopt best practices

- Be bold: people do not know your capabilities as well as you do

- Have faith in your own way of doing things

- Don't allow over-promising; encourage realistic and collective decision-making

- Put people first; give back to employees

NEW HOPE
LIU Yonghao
1951–

DURING CHINA'S CULTURAL REVOLUTION, Liu Yonghao raised pigs in Sichuan. Afterwards, he attended a technical college and was assigned by the state to teach electronics. His salary in 1979 was 38.50 yuan per month – about $25 at 1979 prices. As Liu said to *Asiamoney* in 1999, 'I thought it should be more.'

Encouraged by Deng Xiaoping's movement of 'Reform and Opening Up,' Liu and his brothers sold their bicycles and watches, borrowed from their family and pooled their savings to scrape together 1,000 yuan to start a small livestock business. Recognising that almost every small farmer in Sichuan raised an animal or two – typically pigs, fed on food scraps – Liu started to supply scientifically formulated feedstuffs, marketing direct to small farmers under the company name of Hope.

In 1995, the brothers split the company into four parts. Liu developed New Hope, growing vegetables on an industrial scale on previously unproductive land for export and use in processed foods, and investing in slaughterhouses and food processing plants. Since then, New Hope Group has become one of China's largest private companies, and made Liu one of the country's richest citizens.

The ideas

After the company's early success raising and selling livestock, Liu's idea of moving into animal feedstuffs raised the company's scale and profile dramatically. To **circumvent state regulations** that restricted private enterprises to a maximum of eight employees, Liu argued that the company was involved in 'science and technology,' gaining an exemption.

Liu hired scientists to create **nutritionally balanced feedstuffs** and **promoted these to farmers** with messages posted on farm gates and the walls of buildings in villages: 'If you want to get rich raising livestock, Hope will help you.' 'If it eats one kilo of Hope feed, your pig will grow by two.'

By the late 1990s, according to *The Economist*, Hope had 60 manufacturing plants, 10,000 full-time employees, 90,000 sales agents and sales of over one billion yuan (about $120 million at late-1990s exchange rates).

In 1995, the company was split into four subsidiaries and Liu took charge of New Hope Group. The company began to integrate its food production operations **'from feed to fork.'** The company claims to be China's leading animal feed producer, has leading positions in poultry and pig processing, and owns the largest dairy operation in southwest China, making it one of the country's **leading suppliers of meat, eggs and dairy produce** at a time when consumption of these food items is rising rapidly.

New Hope became the largest shareholder in China's first privately owned bank, Minsheng; the company further **diversified** into chemicals and real estate.

Liu aims to improve the scale of China's food production by offering **financial and technological support** to small farmers and local cooperatives, making money through the supply of feedstuffs and financial services and by buying back mature animals for processing. The company now also owns its own **branded consumer food lines**.

Liu set up his first overseas plant in Vietnam, in 1999, and has expanded his overseas operations to Bangladesh, the Philippines and Indonesia. His goal is to grow New Hope into a **global player in agribusiness**. 'Profit margins in agriculture are thin and it takes a long time to get the payback,' Liu told *Forbes* magazine in 2005, 'but if you have scale, you can make money.'

'A single farmer works on a small farm with his family, and might raise a cow or a pig pretty much in the same way that people did 1,000 years ago,' Liu told *Forbes* in 2005, noting that half of China's pigs were born on farms raising five pigs or fewer. **'You can't have a modern industry with that.'**

In practice

- Develop a product from which many people can benefit

- Grow your business by helping others grow theirs

- Add value; diversify

- Scale up

- Integrate vertically ('from feed to fork')

HYFLUX
Olivia LUM
1961–

OLIVIA LUM'S RAGS-TO-RICHES STORY is the real thing. Abandoned as a baby at a hospital in Perak, Malaysia, she was adopted, along with four other children, by a woman she called 'grandmother' – a devoted carer but also a compulsive gambler whose debts forced the family to leave their house and move into a tin-roofed hut.

Adversity seemed to bring out the best in Lum. Having become the family's sole breadwinner at the age of nine, she was earning enough money by the time she was 12 via an array of odd jobs to move the family into better housing. Lum paid her own way through school, college and university, earning a degree in chemistry and landing a well-paid job as a laboratory technician with Glaxo Pharmaceuticals. After three years with Glaxo, she sold her car and her apartment to raise the seed capital for her own water-treatment business. Lum then built her tiny company, Hyflux, into a global water treatment empire.

The ideas

Given her troubled background, Olivia Lum's first job out of university with Glaxo Pharmaceuticals might have been considered a sufficient achievement. The enterprising Lum saw things differently. Singapore is a city thirsty for water. Lum also noticed that Glaxo had problems dealing with their industrial waste water. She felt that there was money in water treatment. In 1989, after three years with Glaxo, she handed in her notice, **sold her car and her apartment** to raise S\$20,000 and launched a company called Hydrochem, selling water filters and softeners, employing an office administrator and a technician and travelling around Singapore and Malaysia on a motorbike, selling her wares.

After three years, she **moved into manufacture**, creating her own treatment systems based on membrane filtration; the company name changed to Hyflux. Lum took a **course in welding** to enable her to build her first systems, and **won a contract** for a water treatment system at Singapore's Bird Zoo, steadily growing the business with more and larger projects.

She started to win projects in China, where her **Mandarin gave her an advantage** over many larger Western or Japanese concerns. Chinese project managers were also impressed that, if there was a problem with their system, Lum would fly over at short notice from Singapore and, with her welding skills and intimate knowledge of her systems, **fix it herself**.

In 2001, Hyflux went public on the Singapore Stock Exchange. The company now offers a **complete range of water technology solutions**, especially desalination and waste water treatment. It has built projects around Southeast Asia, in China, Algeria and the Middle East. The major desalination plant that Hyflux built in Singapore supplies ten per cent of the republic's fresh water.

The company is spending eight per cent of revenues on research to develop its own technologies, which include products such as a water dispenser that creates **drinkable water from the moisture content of the surrounding air**, purifying it with filters and UV light.

Lum is known to her colleagues as '**The Pressure Cooker**'; Hyflux emails are not allowed to contain the words 'urgent' or 'important' – **everything is urgent and important**.

Lum's defining characteristic is probably her relentless drive to succeed. In the days when she was riding around Malaysia visiting factory after factory in search of new business, Lum would brace herself to the task each morning with a little mantra: 'Today is the day that there will be better opportunities.'

For her efforts, Lum was the first woman to be awarded Businessman of the Year in the Singapore Business Awards of 2004, and the first woman to enter the top 40 Forbes Southeast Asia Rich List the following year. In 2011, Lum was Ernst and Young's World Entrepreneur of the Year.

In practice

- Keep looking for new opportunities

- Acquire skills that allow you to be self-reliant

- Be your own salesperson

- Develop your own technologies

- 'Everything is urgent'

TENCENT
MA Huateng
1971–

MA HUATENG WAS WORKING in the paging division of the telecoms company China Motion in Shenzhen when he was sent on a training course to Florida. There, he found himself in the middle of an explosion of internet technologies, including the instant messaging system ICQ.

When he returned to Shenzhen, Ma left his job and, with the support of his family and the help of four friends, set out to launch an instant messaging system in China. The new company, established in November 1998, was called Tencent, a westernised version of *Tengxun*, which translates as 'galloping message.' The founders hoped to develop an internet-based system that would work with China Motion's paging technology, and then sell the idea to China Motion, or to other parties.

The product, launched in February 1999, was named OICQ, in an unabashed reference to the ICQ technology on which their messaging system was based. It attracted 50,000 users in its first year.

The ideas

The launch of OICQ required funding. Local banks did not see OICQ's user base as an asset against which they could lend money. Tencent then sought outside investors, one of whom offered 600,000 yuan (about $72,500) to buy the technology. Ma held out for one million yuan. 'Fortunately, we failed to reach an agreement,' said Ma. In late 1999, with the internet industry worldwide booming, Ma found **venture capital funding**: $1.1 million from IDG Ventures, one of the first Western investment firms in China, and another $1.1 million from Hong Kong-based PCCW.

In 2000, OICQ was renamed QQ. The company faced competition from Microsoft's Mandarin version of its popular MSN Messenger service, and from other major China internet players, such as the successful portals Sina.com and Sohu.com and the e-business group Alibaba.

Tencent launched its own portal, QQ.com, and began to **sell virtual goods** to its burgeoning user base – especially customised avatars for customers to use as their instant messaging personas. **Ad revenues** and virtual goods sales began to take off. In June 2004, the company launched on the Hong Kong Stock Exchange, raising $200 million. 'This is just the beginning,' said Ma. He was right.

In 2005, Tencent began to generate revenues from its QQ Mobile service. Its cute scarf-wearing, winking Penguin logo became so popular that it began to earn money through **licensing**.

The company moved into **online games**, initially with chess and card games but soon licensing and adapting South Korean-developed games such as Cross Fire and Dungeon & Fighter, promoting the games via its still-growing QQ user base (up to ten million peak simultaneous users by 2005).

Tencent moved into **other internet platforms**: a social networking site, QZone; a consumer-to-consumer auction site, PaiPai; on online payment system, TenPay. The company originally partnered with Google for its search engine, but also began developing its own; in 2005 Tencent switched to its own search engine, SOSO, soon also switching to its own advertising platform and mobile platform. The company had made the right call: Google pulled out of China in 2010.

In 2007, Tencent invested over 100 million yuan (c. $13 million in 2007) in a major **internet research facility**, China's first. In 2010, the company launched a Twitter-like service called Tencent Weibo ('microblog' in Mandarin) in competition with Sina Weibo.

Tencent is now one of the **world's major internet companies**. Its dominant position in China has brought it into conflict with other internet operations. In a 2010 interview with *Corporation* magazine, Ma was asked to comment on the perception that Tencent's huge user base made the company too powerful. 'What are we suppose to do about that?' replied Ma. 'Our users like our product. There's nothing we can do about it.'

In practice

- Don't accept early offers that undervalue your idea
- Be inventive (sales of virtual goods were significant)
- Don't be afraid of major competitors
- Develop your own technologies
- Diversify to compete on many fronts

ALIBABA
Jack MA
1964–

JACK MA WENT FROM being an English teacher at a university in the city of Hangzhou, on the Yangtze River delta, to founding China's largest ecommerce network, making him a billionaire and one of the richest men in China.

Ma launched Alibaba.com in 1999 as a free listing service for Chinese manufacturers looking for overseas buyers. When venture capital funding was put in place in 2002, the website started to charge sellers to place their listings on the site. Ma wasn't particularly happy; he was more interested in attracting large numbers of users.

In 2003, he launched Taobao Marketplace in response to eBay's entry in the China market. This time, Ma would not be deflected from his 'free' model.

The ideas

In 1999, Ma invited 17 people to his apartment and set out his vision of a new Chinese ecommerce website. The group 'put their money on the table' and Alibaba started business with $60,000, encouraging Chinese businesses to **offer products online for overseas buyers**. The following year, Goldman Sachs put in $4 million for a 23 per cent stake. With money running out in 2002 as Ma pursued his 'free' model, Goldman Sachs, Fidelity Investments and Japan's Softbank put in £$25 million and persuaded Ma to 'monetise' the operation. By 2011, according to *Forbes*, Alibaba had 18 million registered users in its international English-language site and 44 million B2B users in China, most of them promoting Chinese-made products.

Ma went on to launch the Taobao retail outlet, in answer to eBay's entry in the China market, and later TMall, an outlet for brand-name goods. Taobao ('digging for treasure') was designed to help individual entrepreneurs and small businesses to **open up a retail outlet on the internet**.

Ma refused to be daunted by the clout of his **giant competitor**: 'eBay may be a shark in the ocean, but I am a crocodile in the Yangtze River. If we fight in the ocean, we lose – but if we fight in the river, we win.' Ma's understanding of the Chinese market allowed him to **outmanoeuvre eBay's 'EachNet' China venture**; Taobao offered its users the opportunity to post photographs and personal details, to exchange instant messages and voicemail, establishing trust in the new and nervous online marketplace. Ma also introduced the online payment service, Alipay, which held back payments until buyers had received and approved goods.

By 2006, Taobao had 67 per cent of China's consumer-to-consumer online user market, to EachNet's 29 per cent; **eBay withdrew from the China online auction market**. The crocodile had eaten the shark.

Taobao has been 'named and shamed' by the U.S. government as being a significant outlet for counterfeit brands, though the U.S. Trade Representative has since acknowledged Taobao's 'significant efforts' – which include an **anti-counterfeiting team** of 400 people – to take down pages offering fake products.

Closer to home, Taobao's sales team were accused of offering 'Gold Supplier' status to fraudulent sellers. Two senior executives' resignations were called for, though they were not accused of any personal wrongdoing, as Ma sought to **retain his organisation's essential trust**.

In 2005, Yahoo invested $1 billion for a 40 per cent stake in Alibaba, also giving the group control of internet search platform China Yahoo, which was not a success. The American company's stake in Alibaba became one of its most significant assets. In 2012, Alibaba bought back half of Yahoo's 40 per cent stake for $7.1 billion, valuing Alibaba at around $35 billion. The company also **re-privatised** Alibaba.com.

Ma has **big plans** for what he still hopes to achieve, both for his enterprise and for his country. His goal is to help ten million companies to start doing business online, to create ten million new jobs and to serve a billion customers worldwide.

In practice

- See new opportunities; launch new ventures

- Challenge major competitors; 'the crocodile can eat the shark'

- Take firm action to maintain trust

- Help other companies do business; create jobs and wealth

WHOLE FOODS MARKET
John MACKEY
1953–

IN THE 1970S, JOHN MACKEY joined a vegetarian collective in Austin, Texas, and later opened a store that would lead to the Whole Foods Market health-food supermarket chain.

According to his philosophy of 'conscious capitalism,' companies should decide on their higher purpose – why they exist and what they are trying to accomplish. The higher purpose may be as simple as offering a service or benefit to others, advancing human knowledge, or creating beauty and excellence.

Mackey believed at first that his company's higher purpose lay in delivering excellence. 'I actually thought we were in some variant of service – that it was really about fulfilling the good,' Mackey told *Harvard Business Review*. 'The team members consistently told me I was wrong, that we had a different purpose. It was this more heroic purpose [of trying to change the world].'

The ideas

Mackey studied at Trinity College in San Antonio and the University of Texas, Austin. He drifted between the two, studying only the courses that interested him – especially philosophy and religion – and never acquired a degree. He **joined a vegetarian collective** in Austin because he hoped he would 'meet a lot of interesting women,' and became the food buyer for the collective.

In 1980, Mackey and his girlfriend teamed up with the two owners of the Clarksville Natural Grocery store to open a 10,500-square-foot store called Whole Foods Market – one of only a handful of **health-food supermarkets** in the U.S. at the time, and an immediate success. New stores were opened in Houston, Dallas, New Orleans and then on the West Coast, in Palo Alto.

In the 1990s, the company fuelled rapid growth by **acquiring other health-food chains** around the country. In 2001, the company opened its first store in Manhattan, New York, followed by stores in Canada and the United Kingdom. In 2005, Whole Foods Market entered the Fortune 500 list of top U.S. public corporations; in 2011, revenues were $9 billion; and as of July 2012, the chain had 331 stores.

Whole Foods Market aims to offer a range of **healthier**, more **environmentally sustainable** and more **animal-friendly** products. The company labels its meat products to show the animal welfare practices of its suppliers, and is committed to selling sustainable seafood. As Mackey told the *Harvard Business Review*, 'You're either committed to sustainability or you're not ... Sometimes that means you do things that might **hurt you in the short term** but will **underscore your integrity** as an organisation.'

Mackey argues that when an organisation's higher purpose is fully understood, a harmony of interests exists in the actions of every involved party: Whole Foods Market wants **staff to be well-informed** and happy in their work, because this makes for loyal customers;

customers would not be happy if the chain offered products that violated its principles, so the company must find suppliers whose products result from sustainable and low-impact farming practices offering high standards of animal welfare; this improves the environment, from which society at large benefits. Each partner enters into these contracts willingly because they benefit in both the short and the long term.

Whole Foods Market employees are given a **high degree of autonomy** in choosing, within the company's overarching guidelines, what their own store should stock. Stores are divided into teams, which are **rewarded by profitability**; teams meet regularly to reach consensus on decisions; profit and reward statements are available for all to see. Even hiring decisions are **made by consensus**: new recruits join a team and, after a trial period, a vote decides whether the new member stays with the team; a two-thirds majority is needed.

The company's adherence to its core principles is the best guarantee of financial success and shareholder value. 'I actually don't think trying to maximise profits is a very good long-term strategy for a business,' Mackey told *Harvard Business Review*. 'It doesn't inspire the people who work for you. It doesn't lead to that **higher creativity**.'

In practice

- Anticipate consumer movements
- Scale up a successful model
- Devolve decision-making ; give more autonomy to those closest to the customer
- Decide on your organisations' 'higher purpose,' which should define your relationships with customers and suppliers

56

MAHINDRA & MAHINDRA
Anand MAHINDRA
1955–

ANAND MAHINDRA'S GRANDFATHER, K.C. Mahindra, co-founded the steel trading company of Mahindra & Mohammad in 1945 with his brother J.C Mahindra and Ghulam Mohammad. Following the independence and partition of India in 1947, Mohammad left the company to become the first finance minister of the new nation of Pakistan, and the two brothers renamed their company Mahindra & Mahindra.

Their steel company moved into manufacturing by acquiring the licence to assemble the iconic WWII Willys Jeep for the Indian market. In 1963, the company entered a joint venture with International Harvester to form the International Tractor Company of India. The partnership came to an end in 1971, and the company merged back with Mahindra & Mahindra. The company diversified into many areas, including finance, technology, energy and defence, but it was by positioning the company as a global player in vehicle manufacture that Anand Mahindra made his most prominent mark on the company.

The ideas

At the beginning of the 1990s, India faced a balance of payments crisis. It received a bailout from the International Monetary Fund, a condition of which was the liberalisation of the Indian economy. A raft of measures introduced in 1991 included the opening up of India to overseas trade and investment, privatisation, deregulation measures and tax reforms.

Mahindra decided that the family group had to **redefine its work culture**, or be left behind as the country faced new, international competition. He had moved to Mahindra & Mahindra from Mahindra Ugine Steel, where **the unions had negotiated a 'workload' system**: once the agreed number of units was completed each day, work stopped; workers played cards or slept for the rest of their shift.

In 1991, Mahindra announced that the bonuses traditionally given at the time of the autumn festival of Diwali would be **linked to productivity**. The workforce demonstrated; Mahindra and the management team found themselves trapped in their offices by angry workers. After three hours, Mahindra went out to talk to the workforce. They heard him out. 'I said there were going to be no more free lunches. I told them change was going to happen.'

Change did happen. Under the old workload system, a workforce of over 1,200 produced the agreed 70 engines per day. By 1994, 760 workers could produce 125 engines per day.

Mahindra set out to **globalise the company**, competing with the world's major automotive manufacturers. In 1995, the company joined a 50/50 venture with Ford Motor Company to create Mahindra Ford India Ltd. The venture was not a complete success: the first product, the Ford Escort, sold poorly and was discontinued after five years. Mahindra gave over control of the venture to Ford, which increased its share of the venture in 1998 to 72 per cent and renamed the company Ford India Private Ltd. Mahindra saw the exercise as an **invaluable learning curve** in modern motor manufacture.

He conceived an ambitious project for M&M: to manufacture its own Sports Utility Vehicle (SUV) in India and launch it onto the global market. Using its strengths in vehicle assembly, the company contracted with suppliers to design, manufacture test and supply the major components of the car to given specifications, **abandoning the accepted practice** by which automotive manufacturers design and engineer every element of a new vehicle, at great expense. The Scorpio was brought to market at a total cost of $120 million, perhaps one-fifth of what a U.S. manufacturer would expect to invest in a new vehicle. It became one of India's leading SUVs, and was exported around the world.

Mahindra embarked on a series of **acquisitions and mergers**. In 2007 M&M merged with Punjab Tractors, doubling its share of the India tractor market and becoming a leading global player; and in 2010 it bought a 70 per cent stake in South Korea's Ssangyong Motor Company, giving the company access to distribution networks in Latin America, Europe and Russia.

In practice

- Challenge outdated working practices
- Form partnerships; learn from the experience
- Use radical new solutions
- Establish global networks
- 'Accept no limits; think alternatively; drive positive change'

PORO
Annie Turnbo MALONE
1869–1957

ANNIE TURNBO MALONE was an early black American entrepreneur and innovator. The daughter of former slaves, she developed a range of hair-care products for black American women, and, since black businesspeople were unable to get distribution through the normal retail channels, pioneered a method of direct selling via a network of agents. Malone's success made her a multimillionaire.

Malone's fortune was dissipated by a divorce settlement, a lawsuit from a former employee and demands from the U.S. government for unpaid excise taxes (hair-care products were subject to a 20 per cent 'luxuries' tax). Malone lost her business and has been eclipsed in history by her previous employee, Madame C.J. Walker – who created (and kept) her own hair care business serving a generation of aspiring African Americans – but it was Malone who blazed the trail. Before her fortune was lost, she gave generously to a range of charitable causes, especially those concerned with the advancement of African Americans.

The ideas

Annie Malone was born in Metropolis four years after the end of the American Civil War. Her parents died when she was young and she was brought up by an older sister. At a time when few houses had indoor plumbing, hair care was rudimentary and scalp diseases were common. Methods for straightening the hair of African Americans were also unsophisticated (goose fat and heavy oils were commonly used); chemical straighteners were harsh and damaging.

Malone developed a **chemical method for straightening hair** without damage, and a range of hair care products including a 'Wonderful Hair Grower.' She sold her products locally, on a small scale.

In 1902, Malone moved to St Louis, Missouri, a city with a large African American population, and sold her products **door to door**, employing three assistants and using **free sampling** to drive sales. In 1904, the year St Louis hosted a World Fair, she opened her **own store** in Market Street.

A favourable response gave Malone the confidence to promote her products on a national scale. She **advertised in newspapers for the black community** and travelled widely through America's southern states, at a time when racial discrimination and racial violence were endemic, building up a **network of sales agents** throughout the black community. A career as a sales agent for Malone allowed many black women to build their own businesses and achieve economic independence.

When one of her agents, Sarah Breedlove (who was also the daughter of former slaves), set up her own hair business and promoted her own 'Wonderful Hair Grower' and other products, using her married name of Madame C.J. Walker, Malone **created the Poro trademark**.

In 1918, she created a Poro College – a **training school** for sales agents, a **research and manufacturing plant** and a **social centre for African Americans** at a time when discrimination denied them access to many forms of public entertainment. In the 1920s, Poro College employed 175 people, while franchised outlets in the Americas, Africa and the Philippines employed some 75,000, mainly black women.

In practice

- Create a good product

- Sell it however you can

- Consider building a network of sales agents

- Identify with your core users

- Invest in research and training

- Build like-minded communities

MARKS & SPENCER
Michael MARKS
1859–1907

WHEN A WAVE OF anti-Jewish riots broke out in southwestern imperial Russia in 1881, Michael Marks, then in his early twenties, fled his country for England. He hoped to find work in the factories of Sir John Barran, a clothing manufacturer in Leeds, an important centre of Britain's Industrial Revolution. Word had spread through the Jewish community that Barran was happy to employ refugees from Eastern Europe. Barran was an early pioneer in the manufacture of ready-to-wear clothing – before the late nineteenth century, wealthier people had their clothes made by tailors; working people made their own clothes or paid a local seamstress. A revolution in the way in which people bought clothes was about to start – and Michael Marks was about to play a part in it.

The ideas

Having arrived, penniless, in northern England, Marks never did get to work in the factories of John Barran. He first approached Isaac Dewhirst, a prominent Leeds wholesale clothier and haberdasher, looking to buy goods to sell as a **travelling peddler**. Dewhirst loaned Mark £5 to buy items from his warehouse.

Marks **opened a stall at the open market** in Leeds. This market was open on Tuesdays and Saturdays; he opened other stalls in other northern towns with different market days, and one in the covered market in Leeds, which was open all week. Marks offered products at a range of prices, but soon found that the cheapest 'penny' items sold best.

Marks's slogan became 'Don't ask the price, it's a penny.' He started to open his **'penny bazaars'** in the cotton towns of northern England, recruiting staff to run his stalls while he focused on buying and distribution. To increase the range of items on offer, he moved beyond clothing, into household goods, toys and stationery.

By the time he opened stores in Bolton (1892) and Manchester (1894), it was clear that Marks **could no longer run the operation on his own**. He approached his original benefactor, Dewhirst, for investment. Dewhirst declined – a bad investment decision – but recommended his financial manager, Thomas Spencer, who had accumulated some capital and was looking for a suitable venture.

Michael Marks and Thomas Spencer put up £300 of share capital each to establish Marks and Spencer in 1894. By 1900, the company had 36 penny bazaars and 12 high street stores. When the firm **went public** in 1902 and Spencer retired, his £300 investment was worth £15,000.

The Marks and Spencer chain went on to become one of Britain's major retailers. Marks's son Simon carried on the family business. In 1928, he introduced the St Michael brand of clothing and food (all, at that time, sourced only from British suppliers) in honour of his father. Several generations of Britons wore shirts, skirts, trousers, jumpers, jackets, coats and underwear bearing the St Michael logo. Michael Marks would have been surprised at the extent to which he had fulfilled the vision of Sir John Barran – the industrialist who welcomed refugees and at whose factories Marks never did get to work – by supplying **affordable, ready-made clothes** for the nation.

In practice

- Start small; work hard; get bigger
- Establish a core value position ('Don't ask the price, it's a penny')
- Expand your range
- Raise investment; grow the business
- Spot consumer trends

PANASONIC
Konosuke MATSUSHITA
1894–1989

IN FEBRUARY 1962, Konosuke Matsushita appeared on the cover of *Time* magazine; the cover story described the emergence of Japan as one of the world's great industrial powers, and attributed the new-found affluence of the nation's citizens to the well-paid jobs in the factories of manufacturers such as Matsushita.

Matsushita must have been proud to see the recognition of his lifelong commitment to affordable quality, but prouder still to read the acknowledgment of Japan's new middle class. As early as 1931, the young consumer goods entrepreneur had realised the true purpose of his company. 'Our mission as a manufacturer,' he said, 'is to create material abundance by providing goods as plentifully and inexpensively as tap water. This is how we can banish poverty, bring happiness to people's lives, and make this world a better place.'

The ideas

At the age of 15, Matsushita took a job at the new Osaka Electric Light Company. Electric power was arriving in Japan, and Matsushita **recognised the future** when he saw it. He was given a managerial role at the age of 22, but became dissatisfied when his supervisor showed no interest in a new electrical socket that he had designed.

He resigned to set up his own business with two colleagues from the Osaka Electric Light Company and his wife's brother, working out of the family's small tenement. Matsushita's electrical sockets did not sell well; his previous colleagues left the company. Bankruptcy loomed. The company was saved by **an unexpected order**: 1,000 insulator plates for electric fans. Konosuke was back in business. Sales of his electrical socket began to pick up; he designed a new, successful, two-way socket. By 1922, he could afford a new factory and office. One of his first designs was **a battery-powered bicycle lamp** that could run for up to 40 hours – ten times longer than other battery lamps.

Early electrical goods were expensive, and Matsushita believed that people would buy them in **large quantities if the price was low enough**. He designed and developed a new electric iron, manufacturing an unprecedented 10,000 per month to drive the price down to just over three yen, at a time when most irons sold at five yen. The company also started to manufacture radios and a wide range of lighting and electrical products.

One day, sometime in the 1930s, Matsushita watched a vagrant drinking water from a tap outside a house, and realised that no one would mind. 'Even though the water was processed and distributed,' he recalled, 'it was so cheap that it didn't matter. I began to think about abundance, and I decided that the mission of the industrialist is to **fill the world with products** and eliminate wants.' By 1933, the company had relocated to Kadoma, near Osaka, and had over 200 product lines.

The company, along with most of Japan's industrial base, was virtually destroyed during WWII, losing 32 factories and offices, though the Kadoma complex survived. The new occupying government set out to break up Japan's imperial era *zaibatsu* – family-owned monopolies that had controlled much of the country's economy since the nineteenth century. Matsushita **spent three years appealing** to have his name removed from the list of company owners whose businesses were due for enforced 'de-concentration.' When it was ordered that Konosuke should step down as president of Matsushita, 15,000 employees successfully petitioned Allied General Headquarters, arguing that he was essential for the company's reconstruction. The company was finally released from the last of its post-war restrictions in 1950.

Matsushita then positioned the company for **international expansion**, forming a partnership with Philips, the Dutch multinational, to benefit from more advanced technologies, and visiting the United States to **set up dealerships**.

Japan's economy started to boom, and electrical goods, from rice cookers to televisions, became essential purchases. Matsushita became the **country's biggest advertiser**. In 1956, Matsushita announced an ambitious five year plan, calling for a **quadrupling of sales**. Matsushita's growing reputation for high quality electrical products drove exports, particularly of televisions, under the Panasonic brand; the company became one of the **world's largest manufacturers of electrical goods**.

In practice

- Get experience in the latest technology
- Have faith in your own ideas: set up your own business
- Innovative products can become mass-market products at the right price
- Form alliances with companies you can learn from
- Think globally; set ambitious goals

BIOCON
Kiran MAZUMDAR-SHAW
1953–

KIRAN MAZUMDAR-SHAW WANTED TO be a brewer, like her father. She earned a brewmaster's post-graduate qualification at Australia's University of Ballarat, becoming India's first master brewer, but getting employment as a woman master brewer in India in the

1970s proved difficult. As she told *Business Today* in 2011, potential employers argued that she would face insurmountable problems: 'The words were: "You're a woman. It's difficult for a woman to deal with labour unions. You are high-risk. Can you command the respect of your male colleagues?"'

Mazumdar-Shaw decided to look for work in other countries and happened to meet an Irish entrepreneur called Les Auchincloss. He convinced her to start up an Indian division of his biotechnology company. Biocon eventually developed into one of India's leading pharmaceutical companies, employing nearly 6,000 staff, of whom nearly 40 per cent are women. Biocon is currently helping to reverse the 'brain drain' of scientists from India to other countries.

The ideas

Having agreed to launch Biocon in India, Mazumdar-Shaw's **attempts to raise finance for the new venture failed**. Biotechnology was in its infancy; she had no business experience; and she was a woman. She launched the company in 1978 from the garage of her rented house, with a bank overdraft of 10,000 rupees – around $7,000 in 2011. Even then, the bank wanted her father to guarantee the loan. Being the managing director of her new company, Mazumdar-Shaw refused, as a matter of principle. By chance, she met the general manager of the bank at a friend's wedding reception and aired her grievances. Company MDs were typically the guarantors of company loans – why was she different? The next day her loan was approved.

Biocon India's first product was an enzyme derived from papaya fruit and used to remove cloudiness from beer in the brewing process. Biocon began to establish itself as a **supplier of enzymes** for industrial processes in brewing, textiles, animal feeds and other industries.

In the mid-1980s, the company got funding from ICICI Bank to build a fermentation plant, which became the foundation of the company's **research and development** activities.

In the 1990s, Mazumdar-Shaw decided that her company's future lay with **biopharmaceuticals** rather than enzymes; Unilever, who had bought Biocon Ireland in 1989, disagreed. Mazumdar-Shaw's husband, John Shaw, used his personal savings to **buy out** the old Biocon Ireland share of the company. Biocon India was now independent.

The company started to **manufacture a generic version** of a cholesterol-lowering drug which came off patent in 2001. Two years later, Biocon began to manufacture insulin for the treatment of diabetes.

In 2009, Mazumdar-Shaw helped to found a low-cost cancer centre in Bangalore. Her company is committed to the search for **less expensive means of drug development**. 'We simply cannot afford to develop drugs that cost $1–3 billion to develop,' she told CNN in November 2012. 'You will only be confining it to a very few people in the world who can afford it. We've got to change this model. I believe that we have enough technology in the world to bring down this cost of innovation.'

When the company went public in 2004 on India's National Stock Exchange in Mumbai, the offering was oversubscribed by 33 per cent, valuing the company at over $1 billion.

In practice

- Be bold; trust in your own abilities

- Challenge prejudice

- Stick to your vision; set up on your own

- Provide a home for local talent

- Look for ways to make innovation easier and cheaper

THE 3M COMPANY
William McKNIGHT
1887–1978

WILLIAM MCKNIGHT joined the Minnesota Mining & Manufacturing Company (soon to become known as 3M) in 1907 as an assistant bookkeeper. He was surprised when he was offered the job of sales manager four years later, at a time when the company was struggling to survive, and would have been astonished to imagine that would go on to serve the company for 65 years, as general manager, president and chairman of the board.

What is truly surprising is that McKnight would turn out to have the leadership qualities that only now, more than 100 years later, we are beginning to accept as the most enlightened and most productive. Management before and after McKnight (and up to the present day) has tended to adopt the 'command and control' model, in which commands cascade down the pyramid and management obsesses with controlling the execution of these commands. McKnight saw his role as a facilitator, as the man who helped other people to deliver the best that they were capable of. 'Put fences around people,' said McKnight 'and you get sheep.'

The ideas

It is a wonder that 3M survived its early years at all. A group of five investors founded the company in 1902 to mine for mineral ores on the banks of Lake Superior, in North America, believing that they had discovered a deposit of corundum, an extremely hard mineral used as an abrasive. They shipped their first delivery in 1904, and it was not discovered for some years that their ore was not corundum, but a similar and far softer ore called anorthosite. In the meantime, the company had raised investment to begin to manufacture sandpaper which, because their ore was not corundum, was of poor quality.

The company struggled. In 1911, the sales manager resigned, and young McKnight was given the role. He was promoted to general manager in 1914; two years later, he became vice-president and, because of the ill health of the president, effectively began to run the company. He began to demonstrate his **unusual management skills**, encouraging people to experiment, forbearing criticism when mistakes were made, creating the conditions that fostered innovation.

3M bought the patent for a new waterproof sandpaper. A young researcher called Dick Drew took samples of the new Wetordry sandpaper to local auto-repair workshops and noticed that they had a problem with their masking tape: the existing tape either tore away bits of paint when it was removed, or left a residue on the car. He promised that 3M had a solution, and spent the next two years trying to find one. At one point McKnight told Drew to leave the tape project and concentrate on developing sandpaper products. Drew **kept working on his tape in secret**; it launched two years later in 1925, generating sales of over $160,000 in the first year, rising to over $1 million ten years later. McKnight's leadership had created a culture in which Drew could be certain that successful innovation would be rewarded, and that 'insubordination' would be ignored.

Similar **unexpected successes** continued to happen. When the company dropped its research into a reflective material for road markings, a researcher followed in the footsteps of Dick Drew and kept working on the idea outside work hours, discovering the basis for Scotchlite reflective material. When another researcher spilled a fluorochemical on her own shoes, she noticed that the area became resistant to dirt, and Scotchgard fabric protector was born.

The **Post-it note** was famously conceived when employee Art Fry found that paper bookmarks kept falling out of his hymn book and melded that idea with the idea of a low-adhesive glue being developed by another colleague.

McKnight began to reinvest an unusually high five per cent of sales into research and development and put in place the 15 per cent rule, encouraging engineers to spend **15 per cent of their time on a project of their own choosing**; he insisted, later in the company's development, that each 3M division should generate 25 per cent of sales from products developed within the previous five years.

In practice

In 1948, McKnight wrote down his philosophy:

- 'As our business grows, it becomes increasingly necessary to delegate responsibility and to encourage men and women to exercise their initiative. This requires considerable tolerance. Those men and women, to whom we delegate authority and responsibility, if they are good people, are going to want to do their jobs in their own way.'

- 'Mistakes will be made. But if a person is essentially right, the mistakes he or she makes are not as serious in the long run as the mistakes management will make if it undertakes to tell those in authority exactly how they must do their jobs.'

- 'Management that is destructively critical when mistakes are made kills initiative. And it's essential that we have many people with initiative if we are to continue to grow.'

MERCK & CO
George W. MERCK
1894–1957

GEORGE W. MERCK'S FAMILY BUSINESS had a longer history than most. Friedrich Merck had set up as an apothecary in Darmstadt, Germany, in 1668. In the nineteenth century, with the development of modern chemistry, the firm achieved the first commercial production of the popular painkillers of the day: morphine, codeine and cocaine.

By the end of the century, North America was a major client for the firm's products and one of the family, George Merck (George W.'s father), was sent to investigate. He settled in the U.S. and founded Merck & Co, manufacturing more or less the same products as the company's German parent, and avoiding import tariffs.

George W. Merck graduated from Harvard in 1915 with a degree in chemistry. The outbreak of the First World War prevented him from travelling to Germany, as planned, to study for his doctorate. His father persuaded him to start work in 'the shop,' arguing that the war would end in a matter of months and that George could travel to Germany to continue his studies. But, as Merck told *Time* magazine in 1952, 'I never did, and I'm still in the shop.'

The ideas

Merck took over the presidency of Merck & Co in 1925, a year before his father's death. Where his father had personally overseen almost every aspect of the company, Merck employed managers and **empowered them to run their departments**.

He split the company into **two divisions**: one internal, responsible for personnel and research and development, and one external, responsible for sales and corporate growth.

Merck steered the company through the worst years of the Great Depression, and as the economy improved, he embarked on his most ambitious and significant project – the creation of a **research facility** at Rahway, New Jersey, that would be the equal of the university laboratories and research institutions, where all significant 'pure' research had previously been carried out.

He encouraged Merck scientists to pursue their interests even where there was **no clear commercial benefit**, and employed another division to look for commercial applications of their work. 'Employees were dedicated in a way we associate with Silicon Valley today,' said Fran

Hawthorne, author of *The Merck Druggernaut*, 'working well into the night and weekends because they felt they were changing the world.'

In the 1930s, there were very few 'prescription drugs'; doctors would prescribe a list of various pills and potions that were hoped to alleviate the patient's symptoms. Merck was about to **lead the revolution in the commercial production** of drugs, vitamins and antibiotics that would transform healthcare by providing targeted solutions to particular ailments and diseases.

The company became a leading manufacturer of the antibiotic sulfonamide and a generation of other 'sulfas,' credited with **saving tens of thousands of lives** in the Second World War in the days before the commercial production of penicillin – which was achieved, on a small scale, by Merck and Co in 1942, leading to the successful treatment of a patient dying from streptococcal septicaemia; this treatment used half of the available supply of the drug.

In 1935, Merck chemists completed the synthesis of the hormone, cortisone. The company also developed the modern antibiotics Streptomycin and Cefoxitin; by 1953, Merck & Co were producing **40 per cent of antibiotics in the U.S.** That year, the company merged with Philadelphia pharmaceuticals firm Sharp & Dohme to create the biggest drug manufacturer in the U.S.

Merck died in 1957. He had focused his company on **discovery and innovation**, putting the customer – the patient – first. 'Medicine is for the patient,' said Merck. 'Medicine It is not for the profits. And if we have remembered that, the profits have never failed to appear. The better we remembered, the larger they have been.'

In practice

- Employ and empower talent
- Focus outside the organisation – this is where the opportunities are

- Encourage 'pure' research, *then* look for commercial applications

- Put purpose before profit: colleagues will be inspired and motivated; profits will follow

ARCELORMITTAL
Lakshmi MITTAL
1950–

IN 2005, LAKSHMI MITTAL was the third-richest person in the world, behind Bill Gates and Warren Buffett. He was still the sixth-richest man in the world in 2011, according to Forbes, though in 2012 he had fallen to the number 21 slot, the value of his global steel corporation having been affected by the downturn in Europe, reducing Mittal's worth to a mere $16 billion. Mittal, who lives in London, was the richest private resident in the United Kingdom for eight consecutive years; his house in London's exclusive Kensington Palace Gardens is so grand that it has been dubbed the Taj Mittal.

Mittal was born in the village of Rajgarh in India's state of Rajasthan. The village had no electricity or basic amenities, and Mittal's career qualifies as a genuine case of 'rags to riches.' It must be said, however, that the enterprise and industry of his father, Mohan, was to give young Lakshmi a good start in life.

The ideas

Lakshmi Mittal's father moved the family from Rajgarh to Kolkata and created a group of several small-scale steel mills called Ispat Industries. As a teenager, Mittal worked for the family business and continued to work part-time while he studied for his degree in business and accounting at St Xavier's College.

Because the Indian state imposed tight restrictions on the output of steel from private mills in India, Mittal set his sights on **international expansion**. In 1975, he persuaded his father to open a small steel mill in Jakarta and to **install him as manager**. One year later, he bought the Jakarta operation from his father and formed his own company, Ispat International, part of the Mittal family business.

Mittal invested in **new technology**: electric arc mini-mills, which manufactured steel from scrap steel, avoiding the need for blast furnaces to extract liquid iron from the ore – meaning lower entry costs and greater production flexibility. He forecast, correctly, that the growing use of mini-mills in the steel industry would force up the cost of scrap steel, and he explored the use of Direct-reduced Iron (DRI) as an alternative raw material. He sourced his DRI from state-run steel plants in Trinidad and Tobago, **reducing the cost of his raw materials** and increasing profits.

In the late 1980s, in a deteriorating global economy, Mittal offered to take over the multimillion-dollar-loss-making steel plant in Trinidad and Tobago, with an option to buy after five years. Mittal **turned the mill into profit** within a year, cutting back the workforce and reducing costs but investing $10 million in new equipment. By acquiring the plant, he also secured his source of cheap DRI and began to produce steel at increasingly competitive costs in the global market.

Mittal went on to **repeat this successful formula** in Mexico, Canada, Germany, Ireland and other countries. He acquired a huge, loss-making blast furnace operation in Kazakhstan, laying off nearly a quarter of the plant's 85,000 workers but announcing plans to invest $500 million over the coming five years.

Increasingly, the company was able to use its **global scale** and its own shipping fleet to route both raw materials and finished product to the most advantageous markets, while Mittal's rigorous management ensured that best practices and efficiencies at any plant in the global network were quickly spread to other plants.

In the United States, the financier Wilbur Ross had begun to buy up failing U.S. plants to create the International Steel Group, which he sold to Mittal in 2005 for $4.5 billion, creating the Mittal Steel Corporation, the **world's largest steel maker**. In 2006, after a hard-fought and bad-tempered takeover battle, Mittal acquired the European steel giant Arcelor to create ArcelorMittal, producing three times more steel than its nearest rival, Nippon Steel.

In practice

- Think globally

- Adopt new technology; think about its likely impact on markets

- Secure sources of raw materials

- Consider acquisition to drive rapid growth

- Turn around failing operations through cost control coupled with efficiency-improving investment

- Choose most advantageous markets for purchase and sale

- Spread best practice

BHARTI AIRTEL
Sunil Bharti MITTAL
1957–

SUNIL BHARTI MITTAL (no relation to Lakshmi Mittal) started off in business with a loan of 20,000 rupees (about $400) from his father. He tried various enterprises – from manufacturing bicycle parts to importing portable power generators and touch-tone phones – before moving into telephone manufacture and then seizing the opportunity to bid for India's first mobile phone licences.

Mittal built his company into a market leader, but to stay in front, it had to grow at an astonishing rate – so fast, in fact, that Mittal thought it was impossible. 'We'd need to hire 10,000 people, maybe 20,000, within two years. Did we have the resources to do that?' Mittal solved his dilemma in a radical way: he got bigger by getting smaller, handing over the running of his networks to major international players and outsourcing billing and customer accounts to IBM, leaving the company, newly named Bharti Airtel, to focus on marketing, innovation and new business opportunities.

Airtel is now India's biggest cellular services provider, with over 180 million subscribers in 2012. The company's operations in 20 countries around the world make it the world's third-largest mobile telecommunications company.

The ideas

Mittal's entry into the world of telephones began at a trade fair in Taiwan when he came across touch-tone phones – phones in India still used rotary dials – and started importing them. The government muscled in on this, however, insisting on manufacture in India and issuing 52 licences, most of them to far larger manufacturers than Mittal.

Mittal entered a **partnership with Siemens**, the German appliances manufacturer, and formed Bharti Telecom Ltd, in time becoming India's **biggest phone manufacturer**, forming further tie-ins with high-tech partners from Japan, South Korea and the U.S.

In 1992, the Indian government invited bids for the country's first mobile networks. Following his principle of forming partnerships with leading overseas companies, Mittal formed a consortium with SFR-France, Emtel-Mauritius and MSI-UK to form Bharti Cellular and **bid for licences**. The venture won four major licences, three of which were overturned after legal challenges from rivals, leaving Mittal with one of the two licences for Delhi.

Bharti launched its **mobile service** in Delhi in 1995, under the Airtel brand. Having only the one licence at this time proved a blessing in disguise: running the networks was far more expensive than bidders had forecast. Operators struggled to make their licence payments. In 1999, the government switched from licences to a revenue-sharing model.

In the same year, Mittal sold an 18 per cent share in Bharti to a U.S. private equity firm. In 2000, SingTel (Singapore Telecoms) invested $400 million. Mittal embarked on a buying spree, **snapping up financially weakened rivals**. In 2002, the company went public on India's stock markets, and Mittal continued to make **high-speed acquisitions**. 'There was a time when we had 16 projects running simultaneously, and our shareholders were jittery,' Mittal told *Forbes Asia*, 'but we had no choice. Either we kept pressing ahead or we became a marginal player.'

In 2004, Mittal made his momentous decision to **outsource most of the business**, signing contracts worth $400 million for Sweden's Ericsson and Finland's Nokia to manage his networks, and a ten-year contract with IBM to outsource billing and data-handling. 'I got calls from around the world saying: "You've gone nuts, this is the lifeline of your business,"' Mittal told *Forbes*. He reasoned differently. 'I don't manufacture [the network]; I can't maintain or upgrade it. So I'm thinking: This doesn't really belong to me. Let's just throw it out.'

Bharti had lost money for every year until 2003, but as of 2004 began to earn improving profits. By 2005, the company had a national mobile footprint. In 2007, Bharti became the fastest private telecom company in the world to reach 50 million subscribers. The company's share price rose five-fold between 2003 and 2007; Mittal became a billionaire. 'One should sense opportunity at the beginning of a curve,' he told the *Times of India*. 'Yes, there will be difficulties on the way – but everything in life is possible.'

In practice

- Keep looking for new business opportunities

- Form alliances to allow you to enter fields where you lack experience

- Think big; small players are marginalised

- Very rapid growth can be impossible to manage: outsource non-essential functions

SONY
Akio MORITA
1921–1999

AS THE ELDEST CHILD, Akio Morita was meant to take over the family's 300-year-old brewing business. But his love of the family's phonograph led instead to a fascination with the latest technology of the day. Morita studied physics at Osaka University, and when the Second World War started, enlisted with the Japanese Imperial Navy, where he found himself working on technology for heat-seeking weapons alongside Masaru Ibuka.

When the war ended, Ibuka invited Morita to join him in starting a new company. The venture, called Tokyo Telecommunications Engineering Corporation, would be renamed Sony, and soon became one of the world's leading electronics companies.

Morita became a tireless international ambassador for Sony, networking with business and political leaders around the world and moving from a post-war 'Japan first' mindset to becoming a vocal advocate of free trade. His marketing genius was driven by innovation, rather than market research. 'Our plan is to lead the public with new products rather than ask them what kind of products they want,' he wrote in his autobiography, *Made in Japan*. 'The public does not know what is possible, but we do.'

The ideas

The company's first product was Japan's first reel-to-reel magnetic tape recorder. In 1955, the company licensed the world's first transistor from Bell Laboratories in the U.S. and produced the **first commercially successful transistor radio**. Two years later, the company introduced the first 'pocket-sized' transistor radio (early versions didn't actually fit in shirt pockets; Sony's salespeople wore shirts with specially designed larger pockets). Portable transistor radios became hugely popular, especially in the United States, when the development of commercial radio stations was coinciding with the early years of rock-and-roll.

Morita led the move to a more **internationally recognisable brand name** for the company, based on the Latin *sonus* ('sound') and tapping into the U.S. slang 'sonny.' He focused on the Sony brand at a time when most Japanese manufacturers where producing goods to be sold under other brand names. Early in the company's history, he turned down an order from the watchmaker Bulova for 100,000 radios to be sold under the Bulova brand – 'the best decision I ever made,' he recalled in his autobiography.

Morita also saw the importance of **overseas markets**, since Japan's retail markets were dominated by established manufacturers. The Sony Corporation of America was founded in 1960. In 1963, Morita and his family moved to New York for a year to experience American life at first hand, and Morita began his relentless round of **socialising** with American businessmen and politicians, turning himself into an ambassador for Japanese business in the U.S. Sony's first U.S. factory opened in 1972.

The success of the transistor radio was followed by Sony's **Trinitron television system** and the world's **first successful home video cassette recorder**, using Sony's Betamax technology. Reluctant to license Betamax to other manufacturers, Sony watched as rivals developed products using JVC's VHS format, and eventually saw the Betamax format destroyed by the market.

Morita's co-founder, Ibuka, was working on a **portable music player**. Morita saw people carrying their transistor radios wherever they went and listening to music in their cars. He decided that this was the right product for the right time, despite internal concerns about a music player without a record function. Sony America didn't like the name 'Walkman' and launched the product as 'Soundabout.' In Britain, the marketing team chose 'Stowaway' and, in Scandinavia, 'Freestyle.' After initially slow sales, Morita **imposed the worldwide brand name Walkman**. The word was included in the Oxford English Dictionary in 1986.

Sony developed the Compact Disc format in association with Philips, upgraded the Walkman to the CD-based Discman, introduced the first consumer video camera recorder (based on Betamax) and later developed its own Video8 compact video cassette format.

Morita took over as Sony president from Ibuka in 1971, and became chairman and chief executive in 1976. Describing Morita's **working schedule** before he suffered a stroke in 1993, Kenichi Ohmae, author of *The Borderless World*, wrote: 'He took trips from his home base in Tokyo to New Jersey, Washington, Chicago, San Francisco, Los Angeles, San Antonio, Dallas, Britain, Barcelona and Paris. During that time he met with Queen Elizabeth II, General Electric chief Jack Welch, future French President Jacques Chirac, Isaac Stern and many other politicians, bureaucrats and business associates. He attended two concerts and a movie; took four trips within Japan; appeared at eight receptions; played nine rounds of golf; was guest of honor at a wedding ceremony; and went to work as usual for 17 days at Sony headquarters ... Whenever there was a small opening, Morita would immediately and strategically fill it by arranging a meeting with someone he wanted to become acquainted with or catch up with.'

In practice

- Create a brand and guard it fiercely

- Think globally

- Try to anticipate markets: 'The public does not know what is possible, but we do.'

- Be a full-time ambassador for your organisation

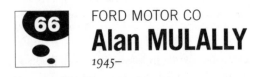

FORD MOTOR CO
Alan MULALLY
1945–

WHEN ALAN MULALLY TOOK on the role of Ford CEO in 2006, the company was looking at a $17 billion loss for the year. Mulally implemented a cost-cutting plan but also raised $23.5 billion in loans to fund his recovery and turnaround strategy, mortgaging most of the company's assets, including Ford's famous Blue Oval logo.

At the time, it was seen as an act of desperation. In fact, it was intended to cushion the company against future shocks and to provide investment for a brighter future. During the 2008 financial crisis, while General Motors and Chrysler (the other two of the 'Big Three' motor manufacturers in the U.S.) accepted their share of an $80 billion automotive industry rescue plan, Ford did not – an act that was seen by Ford employees as 'a badge of honor' and by American consumers as a good reason to buy a Ford.

The ideas

Alan Mulally always appreciated the **force of vision**. As a young man, he heard President John F. Kennedy announce America's intention to put a man on the moon. 'It was not about going to the moon,' Mulally told the *Journal of Management Inquiry* in 2010, 'but it was about what we were going to learn about ourselves. It was about the boundaries that we were going to push.'

Mulally believes that **'to love and be loved'** is at the centre of everyone's personal and working lives. This drives him and makes him happy. As a result, it makes the people he works with feel happy (and inspired) also. Mulally not only **answers every email**, he has a habit of turning up in people's offices in response to their emails, regardless of their status on the company.

He provides his team not just with support and empathy but with **a vision**. Bryce Hoffman, author of *American Icon: Alan Mulally and the Fight to Save Ford Motor Company*, says that Mulally sees himself as the **'cheerleader-in-chief,'** and that, as with many other great leaders, he has found inspiration in getting back to the vision of his company's founder – in this case, Henry Ford. 'Mulally wanted to get back to Ford's heritage,' said Hoffman, 'which was to build a product that made people's lives better.' When asked by *BusinessWeek* in 2011 to comment on why he had been selected for several CEO of the Year awards for his transformation of Ford, Mulally said, 'I think one of the things they're recognising is the fact that we pulled together around a very compelling vision. We also developed a comprehensive strategy to transform Ford. And then, of course, we've been relentlessly implementing it.'

Before the industry crisis, Ford needed to sell 3.4 million vehicles in the U.S. market to break even; after Mulally's **cost-saving programme**, Ford needed to sell 1.8 million vehicles to break even. In the 12 months to March 2012, Ford sold 2.7 million vehicles.

As Ford continued to repay its debt, the ratings agency Moody's returned the company's debt status to investment grade. With this upgrade, Ford **regained control** of the factories, brand names and trademarks that Mulally had mortgaged to achieve his goal – including the iconic Blue Oval logo.

In practice

- Offer a compelling vision and a comprehensive strategy; implement relentlessly

- Invest in the future

- Streamline to ensure profitability

- Reach out to people; make them feel happy and inspired

XEROX
Anne MULCAHY
1952–

THE WORLD'S FIRST plain-paper photocopier, the Xerox 914, was launched in 1959, replacing mimeographs, carbon-paper, Photostats and other early duplicating technologies. The machine, capable of copying a document in less than 30 seconds, was a huge success.

In the 1960s, Xerox technicians managed to link one photocopier to another by telephone; what was scanned on one machine was printed on the other, leading to the modern fax machine. In 1969 Xerox invented the laser printer.

By the 1990s, however, despite an impressive record in innovation, Xerox looked like a dying company: its core products faced fierce competition and the digital revolution suggested that the entire market for paper duplication and transmission would soon disappear.

After an outside CEO failed to turn the company around, Anne Mulcahy, a relatively unknown insider, was given the momentous task.

The ideas

Mulcahy was not even on the board of Xerox when she was put in charge of the company. 'I never expected to be CEO of Xerox,' she told *Fortune* magazine in 2003 with characteristic honesty. '**I was never groomed to be CEO of Xerox.** It was a total surprise to everyone, including myself.'

Xerox had not done enough to plan for a changing future while times were good. Despite its remarkable track record in innovation, the company had failed to bring many of its best ideas to market. Mulcahy set out to reconsider what essential service Xerox supplied to its customers, and decided that it lay in supplying solutions that **made life easier for business**.

She **outsourced manufacturing**, slashing the company's workforce of 100,000 by 30 per cent – a move that many of the company's lenders had expected would be too tough for an insider to make.

Mulcahy's 'insider' status proved, in fact, to be an asset. One lender told her that she would not be able to transform the company's finances until she changed its culture. As *Fast Company* magazine reported in 2003, Mulcahy responded, '**I am the culture.** If I can't figure out how to bring the culture with me, I'm the wrong person for the job.' The whole company was aware of Mulcahy's personal efforts to save Xerox – as her colleague and later successor as CEO, Ursula Burns, told *Fortune*, 'Her mission in life was, "If this place is going to fail, it's not going to be because Anne Mulcahy slept."'

She implored colleagues to '**save every dollar as if it were your own'** but also allowed annual salary rises to go through and made symbolic gestures – like giving every employee a holiday on their birthday –

that sent the message that the company, which had always enjoyed high levels of employee loyalty, still cared about them.

Xerox's share price was at a low of $4.20 in October 2002, but by mid-2003 the company had reported four consecutive quarters of operating profits, debt was down by over 20 per cent, and the company had $3 billion in cash.

Throughout the crisis, Mulcahy continued to spend six per cent of revenues on research and development. With the strategic move into business services as well as business products, the company's accumulated wisdom began to come into its own, enabling a range of **innovative products and services** such as intelligent document readers that would not merely copy documents but analyse them, offering huge efficiencies in information processing.

Mulcahy gave colleagues a **vision of the future** that they could believe in. 'When people ask me how we move things so quickly – in a couple of years, turn a company around – I don't have to think about it,' she told a Society for Human Resource Management Strategy Conference in 2010. 'It was not brilliance or strategy or execution but the fact that our people believed. We aligned ourselves around goals and objectives. We had the **power of the people** behind them.'

In practice

- Decide on the core purpose of the organisation
- Nurture the culture
- Ask for necessary sacrifices; show that the organisation cares
- Spend on R&D; focus on bringing good ideas to market
- Give the team a vision they can believe in; get colleagues aligned

NEWS CORPORATION
Rupert MURDOCH
1931–

KEITH RUPERT MURDOCH – known to the world as Rupert Murdoch – inherited a controlling share in his father's regional newspaper group in Australia and built the business into a national media group. In the 1960s, he began to build a newspaper empire in the UK and, in the 1980s, bought the satellite TV operation that was to become BSkyB. Also in the 1980s, Murdoch acquired the 20th Century Fox movie studios in the U.S., and then bought a TV company that was developed into the Fox TV network, a surprise rival to the three established U.S. broadcast TV networks. Murdoch's 2003 acquisition of a share in the major U.S. satellite TV operator, DirectTV, confirmed Murdoch's News Corporation's arrival as a global media conglomerate, second, at the time, only to Time Warner.

The ideas

Having made a success of the *Adelaide News*, Perth's *Sunday Times* and *The Australian* in the 1950s and early 1960s, Murdoch **switched his attention to Europe**, buying the UK's *News of the World* Sunday newspaper. Soon afterwards, he acquired the popular but financially struggling daily, *The Sun*, enabling him to use the presses of the weekly *News of the World* for the remaining six days of the week.

In 1981, he took over the UK's prestigious *Times* and *Sunday Times*, which had been losing money under the previous owners, after a series of disputes with the UK's powerful print unions had led to the closure of both titles for almost a year in 1978. Murdoch negotiated a new deal with the unions in return for saving the titles from closure, allowing the newspapers to move from the 'hot metal' Linotype method of typesetting to modern photo-composition, but union resistance to the logical conclusion of modernisation – the creation of complete pages on-screen – led to further disputes. Murdoch built a new, modernised newspaper plant in Wapping, east London, supposedly for the production of a new London evening newspaper. When the unions went on strike in early 1986, Murdoch's News International **dismissed all 6,000 striking workers** and moved production to Wapping. Sacked workers demonstrated outside the Wapping plant for a year, sometimes violently, trying to prevent workers from entering the plant and lorries from leaving with finished newspapers. The protest collapsed in 1987 and was a landmark, along with Britain's miners' strike of 1984–85, in UK labour relations.

Murdoch's profits from his newly modernised newspaper operations underwrote his investment in his UK satellite TV venture, Sky Television. Sky Television **gave away the satellite dishes** and set-top boxes needed to access the service and forced rival BSB to agree to a merger, creating BSkyB. The merged venture still struggled until Murdoch acquired the rights, in 1992, for the **exclusive TV coverage** of the UK's newly created Premier League. Any UK viewer who wanted to watch a Premier League football match now needed access to Sky. Murdoch was to repeat the tactic in the U.S.

In 1984, Murdoch **moved into movies** with the acquisition of 20th Century Fox. He also bought the U.S. Metromedia TV stations that were to create the foundations for the **Fox TV network**. In 1993 Murdoch outbid CBS for the rights to coverage of U.S. National Football League games. With the rights secured, Murdoch was able to persuade New World Communications Group, owners of TV stations affiliated to the CBS TV network, to align with Fox TV rather than lose their lucrative football coverage, offering New World the additional incentive of $500 million in new investment. Fox TV was on its way to rivalling established U.S. TV networks ABC, CBS and NBC.

A key element in Murdoch's success was his willingness to invest for the long term in order to **build audience share**. Once he had achieved scale, Murdoch used what *BusinessWeek* magazine described in 2004 as his key competitive tools: '**pricing power, programming clout, and indifference to losses.**'

Murdoch's empire nearly collapsed under the weight of its debts in the early 1990s, forcing it to sell off U.S. and Australian magazine interests. The company acquired the social network service MySpace in 2005, but sold it at a huge loss in 2011. The acquisition in 2007 of Dow Jones, publisher of the *Wall Street Journal*, saw a later write-down of the company's value.

Murdoch runs this sprawling global network of media businesses mainly via the telephone. He receives a **weekly update** on his empire's performance called The Flash. He is said by colleagues to view his business empire 'from 30,000 feet' – always seeing the **global picture**, but diving in to attend to detail when needed. After the announcement of the DirectTV deal in 2003, Murdoch told the magazine: 'Don't worry. We don't want to take over the world. We just want a piece of it.'

In practice

- Build an empire patiently over time, putting vital elements in place

- Challenge vested interests that are damaging the business

- Use major investments (like Murdoch's acquisition of football TV rights) and growing scale to improve your bargaining power

- See the big picture; attend to detail when necessary

INFOSYS
N.R. Narayana MURTHY
1946–

IN THE LATE 1960s, Nagavara Ramarao Narayana Murthy was studying for a master's degree in control theory at the Indian Institute of Technology, Kanpur, when he heard a visiting U.S. professor talking to students over breakfast about the latest developments in computer science, and in particular about how these would change people's lives. 'I was hooked,' Murthy said, some 40 years later. 'I went straight from breakfast to the library, read four or five papers he had suggested, and left the library determined to study computer science.'

In 1981, Murthy and six other computer engineers founded Infosys with 10,000 rupees between them (about $200 at today's exchange rate) and built the company into a global leader in computer technology services and business consulting.

Murthy has remained a firm believer in the opportunities created by chance events. His advice to the students at Stern was that 'the future will be shaped by several turning points with great learning opportunities.'

The ideas

After his master's degree, Murthy went to work as a systems engineer for the Indian Institute of Management, Ahmadabad. 'We used to work 20 hours a day; go home at 3 a.m. sometimes and be back at 7 a.m.,' he told India Seminar 1999. 'There was so much opportunity to learn ... I learnt what it is to be an engineer. It isn't theory but **application of the theory** to solve problems and make a difference to society.'

Murthy **launched Infosys** in 1981 with six other engineers. The team had worked with the New-York based Data-Basics Corporation company at Patni Computer Systems, and Data-Basics now wanted their own India-based software team, but were persuaded that Infosys could take on the task.

Infosys was a pioneer of the **Global Delivery Model**, which argues that work should be done wherever on the planet the best talent is available at the most competitive price with the lowest acceptable risk.

Murthy set his sights on the **global market**, but establishing the company was difficult. There was a waiting list for computers – the company used time-share for its first few years and its first computer was not installed until 1984; it took a year just to get a phone line installed, because businesses were not given priority. Finance was only secured when Murthy happened to share a plane with an official from the state Industrial Investment and Development Corporation and opened the door for a proposal. In 1987, Infosys opened its first overseas office in Boston.

In 1990, the partners received an offer of $1 million to sell the company. His colleagues were tempted, but Murthy reminded them of the challenges and difficulties that they had faced so far. 'If they were all bent upon selling the company,' said Murthy, '**I would buy out all my colleagues**, though I did not have a cent in my pocket.' Murthy's demonstration of faith changed his partners' minds. In 1993, Infosys launched on the Indian stock exchange.

There was another pivotal moment when a major client set up a competitive pitch and drove fees down to a level where Murthy did not believe they could continue to deliver adequate levels of staff training and client service. 'I communicated clearly to the customer that we could not accept their terms, since it could well lead us to letting them down later. But I promised a smooth, professional transition to a vendor of the customer's choice.' The client represented 25 per cent of the company's revenue. Standing firm on its business model was 'a turning point,' said Murthy. He put in place a **de-risk strategy** to ensure that Infosys would never again be over-dependent on one client, country or technology.

In 1999, a listing on the U.S. electronic NASDAQ exchange delivered capital to drive **rapid growth** – Infosys has 67 offices around the world, including 18 in the U.S. The company has also earned a reputation for the **integrity and transparency** in business dealings that Murthy championed throughout his 21 years as CEO.

In practice

- Compete globally with the best companies in your industry
- Have faith in your potential
- Stick to your pricing structure to maintain quality
- Ensure good corporate governance and transparency

COFCO
NING Gaoning
1958–

AS THE CHAIRMAN of China National Cereals, Oils & Foodstuffs Corporation (COFCO), Ning Gaoning, also known as Frank, is effectively running a government department – one of China's State-Owned Enterprises (SOEs). He is charged with supplying essential foodstuffs to nearly 20 per cent of the world's population – over 1.3 billion people. Ning, however, sees himself not as a bureaucrat but as an entrepreneur. He has called himself 'a cowboy for state assets,' and is often cited as one of China's most influential business leaders.

The ideas

On graduating from the Katz School of Business, University of Pittsburgh, with an MBA in 1987, Ning took a job with China Resources (Holdings) in Hong Kong, a company which had previously been the sole agency for the import into Hong Kong of goods and power from mainland China, but which was now acquiring its own interests in brewing, textiles, chemicals, real estate and other industries on the mainland.

Ning rose steadily though the organisation, becoming chairman within 17 years, and began to focus on achieving leading positions in the key industries represented by the group, financing the deals with the holding company's retained earnings but also from listings on the Hong Kong Stock Exchange and from bond issues. Ning's activities began to **create efficiencies**, taking over poorly run businesses, often owned by local government, and introducing **modern management disciplines**.

In 2004, he was appointed to head COFCO, and to oversee a restructuring programme. He set out to improve the food giant's **vertical integration**, taking control of every aspect of food production and processing. 'As we control every link of food production, quality is assured,' Ning is reported as saying during the Communist Party's 18th National Congress in November 2012. 'Also, efficiency is improved.'

Ning focused on the more profitable aspects of COFCO's business, **dropping poorly performing areas**. In the seven years since Ning took over as chairman of the group, profits rose from 1.58 billion yuan in 2004 to ten billion yuan in 2011.

He defended the role of China's SOEs, arguing that they improved living standards by offering **products and services of higher quality** and, in the face of concerns that SOE's were squeezing out smaller, private companies, countered that weaker companies would always be challenged by mature market leaders, regardless of whether these were state-owned or private, arguing that competitive state-owned enterprises can be as much a part of the process of **'creative destruction'** as private companies.

Speaking one year earlier at the 10th China Entrepreneur Summit, Ning stressed the need to add value by **building strong brands**. Commenting on the fact that many of the major retail tenants of COFCOs Commercial Real Estate Division were foreign brands, Ning said that China, as a major garment producer, was failing to 'build brands that could truly impress the consumers and continuously influence people's lives,' in the way that established foreign-based clothing brands were doing. COFCO, said Ning, 'truly hopes to move towards innovation and technology, nutrition and health, and strives to **promote life quality**, increase life expectancy, reduce diseases, increase vitality, and enhance the health of Chinese people.' The company established a Nutrition and Health Research Institute, staffed with over 40 PhD-holding scientists.

Ning cautions against businesses competing always on price, and of 'me-tooism' (producing products for a market that has been established by an innovative brand). 'We should **worship technology**, R&D, innovation, industry, brands, superior products, and good enterprises able to achieve sustainable development through technology.'

In practice

- Introduce modern management disciplines
- Consider vertical integration to guarantee quality throughout the supply chain
- Drive efficiencies; compete with less well-run businesses
- Build brands
- Focus on innovation and technology
- Improve customers' lives

PEPSICO
Indra NOOYI
1955–

As GLOBAL CHAIRMAN AND CEO of PepsiCo, Indra Nooyi faced a consumer-driven campaign in her home country of India, following concerns that water extraction for bottling plants of soft drinks manufacturers such as Pepsi and Coca-Cola were causing water tables to fall and local wells to run dry. In addition, there were associated concerns that residues of agricultural fertilisers and pesticides were accumulating in soils and in groundwater and contaminating even PepsiCo's own bottled drinks.

Nooyi rebutted the idea that PepsiCo would allow its global standards to drop: 'For somebody to think that Pepsi would jeopardise its brand – its global brand – by doing something stupid in one country is crazy,' Nooyi told *BusinessWeek* in 2007.

But public concern about the responsible use of water by global corporations struck a chord. She made a promise that the company would 'deliver sustainable growth by investing in a healthier future for our consumers, our planet, our associates and external partners and the communities we have.' And core to this promise was the principle of water stewardship.

The ideas

Indra Nooyi was aware from an early age that water was a precious commodity. When water was scarce in her home town of Chennai, the local supply was turned on only between three and five in the morning. Families filled every available receptacle to get enough water for the day. Nooyi and her brother and sister were given two buckets for their personal needs. 'You learned to live your life off those two buckets,' recalled Nooyi.

Nooyi earned a Bachelor of Science degree in Chennai and went on to earn her MBA from the Indian Institute of Management in Calcutta, still finding time to be the lead guitarist in an all-girl rock band and to play women's cricket. She worked as product manager for Johnson & Johnson and other companies in India before moving to the United States to take a master's degree at Yale School of Management, subsequently spending six years with the Boston Consulting Group.

Nooyi joined PepsiCo in 1994 as chief strategist, and led the move to **take the company out of fast food restaurants** (KFC, Pizza Hut, Taco Bell) to concentrate on beverages and packaged food, with a new focus on healthier foods and drinks. She led the 1998 acquisition of the fruit juice company Tropicana, and the 2001 acquisition of Quaker Oats, with an eye not only on the company's sports drink, Gatorade, but also on its core heritage in oats and its new granola bar snack range.

Under Nooyi's leadership, PepsiCo dramatically **reduced its usage of water** in manufacturing processes, instilling a culture of 'water stewardship' in all of their global operations. The company undertook to work within the spirit of the UN's 'Human Right to Water' policy in every country in which it operated, and invested in a research programme to develop **innovative agricultural techniques**, aimed at reducing water consumption by the farmers who supply the ingredients for PepsiCo products. Pepsi's 'direct seeding' technique of rice cultivation, removing the need to grow rice saplings in flood-irrigated fields as an intermediary stage in rice cultivation, resulted in a **30 per cent saving in water usage** and a reduction of 50 per cent in labour per acre.

Nooyi's vision for the role of global corporations and 'Performance with Purpose' argues that corporations can become **a force for good**. In India, the company's reductions in its own use of water and its contribution to water-saving initiatives by its agricultural suppliers have resulted in a 'positive water balance' – giving back more water to the community than it has consumed.

Nooyi blames the 2008 financial crisis and the subsequent credit crunch on 'capitalism run amok.' As she said in a 2011 BlogHer interview, 'Capitalism is fantastic, it spurs innovation, capitalism spurs growth and it creates wealth ... but **capitalism without conscience is dangerous** ... Today's problems of the world cannot be solved by governments alone, cannot be solved by people alone, it has to be solved in partnership between a company and government.'

In practice

- Anticipate consumer trends

- Move your business into the areas where you feel it should operate

- Be responsible: if your business uses a vital resource, use it carefully

- Put something back: try to make your activities 'net positive'

- Encourage a corporate conscience

ASDA; and others
Archie NORMAN
1954–

ARCHIBALD 'ARCHIE' NORMAN HAS a reputation as a 'change master.' Famous for his turnaround of the failing British supermarket chain Asda, taking it from near bankruptcy to profit within two years, and later negotiating its successful sale to the American retail giant Wal-Mart, Norman went on to become a Member of Parliament and then chief executive of the Conservative Party.

Norman believes that his success is based on changing people. 'I'm much more interested in people and motivation than I am in financial engineering,' he told *The Telegraph*. 'My focus has always been in providing a robust long-term business.'

The ideas

When Archie Norman was persuaded to take on the role of Asda's CEO in 1991, the company was felt by most informed observers, according to *The Independent* newspaper, to be 'little better than a basket case with **virtually no recovery potential**.' In 1989, the company had bought 62 superstores from rival Gateway chain for £705 million, increasing its retail floor space by 50 per cent and becoming one of the largest superstore operators in the UK, but the massive debt crippled the company. An emergency £357 million pounds rights issue looked certain to flop with investors, until it was announced that Norman had accepted the task of turning the company around.

The group needed to reduce costs, and Norman **felt that it had lost touch with its core promise to consumers of lower prices**. Critically, he felt that management had also lost touch with the workforce. As he told *Director* magazine in 1999, 'It was a very hierarchical company which had gone from adolescence to senility in the space of five years. It had been a great entrepreneurial Yorkshire company but it had burgeoned in size, diversified, brought in legions of corporate managers and just lost touch with the front line.' Norman discovered a range of management perks and privileges and a disciplinary approach to staff relations. People working in Asda stores saw their jobs as a disappointment, a failure to do better.

Norman set out to create a culture in which people gained a sense of **pride and achievement from their work** and in which everyone's contribution was equally respected. He froze pay and cut 5,000 jobs, but set in place a **growth strategy** that was to see the company return to profit within two years. Individual stores would drive the business, because they were closest to the customer.

Norman assembled an array of **retail management talent**, including Alan Leighton, who took on the role of CEO when Norman became chairman in 1996; together they turned Asda from a 'basket case' into a thriving retail business. Norman sold the group to Wal-Mart in 1999 for £6.5 billion, creating a **1,000 per cent return for shareholders** who had stayed with the company for the duration of his tenure.

Norman refuses to take the credit: 'Asda is not me and Alan Leighton, it is 85,000 colleagues,' he told *Director* magazine. His management philosophy, as he told *The Telegraph*, was 'to **treat all people with respect**, to **listen to the front line**, to deliver action and to energise the company.'

In 2002, while an MP and shadow minister, Norman was asked to rescue the telecommunications company, Energis, which had gone into administration. His **financial restructuring** of the company is seen as a classic case-study, preventing a sell-off that would have seen hundreds of millions of pounds written off, and giving the company's bankers the confidence to finance a long-term recovery plan. The company was turned around within three years and sold to Cable & Wireless.

In recent years, Norman has been asked to lead the turnaround of Australia's second largest food retailer, Coles Supermarkets, in what *The Telegraph* described as 'probably the **largest turnaround project in food retailing in the world**.'

In practice

- Abandon a hierarchical, critical management approach
- Generate a sense of pride and achievement at all levels of the company
- Ensure everyone's contribution is valued
- 'Treat all people with respect; listen to the front line; deliver action; energise the company'

NOKIA
Jorma OLLILA
1950–

IN THE EARLY 1990S, the Finnish conglomerate Nokia, manufactured many diverse products: toilet paper, tyres, rubber boots, chemicals, consumer electronics – and mobile phones. Finland had just entered a deep recession, caused by the collapse of its most important trading partner, the former Soviet Union, together with a banking crisis and a worldwide downturn. *Forbes* magazine described Nokia at the time as 'gushing blood.'

Jorma Ollila, newly appointed CEO, bet the company's future on a radical move: he positioned the company as a pure-play mobile phone manufacturer, and restructured and sold off all of the company's other operations. He invested heavily in research and development and honed the company's production processes, bringing people from different functions together into teams so that people in sales, sourcing and manufacture could make an input to design in a drive to deliver the desired effect at the lowest cost. Ollila led Nokia through a period of spectacular growth to become the world's biggest mobile phone manufacturer and Europe's most valuable company.

The ideas

Before becoming CEO, Ollila's first role at Nokia was to set up international investments, as the company sought to expand globally and reduce its reliance on trade with the Soviet Union. He became finance director in 1986, and in 1990 was made head of the loss-making mobile phones operation, where he worked on getting phones for the **new GSM standard** ready for market. Demand for mobile phones was growing significantly, but Nokia was struggling to gear up its production.

When he was made CEO in 1992, Ollila made his dramatic move to **jettison all of the conglomerate's other activities**. Within six years, Nokia had taken over from Motorola as the **world's largest manufacturer of mobile phones** (a position it lost to Samsung in 2012). Revenue growth for 1997 to 2000 approached 50 per cent per year.

In 2000, Nokia had 31 per cent of the global handset market and was briefly Europe's most valuable company. As a sign of tough challenges ahead, as the world geared up for the move to 3G, Nokia's stock fell 70 per cent in March 2001. Ollila's main worry was always complacency resulting from early success. In 1998, he had **swapped the jobs** of each of his top five managers, insisting that executives stretch themselves and, if necessary, learn through their mistakes. 'If you don't fail throughout your career at certain points,' he told *Industry Week*, 'then you haven't stretched yourself properly.'

Ollila focused on **streamlining the process** of designing and manufacturing phones, **bringing people together** from all disciplines to work as teams.

The company built manufacturing plants in China that were surrounded by major components suppliers as Ollila pursued a vision of **'zero inventory'** based on **'next door service.'** A key part of this process is a commitment to transparency of information between the company and its suppliers. At one China plant, Nokia built restaurants designed to encourage **casual encounters** between its employees and the suppliers on the same site.

Ollila encouraged debate, but would then take **decisive action.** 'We don't analyse problems to death,' he told *Industry Week*. 'We're pretty determined about timelines [and] about getting things done. Somebody has to take the responsibility and say, 'O.K., this is it. This is what we are going to do. Otherwise you just have a lot of fun in discussing things – and nobody takes the ball and carries it. It's all very well passing it around in a circle. But somebody, at the right point in time, has to grab it and run.'

The company's position has been challenged over the last decade with the advance of smartphones, but Ollila also positioned the company for change and adaptation. '**This organisation loves discontinuity**,' he told *Economist* magazine in 2000. 'We can jump on it and adapt. Finns live in a cold climate: we have to be adaptable to survive.'

In practice

- Think the unthinkable; move in radical new directions

- Streamline processes

- Bring people together from every discipline

- Move people around; allow them to learn from mistakes

- Work closely with suppliers

- Pursue zero inventory

- Encourage debate, then take decisive action

GOOGLE
Larry PAGE
1973–

LAWRENCE 'LARRY' PAGE CO-FOUNDED Google with his Stanford University friend and colleague, Sergey Brin, after the two computer science students worked together on Page's idea for his doctoral thesis, which involved crawling the entire World Wide Web to map the links between individual sites.

It occurred to Page (as it did to Robin Li, creator of China's Baidu search engine) that the number and quality of links into a site were a good measure of its usefulness, in the same way that the most frequently cited academic articles are shown to be the most influential. Existing search engines based their results only on the appearance of keywords in the text of any site, giving rise to many irrelevant results; adding an analysis of the links to any site gave a vastly improved measure of relevance.

Page and Brin initially called their new search engine PageRank, a pun on Page's name, but eventually settled on Google, based on the scientific term 'googol' – a one followed by 100 zeros – because, as they said at the time, 'our goal is to make huge quantities of information available to everyone. And it sounds cool and has only six letters.'

The ideas

Google Inc was incorporated in September 1998 and, in the best tradition of Silicon Valley start-ups, was **initially housed in the garage** of a friend of Page's in Menlo Park, California. The company's first investment of $100,000 came from Andy Bechtolsheim, co-founder of Sun Microsystems. In 1999, venture capital firms put up $25 million of funding.

By 2000, Google had developed 15 foreign-language versions and indexed one billion web pages, making it the **world's largest search engine**.

Page and Brin resisted the idea of funding the site via display advertising but compromised with simple text advertisements linked to keywords being searched for by web users. Advertisers paid only when visitors 'clicked though' to their own websites; an electronic auction system dictated the price of each click – a system pioneered by Goto.com, which was later acquired by Yahoo. Google Adwords launched in October 2000 with 350 advertisers. As the new search engine increased in popularity, revenue from these simple **'pay per click' advertisements** created huge income.

The company's venture capital investors put pressure on Page and Brin to hire a professional CEO: they chose Eric Schmidt, a veteran of Sun Microsystems and Novell. The two founders and Schmidt ran the company as a **power-sharing troika**. Google went public in 2004, offering shares at $85. Shares closed at around $100 on the first day of trading, making many Google employees millionaires.

The company at first **licensed its search facility** to partners such as Yahoo and AOL, before establishing Google search as a brand in itself. Google became famous for its motto, **'Don't be evil.'** It established a relaxed working culture, where engineers were encouraged to use **20 per cent of their time to explore any idea** that interested them. Projects tended to grow organically as the most interesting ideas were picked up, developed, and sometimes dropped, or left, unfinished, in beta testing.

Following its mission, the company took on **ambitious and often controversial projects**, such as Google Earth and Google Maps, allowing users to explore the surface of the planet and even individual streets. Google Books set out to digitise 15 million books and make them available, running into opposition when the project included books that were still under copyright. Google Translate, a server-based device for translating any language into another, can currently translate between 35 different languages.

Page came to feel that Google's focus on information had caused the company to miss the new trend towards social networking. 'Our mission was to organise the world's information and make it universally accessible and useful,' Page told *BusinessWeek* in 2012, 'I think we probably missed more of the people part than we should have.' In 2011, Google launched **its own social network, Google+**.

The company moved into the world of mobile computing with the acquisition of the open-source Android operating system and into video sharing with the acquisition of YouTube. The integration of YouTube with Google+ and the Google Chrome browser, allowing videos to be watched within the Google+ interface, is a step towards Page's dream of bringing together information about people's preferences to **offer people things they haven't asked for, but may find that they want**.

In practice

- Concern about customers' experiences can lead to higher profits (Google resisted display advertising in favour of less obtrusive, search-related text advertisements)

- A clear vision ('organise the world's information and make it accessible') will inspire colleagues to create new and relevant projects

- Focus on products that become part of people's lives

WIPRO
Azim PREMJI
1945–

AZIM PREMJI'S GRANDFATHER WAS known as the Rice King of Burma, and his father was the founder of the Western India Vegetable Products company, whose main product was sunflower oil *vanaspati* – a hydrogenated oil used in cooking.

Premji was studying engineering at Stanford University when his father died at the age of 51. He was just six months short of graduation and 21 years old, but went back to India to take over the running of the business. In a 2010 interview with *Businessweek* magazine, Premji recalled his first shareholders' meeting: 'Someone stood up and said, "Young man, my strong advice is that you sell your shares to a more mature holder. There's no way you can run a complex company like this."' As Premji confessed, 'I was nervous, but I held on.'

Premji modernised and diversified the company. Then when IBM left India in the late 1970s, he spotted an historic opportunity. Premji had been looking for a way to diversify into high-tech areas that could create opportunities for sustainable growth. Now he moved the family business into computer manufacture, software programming and IT services, creating one of India's leading technology companies.

The ideas

When Premji returned to India, the family's cooking oils were still sold in the traditional way. 'A customer would go to a retail shop and ask for 50 grams, 100 grams of *vanaspati*,' Premji told *Forbes* magazine in 2010. 'The retailer would scoop it up from an open box – in which there were crawling mosquitoes and flies – and put it in a plastic container.' Premji introduced **single-use consumer packaging** – 'We were the pioneers in packaging for the mass market' – and also led **diversification** into bakery fats, as well as into shampoos and toiletries and then lighting and hydraulic cylinders, constantly seeking to move the company into higher technologies.

A unique opportunity was presented when IBM decided to leave India rather than accept partial Indian ownership of its India operations when the Janata Party alliance government, which emerged after the defeat of previous Prime Minister Indira Ghandi's Congress Party in 1977, vigorously enforced the country's 1973 Foreign Exchange Regulation Act. Premji was quick to **take advantage of IBM's absence**. 'That created a vacuum,' he told the UK's *Telegraph* in 2010. 'We got our act right. We took the right bets, invested in people, research and development, after-sales service and IT solutions and were extremely successful.'

Wipro started to **build microcomputers**, using technology licensed from Sentinel Computers in the United States. The company sold directly to corporate customers and provided after-sales service, stressing reliability and establishing the brand before establishing a dealer network. The company **assembled products** for major manufacturers such as Canon, Epson, Hewlett-Packard and Sun, and **distributed software** from companies such as Adobe and Netscape.

In 1985, Wipro teamed up with Taiwanese personal computer manufacturer Acer, and then went its own way to produce **India's first indigenous PC**.

In the 1990s, Premji led the company in the development of IT services to clients in many industry sectors in India but also to overseas clients: improvements in telecommunications meant that a high-tech service such as software development and R&D could be delivered to clients anywhere in the world at competitive costs, **taking advantage of India's lower cost of living**. Wipro became a pioneer of the Offshore Development Centre and grew into one of the **world's leading software and outsourced service providers**.

Premji's 79 per cent shareholding in Wipro has made him one of the world's wealthiest people. In 2001 he founded the Azim Premji Foundation Trust, devoted to the goal of achieving **universal educational opportunities**. In 2010, Premji pledged to donate $2 billion to improving school education in India – the largest charitable donation ever in the country's history.

In practice

- Have faith in your own skills and competence
- Diversify
- Move your business towards higher technologies
- Seize opportunities
- Work with major brands; launch your own products; export

76

HANCOCK PROSPECTING
Gina RINEHART
1954–

GEORGINA HOPE RINEHART'S COMPANY, Hancock Prospecting, owns leases to some of the world's richest iron-producing regions in Australia. Her wealth was estimated by Forbes in 2012 at $18 billion, making her Australia's richest person.

Although she inherited the company from her father, with substantial annual royalty payments on an existing mining operation, it was Rinehart who steered the company to develop other mining leases as joint ventures with mining conglomerates, turning what she described as a legacy of 'a mess and debts and liabilities' into a series of real iron mines and a figurative gold mine.

Rinehart, who clearly has mining in her blood, once responded to a question about her definition of beauty with the answer: 'an iron mine.'

The ideas

Legend has it that Gina Rinehart's father, Lang Hancock, a sheep and cattle farmer and mineral prospector in Australia's northwest, was flying his light airplane from the north of Western Australia to Perth, in the south, when storm clouds forced him to keep low. He followed the course of the Turner River through the Hamersley Range, in the sparsely populated Pilbara region. 'Flying low, I followed the gorge,' he remembered. 'I noticed the walls. They were made of iron ore, but I figured it had to be poor grade. At the time, they said Australia didn't have any grade iron ore. I followed the iron ore in the walls for 70 miles.' The ore was not poor grade; Western Australia proved to be one of the richest iron territories in the world. After a decade spent lobbying the government of Western Australia to lift a ban on exports of iron ore, Hancock was able to stake his claim. He and a friend from his schooldays formed a partnership and persuaded Rio Tinto to set up a mining operation in the Hamersley Range from which he and his partner would **share a royalty of 2.5 per cent in perpetuity of all iron ore shipped**. The two partners began to split an annual income of A$25 million.

Hancock's only daughter, Gina Rinehart, now has sole control of her father's company, Hancock Prospecting; in 2012 the royalty from Rio Tinto generated an annual income of $105 million. Following Hancock's death, the income kept the company afloat while Rinehart battled through the courts in a **dispute about ownership** of her father's estate. Once Rinehart had established her ownership of the company, that income was dwarfed by the wealth that Rinehart created by **developing new mines as joint ventures**, turning the leases that her father had acquired into revenue.

Under Rinehart, Hancock Prospecting has developed another iron ore operation with Rio Tinto at Hope Downs (named after Rinehart's mother) and at Roy Hill, with South Korean iron and steel company POSCO. With the Australian-based Mineral Resources Ltd, Hancock Prospecting has developed a **manganese ore mine** at Nicholas Down. The group has also moved into **coal mining**, developing the Alpha Coal Project, in the Galilee Basin region of Central Queensland in eastern Australia, with Indian conglomerate GVK.

Rinehart has recently bought stakes in Australian **media owners** Ten Network Holdings and Fairfax Media, raising concerns that she may use this to promote mining interests. She has also promoted a **political agenda** of lower taxes, lighter regulation and tougher policing, controversially proposing that Australia should use **'guest workers'** as a source of lower-cost skilled labour.

One of Rinehart's mining partners, Rio Tinto, are in no doubts about her qualities and abilities. 'We have a wonderful relationship,' a Rio Tinto official told *Forbes*. 'She is a person who just keeps pushing and keeps stretching, **trying for a better deal**. And I think she's learned by doing this that sometimes it does actually happen.' As Rinehart once told a group of friends, according to *Newsweek* magazine, 'Whatever I do, the House of Hancock comes first. Nothing will stand in the way of that. Nothing.'

With the rising demand for iron, especially from China, iron ore prices are ever rising, and Rinehart is on course to become the richest person in the world.

In practice

- Make the most of what you have; turn potential into reality
- Use joint ventures to supply skills and technology
- Promote your agenda
- Keep pushing for a better deal
- Fight your corner

STANDARD OIL
John D. ROCKEFELLER
1839–1937

THE WORD 'PETROLEUM' means 'rock-oil.' Pools of rock oil seep to the surface in various parts of the world. Where people drilled wells near salt springs to extract brine, from which salt could be produced by evaporation, as they did along the banks of the Ohio River in north-eastern America, the oil was seen as a nuisance, polluting the brine.

A salt well owner called Samuel Keir experimented with various distillations of the oil, producing a medicine and an ointment, but then discovered that he could also distil kerosene, a substance that had recently first been distilled from coal. Kerosene makes an excellent fuel for lamps: at that time, whale oil was the principal source of lighting oil, but the over-hunting of whales was making this a scarce and more expensive product. Kerosene lamps became the most popular form of domestic lighting, and rock oil became valuable.

The oil regions of western Pennsylvania became the scene of a new kind of Gold Rush as prospectors rushed to the region and started drilling for oil. The American oil industry was born, and it would soon make a young man called John D. Rockefeller the richest American of all time.

The ideas

While Rockefeller was at his first job as an office clerk and book-keeper for an agricultural wholesaler, an Englishman called Maurice Clark, who worked for another produce commission company, suggested that they form their own shipping company. The firm of Clark & Rockefeller made a profit of $4,000 in its first year; the outbreak of the American Civil War created a boom in business.

In 1863, Samuel Andrews, a friend of Clark's, persuaded the two partners to **invest in refining oil into kerosene**. Two of Clark's brothers joined the new business and Rockefeller became concerned that the three Clarks would always be able to out-vote him and Andrews. The partners were persuaded to put the company up for auction. Rockefeller **secured the company** for $72,500 – the very limit of his finances – creating the new business of Rockefeller & Andrews, and giving him control what was already the **largest oil refinery in Cleveland**.

Within months, Rockefeller had borrowed from the banks and opened a second refinery. In 1870, the company went public, with a capitalisation of $1 million, **raising finance for further expansion**; the new corporation, Standard Oil, initially controlled ten per cent of all of America's refining capacity. It was to acquire more.

Refineries could be set up near railroads, but oil wells were in remote locations. The erratic production of the many independent oil producers meant that the railroads struggled to run a profitable service. Rockefeller colluded with the railroads to form a **cartel**. Thomas Scott, president of the Pennsylvania Railroad, set up a new company, the South Improvement Company, to ship oil for Standard Oil and other major refineries. The Pennsylvania, Erie and New York Central railroads doubled freight charges for oil shipped from Cleveland to New York to $2.56 per barrel, but oil shipped with the South Improvement Company would receive a **secret rebate** of $1.06. South Improvement would also receive a payment of $1.06 per barrel for any oil shipped that did not come from its own suppliers, to remove any incentive for railroads to ship competitive oil at the higher price. When news of the secret deal leaked out, there were public demonstrations; Standard Oil property and employees were attacked; the newspapers called the episode 'Oil Wars.'

The affair had no effect on Rockefeller's grand plan; he bought more competing refineries, using his increasing buying power to get low prices from the oil suppliers and **undercut the competition**. In a four-month period in 1872, Standard Oil **bought out 22 of its 26 competitors** in Cleveland. Rockefeller had established a **virtual monopoly** of the Cleveland refining business. By 1880, Rockefeller was refining some 90 per cent of U.S. oil, at a time when the U.S. was the world's only oil producer.

In the 1880s oil was discovered in Ohio, but also in Russia and in Asia. Standard Oil had never owned its own oil wells. The company started to **buy oil fields** around the country, eventually controlling 25 per cent of U.S. oil production.

The company began to control every aspect of the oil business, including railroad tank cars and a home delivery network. It started to develop pipelines and came into conflict with its main haulier, the Pennsylvania Railroad, who started to acquire its own refineries and pipelines. Standard Oil withheld payments and colluded with other railroads to start a **price war** until the railroad backed down and sold their pipelines to Standard Oil. The Commonwealth of Pennsylvania indicted Rockefeller for **monopolising the oil business**, starting a flood of actions in other states.

Because American corporate law made it difficult for companies incorporated in one state to operate in another, Standard Oil had formed a **holding company** called the Standard Oil Trust. Eventually, in 1911, 'anti-trust' regulations were used to disband the central Trust, breaking it into a 34 separate companies based in individual states around the country. These new companies went to become Exxon, Mobil, Conoco, Chevron and others, which were in turn to merge and develop into the oil corporations of today. Ironically, Henry Ford had introduced the first Model T Ford in 1908, and demand for another oil-derived product – gasoline – was about to boom. The value of shares in all of the newly devolved Standard Oil companies rose sharply, and Rockefeller **owned a quarter of the shares in all of those companies**. His wealth grew even further, and Rockefeller became the first American to be worth more than $1 billion and, in relative terms, the richest American of all time.

In practice

- Establish a position in a growth industry
- Grow by investment and acquisition to achieve a dominant position
- Use your position to strike advantageous deals with suppliers, improving your market dominance
- Integrate vertically to control all aspects of your business
- Act within the law

THE BODY SHOP
Anita RODDICK
1942–2007

ANITA RODDICK OPENED THE first-ever Body Shop in Brighton, on the south coast of Britain, in 1976. She hoped to make a living from the shop while her husband, Gordon, was away fulfilling his dream to ride on horseback from Buenos Aires to New York – a trip that would take two years.

Roddick raised a bank loan of £4,000 (taken out in her husband's name, because the bank did not feel she was sufficiently business-like), and opened a rather dilapidated store, selling homemade soaps, shampoos and lotions made from natural ingredients, some sourced directly from producers – aloe vera from Guatemala; marula oil from Namibia. Customers took to her concept from the get-go, and within a year, Roddick had opened a second store.

The ideas

The first stores set the tone for what would become a global business within the next decade. Customers felt that The Body Shop was a place where they could buy a new, sensual range of cosmetic products that did not damage the environment and helped producers in poor communities around the globe. Shopping at The Body Shop became more of a **political and environmental statement** than an act of consumption.

Sales materials in the shop enthused about the natural **health-giving properties** of the ingredients and the history of the people who harvested and used them in their own lives. There was a promise that none of the ingredients had been tested on animals. Products were unperfumed, and customers could add their own scents from a range of perfume oils if they chose to do so. Bottles were **recyclable**, and customers were encouraged to bring back their empty containers to be refilled.

Roddick was a tireless and enthusiastic campaigner for a range of social and environmental causes; newspaper interviews in support of her chosen causes generated **good publicity** for the store.

When her husband returned from his trek, he found that Anita had created a small but thriving business and saw the potential to **franchise the operation**. Many of the new franchisees were women, keen to be involved in the exciting new venture. By 1982, two new Body Shop franchises were opening every month.

In 1984, the company **went public**. Hundreds of new franchises opened across Europe and then North America. By 2005, the company would have 2,000 stores in 50 countries around the world, generating $986 million in revenue.

The Roddicks came to regret the decision to take their company public, however. There is an inevitable tension between running a multinational and espousing a relatively radical **social agenda**.

As The Body Shop prospered, the percentage of ingredients that were purchased under **genuine 'fair trade' conditions** was estimated by one source at under one per cent. Green activists pointed out that, like other cosmetic manufacturers, The Body Shop used synthetic colours, fragrances and preservatives in its products. The company's **stance against testing cosmetics on animals** was robust and genuine; nevertheless, some basic ingredients had been tested on animals in the past before becoming commonplace commercial ingredients. In 1994, The Body Shop committed itself to an **audit of its environmental, social and animal protection activities**, one of the first companies to do so.

In 1996, Roddick and her husband stepped down from the day-to-day running of the company and in 2006, to the dismay of some die-hard supporters, The Body Shop was sold to the L'Oréal Group for $1.3 billion. L'Oréal paid a premium price for The Body Shop, in recognition of the **set of values** and the association with Roddick herself that it was acquiring along with the brand and assets. L'Oréal's 2011 annual report said that, 'True to its pioneering spirit, The Body Shop successfully combines innovation, sensorial products and performance while defending its values, in particular, Community Fair Trade and environmental protection.'

In practice

- Set up a business that reflects your own interests; be unconventional

- Being unconventional generates good PR; exploit it

- Scale up; consider franchising

- Going public can lead to difficulties, especially if you are unconventional

- It is better to have principles and to struggle to live up to them than to have no principles

STARBUCKS
Howard SCHULTZ
1953–

HOWARD SCHULTZ CAN BE credited with building his coffeehouse empire not once, but twice. Having grown his company from a few shops in Seattle into a global phenomenon, Schultz stepped down as CEO in 2000, staying on as the company's chairman.

In 2008, the Great Recession was about to begin and not buying an expensive cup of coffee was at the top of most people's list of simple ways to save money. To get the company back on its feet, Schultz went back to the principles that had guided him when he first launched the company in 1987. Starbucks had stopped innovating, Schultz felt. 'If Frappuccino is a hot category and you introduce a new flavour, and it moves the needle a lot, the organisation comes to believe, "That was a great thing we did," and it imprints a feeling of, "That was innovation,"' he told *Fast Company* magazine. 'But that's not innovation. In fact, it's laziness.'

The ideas

Schultz was working for the Swedish coffee-machine maker firm Hammarplast in the early 1980s when he noticed that a coffee bean retailer in Seattle called Starbucks was buying more of their coffee machines than any other retailer, and paid them a visit. Starbucks at the time had five stores and sold only roasted coffee beans and coffee-making equipment, but they proved that there was a market for speciality coffees. Schultz joined them as **marketing director**.

While on a visit to a trade fair in Milan, in northern Italy, Schultz was struck by how the city's **espresso bars functioned as social hubs**. Inspired, Schultz left Starbucks to set up his own coffeehouse, Il Giornale. Two years later, he and a group of investors bought the Starbucks business, with its six Seattle outlets, rebranded Il Giornale as Starbucks, and turned all of the locations into **coffeehouses**.

By 1989, there were 46 Starbucks across the north- and mid-western United States. In 1992, when the company sold 12 per cent of its shares in an initial public offering, there were 140 outlets and turnover stood at $73.5 million. The capital raised in the public offering allowed the chain to **double its number of stores**. In 1996, a Starbucks was opened in Tokyo, with others following in Europe and South America. Chains of coffee shops or restaurants were **acquired and turned over to the Starbucks format**.

The company chose its locations carefully to follow its guiding principle of offering people **'a third place between work and home.'**

Schultz embraced a spirit of responsibility to the company's various communities, committing to '**helping neighbourhoods thrive** wherever we do business.'

Even before the financial crisis of 2008, Starbucks stock was sliding, partly, at Schulz's own admission, because the company had become **obsessed by growth**. Schultz was urged to cut back on employee health benefits and to drop prices; he did neither. He **closed 900 underperforming stores**, and set out to trial a range of **innovations** to increase profitability. His R&D team began searching for a lighter-tasting coffee because their research told them that 40 per cent of U.S. coffee drinkers preferred their coffee that way.

Schultz led the acquisition of a fresh juice company and a specialist bakery to experiment with new offerings. In 2008, he bought a coffee-making equipment company; the machines cost over $10,000 each but, even if you have the money and would like to have one at home, you can't buy one: they are manufactured exclusively for Starbucks as part of what the company calls the 'theatre of experience' that its outlets try to create. 'We understand how to **elevate and romanticise an experience** built around a beverage,' Schultz told *Fast Company*.

Schultz's return to the CEO's role has resulted in a dramatic restoration of the company's fortunes: 2012 saw the company delivering best-ever results, with global sales in the region of $13 billion. The company is rapidly **expanding in China**, hoping to triple its current number of outlets to 1,500 by 2015.

Schultz maintains that the key to Starbucks's continued success lies beyond turnover and profit. 'Profit as a singular goal is a fairly shallow aspiration, and it's not enduring,' says Schulz. 'I've always said that you can't create long-term value for the shareholder unless you create **long-term value** for the employees and the communities you serve.'

In practice

- If people want good coffee, sell good coffee

- Create environments where people want to spend time

- Contribute to the community

- Focus on innovative services

- Create value for the communities you serve

GENERAL MOTORS
Alfred P. SLOAN
1875–1966

ALFRED SLOAN WAS AN engineer who started his working life in the late nineteenth century with a company manufacturing roller bearings. He later bought a controlling share in the business, and convinced the Olds Motor Company of the benefits of roller bearings; Ford and other manufacturers soon followed.

In 1916, Sloan sold his roller bearing company to General Motors (GM), who created a new division and made Sloan its president. When the new division was re-merged with GM, Sloan became a board member and vice-president, becoming president in 1923 and chairman in 1937. In 1920, GM accounted for less than 12 per cent of U.S. motor sales; when Sloan retired in 1956, that share was over 50 per cent and GM was the world's largest corporation.

Sloan is credited with having created key aspects of modern corporate management, focusing on decisions based on information. According to his *New York Times* obituary, Sloan was on record as saying, 'I never give orders. I sell my ideas to my associates if I can.' One associate described Sloan with a metaphor drawn from Sloan's earlier roller bearings: 'self-lubricating, smooth, eliminates friction and carries the load.'

The ideas

When Alfred Sloan died in 1966 at the age of 90, Henry Ford II, chairman of the Ford Motor Company and the eldest grandson of Henry Ford, described Sloan as 'one of the small handful of men who actually made automotive history,' and said that 'under his leadership, General Motors developed from a loosely organised group of companies into the present **highly efficient giant corporation**.'

In 1923, when Sloan became president of GM, the manufacturer was a hotchpotch of different brands and divisions that had been accumulated in the company's early history, including Buick, Oldsmobile, Cadillac, Chevrolet and others. Each had its own infrastructure.

Sloan **centralised policy, finance and aspects of central purchasing**, introducing key financial measures such as return on investment. The divisions were reluctant to relinquish control of their own cash but, with his hands on the key levers of corporate control, Sloan was then keen to **delegate operational control** to divisional managers.

Sloan organised and rationalised the company's disparate car range into **non-competing brands** that would offer consumers **a car for every stage of their life**: 'mass producing a full line of cars graded upward in quality and price' from the Chevrolet, which competed with the Ford Model T, up though Oakland, Buick and Oldsmobile to the luxury Cadillac.

He also introduced the idea of **planned obsolescence** – creating new styles that would replace the old, fuelling continued demand. Since old Henry Ford was beginning to think that his Model T did not need replacement or development, GM began to win share, especially since it refreshed its styles on an annual basis, constantly offering consumers something new.

By 1929, GM had overtaken Ford as market leader, and was to hold that lead for over 70 years. The company survived the Great Depression of the 1930s by **closing plants**, **increasing efficiencies** and **lowering costs**, leading to greater market share.

In 1937, GM faced a 44-day sit-down strike by workers seeking union recognition. The patrician Sloan **refused to negotiate**, but lost public sympathy and backed down, handing over negotiations to his vice-president of operations, William Knudsen. Soon afterwards, Sloan handed the presidency to Knudsen and took on the role of chairman.

Sloan the engineer has been accused of over-emphasising rationality in business at the expense of the human aspect of large organisations, but he himself acknowledged the key role of **emotional input**. 'An essential aspect of our management philosophy is the factual approach to business judgement,' Sloan wrote in his autobiography, *My Years with General Motors*, '[but] the final act of business judgement is of course intuitive.'

In practice

- Pull disparate operations together to make a cohesive unit

- Centralise policy and core functions but delegate decision-making to divisions

- Offer a coordinated range of products

- Constantly introduce new products

- Be informed by data; but use your intuition in making the final decision

KIMBERLEY-CLARK
Darwin SMITH
1926–1995

SOON AFTER DARWIN SMITH was made chief executive of the paper products company Kimberley-Clark, he was diagnosed with cancer of the nose and throat and told that he had less than a year to live. When he attended his first annual meeting as CEO, he was receiving radiation therapy. But he told the board of directors that he had no plans to die for some time – and he was right. He lived for 25 more years, 20 of them as CEO of the company.

Smith took the company in a radical new direction. He closed down the paper mills that had been the foundation of the 100-year-old company and sold off timberland, using the proceeds to re-launch the company's diaper range, going head to head with the mighty Procter & Gamble Company, whose leading Pampers brand had created the market for disposable diapers. 'Wall Street said: You're writing Kimberley-Clark's obituary,' a former vice-president of the company told *Investors Business Daily*. 'You can't compete with Procter & Gamble, they're too big and powerful.'

The ideas

After graduating cum laude from Harvard in 1955, Darwin Smith went to work for a legal firm in Chicago before joining Kimberley-Clark as a lawyer, intending to gain some corporate experience and then go back to practising law. Instead, he rose steadily through the ranks of the company until his appointment in 1971 as CEO.

Kimberley-Clark had been founded in 1872 as a paper manufacturer, and later launched paper-based products such a Kotex, a disposable feminine hygiene product, and Kleenex, the first disposable paper tissue. Smith's decision to close or sell the company's six paper mills was a **complete break with the past**. When Smith told his wife that he had made the decision to close the mills, he said, 'If you have a cancer in your arm, you've got to **have the guts to cut off your arm**.'

The decision to go **head to head with Procter & Gamble** and re-launch Huggies was equally controversial. Kimberley-Clark had come close to leaving the diaper market because it couldn't keep pace with P&G's innovations to their Pampers brand. Smith increased his research and development budget from just under $20 million in 1975 to $110 million by 1987, creating a team of 1,200 researchers, almost one-third of whom had doctorate degrees. The researchers developed a **unique paper fabric** that allowed liquids to pass in one direction only, trapping liquid and keeping babies' skin dry.

Smith invested heavily in **TV advertising** to take on the established Pampers brand. By 1992, Smith's last year as CEO, Huggies had 50 per cent of the U.S. disposable diaper market, and accounted for 23 per cent of Kimberley-Clark's $7 billion turnover.

Smith was known as a robust and challenging leader. 'The higher you moved up in the executive ranks, the harder he was on you,' the former senior VP told *Investors Business Daily*. 'He was tough and blunt ... He would ask you a question about your part of the business – it might be at a meeting, it might be at a cocktail party. You had to answer right away; you couldn't say, 'Well, that's a good question.' If you did that, you were dead. He wanted to see if you were really **plugged into your part of the business**.'

During Smith's 20 years as CEO, Kimberly-Clark was transformed from a sluggish, largely commodity-based business into a highly successful consumer products enterprise. The company's cumulative stock returns over this period **outperformed the market by a factor of four**, beating leading companies such as Coca-Cola and General Electric. When asked about his stellar performance as CEO, the modest Smith replied, 'I never stopped trying to become qualified for the job.'

In practice

- Take tough decisions: 'If you have a cancer in your arm, cut off your arm'

- Invest in research; create innovative technologies

- Build winning brands

- Take on the competition

- Be demanding; let colleagues know what you expect

FEDEX
Fred SMITH
1944–

FRED SMITH HAD A BIG IDEA while he was an undergraduate at Yale University. At the beginning of the computer revolution, manufacturers were persuading companies that machines could replace some of the functions carried out by people. It occurred to Smith, however, that this idea was only viable if the machines never broke down. The idea, Smith said, 'was that simple.' But his point was subtle. A manufacturer based in New York State could easily get a replacement part to a customer in New York City, but to service clients in, for example, the state of Texas, over 2,500 kilometres away, the company would need to be able to deliver spare parts, not in a few days, but overnight.

After university, Smith served with the U.S. Marines in Vietnam, and then joined his father-in-law's aircraft maintenance business. His experience with the company reinforced his belief in the need for a service that could guarantee rapid delivery of spare parts. He went on to found Federal Express (FedEx), using an integrated system of airplanes and company-owned trucks, and started a revolution in the way that companies were able to service customers at a distance.

The ideas

In the early 1970s, most existing couriers shipped packages on passenger airlines, putting them at the mercy of airline schedules and available cargo space. Airlines were also reducing the number of their night flights, making genuine overnight delivery almost impossible.

Smith worked with the concept of **hub-and-spoke distribution** – a network of ten destinations creates 45 possible routes connecting each destination to the others; but as long as one of the ten destinations is selected as a hub, only nine routes are needed. If the journey from one destination to the other could be achieved within the deadline, it did not matter if it did not take the shortest route; efficiencies in the system outweighed inefficiencies created by the longer routes taken by some packages.

Smith first **pitched his idea** to the U.S.'s central banking system, for the transport, sorting and rerouting of cheques, arguing that this system could save the banking system $3 million per day. There was interest, but also scepticism as to whether Smith's system could work in practice. Smith used his $4 million inheritance (his father had started a coach company, sold a controlling interest to Greyhound Lines, and started a nationwide chain of short-order restaurants) and $250,000 of personal money, and raised $91 million in venture capital. As Smith told *Fortune* magazine, 'You couldn't start small and expand, as you could with most businesses. From the very beginning, you had to **build an entire network**.' Federal Express was created in 1971.

In 1973, the system went live, with a fleet of 14 jets serving 25 cities, based on a hub in Memphis, Tennessee, using road vehicles for collection and delivery to the final destination. On its first night, the company carried only 186 packages.

High-profile **advertising campaigns** targeted not only business owners but also executives and secretaries with responsibility for urgent deliveries – an early slogan was, 'When it absolutely, positively has to be there overnight.'

Running cost were high, exacerbated by rising fuel prices and the depreciation of the company's substantial assets; Smith struggled to **keep enough funding in place**. After two years and losses of $26 million, the company turned a profit, delivering urgent packages ranging from computer parts to legal documents and human organs for emergency surgery.

Smith argued the case with government for a **relaxation of restrictive regulations** for air cargo operators; these were lifted in 1977, allowing Federal Express to use larger aircraft, spurring rapid growth for the company, which went public in 1978. In 1984, Federal Express recorded a **profit of $1 billion**, the first U.S. company to do so in less than ten years without mergers or acquisitions.

In 1989, Smith acquired Flying Tigers, a scheduled-cargo airline, making the company the world's **largest all-cargo airline**. Analysts questioned the acquisition, but Smith saw Flying Tigers' licence to fly to several major Asian destinations as a major asset. In 1995 FedEx (as the company was re-named in 1994) became the only U.S. cargo-only carrier with **aviation rights to China**.

Smith espoused a company philosophy of **People, Service, Profit**, based on employee satisfaction and customer service as the foundations for corporate success. The primacy of customer service is a basic corporate tenet. 'Ask any FedEx team member anyplace what the Purple Promise is,' says Smith, 'and they'll tell you: "I will make every FedEx experience outstanding."'

In practice

- Stick with your idea; make it happen

- Lobby against regulations that damage your business

- Think of ways to reach global markets

- Focus on employee satisfaction and customer service

WPP GROUP
Martin SORRELL
1945–

In 1977, MARTIN SORRELL went to work for the advertising firm Saatchi & Saatchi as finance director. The advertising agency was about to become one of the most famous ad agencies in the UK, and would subsequently launch a series of acquisitions of other agencies and consultancies on a worldwide scale, becoming one of the largest advertising agency networks in the world. The financial arrangements for the acquisitions were masterminded by Sorrell, who became known as 'the third brother.'

In 1985, Sorrell left Saatchi & Saatchi and started his own advertising business. He began by acquiring a number of sales promotion agencies, and then shocked the world by making a hostile bid for one of the most prestigious advertising agencies of all, J. Walter Thomson (JWT). Created in the U.S. in the late nineteenth century by its eponymous founder, JWT was the agency that created the world's first TV commercial. The industry had perhaps forgotten that JWT was no longer wholly owned by its partners, as it was in 'the old days': it was now a publicly traded company. It could be bought.

The ideas

When he left Saatchi & Saatchi, Sorrell bought a **shell company** called Wire & Plastics Products (WPP) and used it as a vehicle to build his empire. The advertising world was shifting; mass media no longer necessarily commanded vast audiences; clients were increasingly keen to be able to measure the results of their marketing activities. After the **acquisition** of various sales promotion, graphic design and video operations, which Sorrell felt would prosper in the new climate, he set his sights on JWT.

The agency was one of the strongest brands in the advertising world, with a global reach, but it was delivering poor earnings. Sorrell built up a five per cent stake in the agency, leading to the advertising industry's **first hostile takeover bid** in 1987. His war chest of cash allowed him to outbid other potential buyers and JWT's supporters, finally acquiring the company for $566 million.

Two years later, Sorrell bought another iconic U.S. agency, Ogilvy & Mather, for $860 million. David Ogilvy, the British-born copywriter and founding partner of the agency, by then in his seventies, memorably called Sorrell 'an odious little shit who has never written an advertisement in his life.' The two were later reconciled.

In the early 1990s, Britain entered a recession. Sorrell had bought Ogilvy and Mather with debt and preferred stock rather than equity and was suddenly struggling. 'I made a mistake,' Sorrel told Mark Tungate, author of *Adland: A Global History of Advertising.* 'If I'd done the deal with half-debt, half-equity, it would never have reached that stage. It was a dreadful period.'

WPP did recover, **swapping debt for equity** with banks such as J.P Morgan and Citibank, and went on to win IBM's global business. In 2000, WPP acquire Young & Rubicam for $4.7 billion, the largest acquisition in advertising history. Sorrell continued to buy, building WPP into one of the world's **leading communication services companies**.

He organised the group into a **coherent organisation**, bringing together all of the group's resources to pitch successfully for the global accounts like HSBC, Samsung and Vodafone. Conversely, the group's diversity allowed it to **handle conflicting clients**, such as Unilever and Procter & Gamble, managing accounts from these clients in separate parts of the empire.

In an interview with CNN in 2005, Sorrell acknowledged that he had a **reputation as a micromanager**, but said that he took that as 'a compliment not an insult ... I just think detail's important. I think accuracy's important.' He described his commitment to the company that he built as being like an obsession: 'WPP will always be more important to me than to anybody else ... because we started it 20 years ago with two people in one room ... And this is not a job, this is fun ... This is my way of life.'

In practice

- Build an empire by acquisition

- Create a coherent organisation; put the right pieces in place

- No target is unassailable

- Watch your debt level

- Stick with the detail

TATA GROUP
Jamsetji Nusserwanji TATA
1839–1904

JAMSETJI TATA'S VISION WAS to make a difference for his fellow countrymen – to create employment, raise living standards, and create wealth for his nation.

He began in textiles, introducing new technologies, modern management techniques and enlightened employment practices to the Indian market. Then he went to work on a grand vision to create the foundations for a modern industrial and technological economy in India, setting in motion projects to launch India's (and Asia's) first iron and steel company, a hydroelectric power supply company and a national institute of science. His sons and other relatives were to complete these grand projects, leading to the creation of the modern Tata Group – the Mumbai-based conglomerate with operations in over 80 countries – and helping to launch India on its way to becoming a major economic power.

The ideas

Jamsetji Tata was born in 1839, in Navsari, in the western Indian state of Gujarat. India had been ruled by Britain's East India Company since 1757; the Indian Rebellion of 1857 would lead the British Government to assume control of India; the British Raj would last until India regained its independence in 1947. Tata was to name one of his cotton mills 'Empress,' in recognition of the fact that the mill was opened on 1 January 1877, the day on which Britain's Queen Victoria was proclaimed as Empress of India, and to name a second mill 'Swadeshi' ('own country') as part of a growing movement to see India create its own manufacturing industries. Tata's efforts to create a **modern industrial base** for India can be seen as an essential part of India's progress towards independence.

Tata's **first cotton mill** began production in 1877. Tata had visited the cotton mills of Lancashire, in England, to study their production techniques. Whereas most Indian cotton mills used native-grown short-staple cotton to produce a coarse cloth using relatively simple machines, Tata imported long-staple cotton from Egypt and used **more advanced machinery** to produce a cloth that could **compete with the best imported cloth** from Lancashire.

He also demonstrated an enlightened **concern for the welfare** of his workforce, supplying clean water and sanitation, as well as fire extinguishers and sprinkler systems to guard against the ever-present risk of fire. He introduced **performance-related pay**, retirement benefits, medical care, accident compensation and childcare schemes.

In 1903, Tata opened the spectacular Taj Mahal hotel in Mumbai, the first building in the city to be **lit with electricity** from the hotel's own generators. The hotel was the grandest and most modern in India: Tata built it partly because he, despite being a wealthy man, was refused entry to other hotels run by British owners; the Taj Mahal would be the best hotel in India – and it would be **open to Indians**.

At the end of the nineteenth century Tata had begun to plan for the creation of **three great enterprises**: the Tata Iron and Steel Company; the Tata Hydro-Electric Power Supply Company and an Indian State Institute of Science. Tata's surveyors spent several years locating an ideal site for an **iron foundry**; they settled on a village called Sakshi, west of Kolkata, with access to local coalfields, ore and a plentiful supply of water. His **hydroelectric scheme** was based on building dams to catch the annual monsoon rains, providing electricity for the city of Mumbai.

But before he could undertake these projects, Tata died in 1904, in Germany, after a sudden illness. His sons, Dorabji and Ratanji, with other family members, developed the iron foundry and built the dams, creating the beginnings of what are now Tata Steel and Tata Power. They also ensured that their father's vision of an Indian Institute of Science became a reality. Dorabji and his family associates further **diversified the company into consumer goods and aviation**, creating the foundations of today's Tata Group.

In practice

- Be well-informed and well-connected
- Stay at the leading edge of industrial progress

- Use the latest technology

- Look after employees' welfare

- Start grand projects

- Benefit your communities

TATA GROUP
Ratan TATA
1937–

RATAN TATA HAD THE misfortune to step into shoes of giants. The great-grandson of Tata Group's founder, Jamsetji Tata, he was also the nephew of Jehangir Ratanji Dadabhoy ('JRD') Tata, the group's fourth chairman, under whose leadership the Tata Group had become a major conglomerate with assets of over $5 billion.

Ratan, in contrast with his illustrious and dashing uncle, was a reserved young man who had been happy studying architecture at Cornell University in the USA. In 1962, after graduating, he returned to India and joined the family business, working on the factory floor at Tata Steel. When JRD named Ratan as his successor in 1981, opening a clear route for him to become chairman of the Tata Group at a later date, there was nearly a revolt. As reported in India's *Outlook Business* magazine, Ratan recalled that his uncle, JRD, 'came to my rescue and slowly turned around the whole conversation.'

The ideas

As early as 1983, Ratan Tata spelled out his strategic vision for the Tata Group's future, which included a move into **high-technology industries**, growth through appropriate **mergers and acquisitions**, and a leveraging of **group synergies**.

In 1991, Tata became chairman of Tata Group and faced a formidable management task: each of the established directors of the main Tata divisions was like the **ruler of their own kingdom**; some believed that they were better placed to run the group than Tata himself. The resignation in 1993 of Russi Modi, head of Tata Steel, was seen by many as a sign that Tata had succeeded in **establishing his leadership** of the group.

With advice from management consultants McKinsey & Co, Tata **rationalised** the group's activities, moving out of areas such as oil mills, pharmaceuticals, cosmetics and cement.

Tata had become chairman of the group in the year that India began its process of economic liberalisation. As former Tata Sons executive director Alan Rosling told *Management Today* in 2009, 'It became obvious that, whether or not Tata ventured beyond its borders, it would face foreign competition. It was a strategic imperative of many of our businesses to internationalise, or they would struggle to remain competitive.'

Tata took up the challenge and launched what would become a **$20 billion campaign of global acquisitions**. In 2000, Tata Tea (now Tata Global Beverages) acquired the UK's largest tea company, Tetley; in 2004, Tata Motors bought the heavy vehicle division of South Korea's Daewoo Motors ; in 2005 Tata Steel acquired Singapore-based NatSteel, and in 2007 took control of Corus, the Anglo-Dutch steel giant; in 2008, Tata Motors bought UK-based Jaguar Land Rover from Ford and stunned the car industry with its success in turning the company around.

Ratan Tata became famous for championing the production of the Tata Nano 'people's car,' the **world's cheapest car**, originally sold at the symbolic price of one lakh (100,000 rupees; about $1,800).

According to *Outlook Business*, when Tata handed over the chairmanship of the group to Cyrus Mistry, group revenues were 40 times greater than in 1991, and net profit had increased fourfold.

In practice

- Establish your leadership

- Set out your core vision

- Compete internationally; get big

- Champion iconic projects

TOYOTA
Kiichiro TOYODA
1894–1952

KIICHIRO TOYODA'S FATHER, Sakichi Toyoda, the founder of Toyoda Automatic Loom Works, was a famous Japanese inventor and industrialist. The holder of over 100 patents, Sakichi Toyoda's most famous invention was an automatic loom involving the principle of *jidoka* – 'intelligent automation' or 'automation with a human touch.' The machine would stop itself if a thread broke or ran out, allowing its operator to rectify the fault and thereby to supervise several machines – an efficiency that became increasingly important in the recession of the 1920s. Referred to as the 'father of Japanese industry,' and 'king of Japanese inventors,' many of Sakichi Toyoda's far-reaching and profound observations on the industrial process saw their full development through his son, Kiichiro.

The ideas

The elder Toyoda had little interest in formal education and wanted Kiichiro to start to learn his trade in the family loom factory. Thanks to the intervention of Kiichiro's stepmother, Sakichi's second wife, Toyoda did attend high school and then university, earning a degree in mechanical engineering from Tokyo Imperial University, becoming one of a **first generation of technologically educated young people** in Japan as the country's industrial revolution was gathering pace. He started work in the loom factory, and soon travelled to the U.S. and Europe to study manufacturing, spending two weeks with the leading British textile machinery manufacturer, Platt Brothers, before returning to Japan.

One of Toyoda's father's patents was for an automatic shuttle changer that would replace a shuttle that had run out of yarn without stopping the weaving process. It was a brilliant device, but extremely difficult to manufacture to a sufficient degree of precision. Kiichiro **refined his father's invention** and was granted his own patent.

Toyoda now had the blueprint for a **perfect automated loom** – one that could change shuttles seamlessly, even at high operating speeds, and that would automatically sense a broken thread, preventing wasteful production of flawed material. Platt Brothers offered to buy the **worldwide licensing rights** to manufacture the revolutionary machine, and Toyoda visited them again to negotiate a deal, which would grant Platt's a licence for all territories apart from Japan, China and the U.S.

On the same trip, Toyoda again visited the U.S. and the new factories for producing the increasingly popular automobiles. He noticed that the Platt Brothers loom-making business was struggling while the automobile manufacturers were booming. He persuaded his father to allow him to use space in the loom factory to dismantle and **reverse-engineer American-made engines and automobiles**. After his father died in October 1930, Toyoda convinced the board to invest in automobile manufacture.

The company's **first passenger car**, the AA, was launched in 1936 under the Toyoda name. In 1937, the car business split off from its parent company as the Toyota Motor Corporation (the family name Toyoda, literally 'fertile rice paddies,' was felt to reflect old-fashioned agricultural values).

The concept of *jidoka* was fully developed, dictating that it is better to stop the production process, despite the cost, than let faults enter the process and create problems further down the line. Production workers were **empowered to stop the production line** if they detected a fault; the process then was not merely to rectify the individual fault but to get to its source, eliminating future faults.

This philosophy underpins a further, radical aspect of what is now known as the Toyota Production System: '**Just In Time.**' If errors have been ironed out of the system early in the production process, then the final assembly can proceed like clockwork, with parts arriving 'just in time' to be assembled, removing the need for costly inventories of parts waiting to be used. The Toyota Production System led to the general manufacturing philosophy now known as **lean manufacturing**.

In practice

- Absorb the lessons of your mentors

- Be open to new ideas; watch out for developing trends

- Bring people with you; take them in new directions

- Adapt and develop revolutionary ideas

Steamships and railways
Cornelius VANDERBILT
1794–1877

CORNELIUS VANDERBILT BUILT AN empire of steamships and railways at the dawn of North America's industrial age, and became one of the country's richest men. At his death, his net worth of $105 million was equivalent to one per cent of the country's GDP.

Hardworking and far-sighted, Vanderbilt started out sailing a ferryboat in the waters of Upper New York Bay. He saw the potential of steam power and played a significant role in the development of a modern transport system for America, accelerating the nation's economic growth.

Vanderbilt was also a great competitor, taking on established monopolies and undercutting their prices. His obituary in the *New York Times* describes how Vanderbilt, in his steamship days, 'pounced down upon the [monopolising] offenders and literally drove them from the waters. Nor did he, when he had vanquished them, establish a monopoly of his own. His principle of low rates ... was never violated, so that in every way the public were the gainers.'

The ideas

Vanderbilt created a **successful ferry business** in the waters around New York, taking advantage of the 1812 conflict between the United States and the British Empire to supply the forts of New York Bay with provisions at night, while he continued his passenger business by day. By 1817, at the age of 23, Vanderbilt had amassed $9,000. He invested his profits in more sailing boats, but saw that the new steamships, able to navigate regardless of tide and current, were the future.

Vanderbilt kept his sailboat business, but joined one of the new **steamboat entrepreneurs**, running services from New York to New Jersey and Pennsylvania, in the days when rivers, lakes and coastal waters represented America's main transport network.

Vanderbilt and his employer came into conflict with the New York legislature, who had granted a monopoly of ferry services to another operator. Vanderbilt **avoided arrest** by varying the timings of services and landing stages used and, on occasions, by hiding in a secret compartment of his boat when the authorities attempted to arrest him at sea. The monopoly of New York's waters was finally overturned in the U.S. Supreme Court in 1824. In 1829, Vanderbilt left his employer to set up on his own, having built up capital of $30,000.

He bought two steamboats, designed and built a third and started operating along the same routes. The new owners of Vanderbilt's previous employer's business **paid him to stop competing** with them; he began to operate services in the Hudson River instead. At this time he both bought out competitors and was himself paid off for ceasing to compete. At times Vanderbilt **subsidised low fares with higher prices for food and drink** on board his boats – an early model for 'budget' travel operators.

In 1838, Vanderbilt took over the Staten Island Ferry Service. He also began to **buy stock in the early railroads** that were beginning to link the rapidly industrialising towns of Boston and other New England towns to the ports of New York and Long Island, becoming president of the New York, Providence & Boston Railroad in 1847.

When the California Gold Rush began in 1849, Vanderbilt opened a steamboat service with a short overland stage to America's west coast via the rivers and lakes of Nicaragua, avoiding the dangerous journey around the Americas via Cape Horn, and offering a **faster journey time** than the sea route, using mule trains across the isthmus of Panama (the Panama Railway would not be opened until 1855, and the Canal not until 1914).

He sold his controlling interest in this business to take his family on a tour of Europe in the *North Star* – the first ocean-going steamboat built by a private individual – but returned to find that the new owners of the Nicaragua venture had failed to pay him money owed. He wrote a memorable letter: 'Gentlemen, you have undertaken to cheat me. I won't sue you, for the law is too slow. **I'll ruin you.**' Vanderbilt opened new services to America's west coast, undercutting his previous colleagues' fares and forcing them eventually to buy him off, making all outstanding payments and buying ships from Vanderbilt at prices set by him.

Vanderbilt opened a transatlantic service using the fastest steamships yet seen and continued to **buy shares in railways**, including the two railways that provided access to Manhattan itself. Vanderbilt's transport empire made him one of the richest Americans ever.

In practice

- Start off small, work hard, and build up your capital

- Compete fiercely

- Undercut established services if necessary

- Subsidise low headline prices with profits from related services

- See new opportunities; quickly offer new services

- Build for the future

WAL-MART
Sam WALTON
1918–1992

THE FIRST WAL-MART STORE opened in 1962 in Rogers, Arkansas. It was the nucleus from which Sam Walton grew a business empire that now has almost 4,000 stores in the U.S. and operations in more than 15 countries around the world. Wal-Mart was the largest corporation by revenue in the world in 2010 and 2011. 'If I had to single out one element in my life that has made a difference for me,' said Walton, 'it would be a passion to compete. That passion has pretty much kept me on the go, looking *ahead* to the next store visit, or the next store opening, or the next merchandising item I personally wanted to promote out in those stores – like a minnow bucket or a Thermos bottle or a mattress pad or a big bag of candy.'

The ideas

In 1945, 26-year-old Sam Walton took a loan from his father-in-law to buy a Butler Brothers 'Ben Franklin' **variety store franchise** in Newport, Arkansas. Variety stores sold a wide range of everyday household items at low prices. Franchisors supplied merchandise at fixed costs and set the retail price; franchisees were obliged to buy 80 per cent of their merchandise from the parent company.

Walton began to look for suppliers who would offer him better deals, and found some. 'I've got to tell you, it drove the Ben Franklin folks crazy. Not only were they not getting their percentages, they couldn't compete with the prices I was buying at.' Walton had discovered the principle that was to guide his career in retail: source goods at exceptional prices and **accept a lower margin** to drive higher sales and achieve higher overall profits. His other guiding principle was equally simple: **give your customers what they want**.

Walton made a great success from his franchise, increasing annual sales from $72,000 to £250,000 over five years. But he had failed to ensure that the lease on the store was renewable – the store owner refused to renew the lease, bought the franchise, fixtures and inventory from Walton and passed the business on to his son. Walton took it badly. 'I had built the best variety store in the whole region ... and now I was being kicked out of town.' He **blamed himself for buying a bad lease**, but picked himself up and used the proceeds from the sale to buy another Ben Franklin franchise in nearby Bentonville, Arkansas, which he set up as Walton's Five and Dime.

In 1962, Walton broke from the franchise model and opened the first Wal-Mart store in Rogers. Wal-Mart was to be a fully-fledged discount operation. Store number one carried two signs: **'We Sell for Less'** and **'Satisfaction Guaranteed.'**

After two successful years, Walton started to open more stores. Within five years, there were 24 Wal-Mart stores, all in the state of Arkansas. In 1968, stores were opened in Missouri and Oklahoma.

Walton learned to fly a light aircraft to cut down on the amount of time he was spending driving, and started to **scout for promising new store locations from the air**.

Many things set Sam Walton's business leadership apart: his genuine love of 'merchandising'; his **passion to compete**; and his **hunger for information** about any aspect of his and his competitors' business. He was a great **believer in change**, to stop colleagues from getting into routines and to stop the competition from being able to predict what Wal-Mart would do next.

He was incredibly hardworking, often **starting work at 4.30** in the morning, when the uninterrupted time allowed him to 'think and plan and sort things out.' On a Saturday morning, he would go into the office even earlier to go through the week's figures for every store to prime himself for the routine Saturday morning meetings.

Perhaps the most impressive aspect of Walton's leadership was the way in which he **instilled a distinctive culture** throughout the organisation. Part of this was his commitment to 'partnership' – to sharing the company's success via **profit-sharing** and other incentives.

Another part of it was the infectious delight that Walton took in retailing. 'It's sort of a **"whistle while you work"** philosophy,' he wrote, 'and we not only have a heck of a good time with it, we work better because of it ... we make people feel part of a family in which no one is too important or too puffed up to lead a cheer or be the butt of a joke.'

In practice

- Be hungry for information; take up the best ideas
- Source at low prices; consider lower margins to drive higher volumes
- Stay in touch; change constantly; share success
- Take delight in what you do; create a happy working environment

HTC
Cher WANG
1958–

CHER WANG'S FATHER, Wang Yung-Ching, founded a business empire in Taiwan – Formosa Plastics Ltd – and became one of the world's richest men. Several of his nine children went on to found their own businesses – not in plastics, but in computer technology. Cher co-founded High Tech Computer Corporation, now HTC Corporation, in 1997, to manufacture a combined personal digital assistant and mobile phone. The first product was not successful, but she persisted, investing millions in design and engineering, and created a research department that put the company at the forefront of touch and wireless technology.

The ideas

Wang went to school in Oakland, California, and then went on to the University of California, Berkeley, as a music major, with the dream of becoming a concert pianist. After three weeks, however, she decided to switch to economics: 'I had the dream,' she told the *New York Times* in 2008, 'but I am also **very realistic.**'

Wang's sister, Charlene, had set up a company manufacturing motherboards; Wang went to work for the company in 1982 as a salesperson. In an interview at the 2011 AsiaD digital conference, she said that it was dragging heavy PCs around the train stations of Europe in order to be able to demonstrate the performance of the company's motherboards that led to her **'daydreaming' about future mobile devices**.

In 1997, Wang and her husband, Chen Wen-Chi, founded High Tech Computer Corporation, but 'the market just wasn't ready for a PDA phone that behaved like a minicomputer,' Wang told *BusinessWeek* in 2005. She also admitted to software and design weaknesses in the product.

Her response was to invest in more research and development, building up an **R&D team of nearly 1,000 people**, determined that HTC would represent the cutting edge of technology. In 2000, the company landed the **vital contract with Compaq** to build the iPAQ handheld computer.

HTC began to build its reputation as a leading manufacturer for mobile phone companies, supplying **custom products** offering higher functionality. HTC produced one of the world's first touchscreen smartphones, quickly saw the potential of 3G and GPS, and drove advances in **'intuitive' touchscreen functionality** after researching people's instinctive hand gestures.

A key early decision was to work almost exclusively with the Microsoft operating system for wireless devices. Wang cultivated what was to become a **core strategic partnership with Microsoft**, meeting regularly with Bill Gates and Stephen Ballmer, impressing both with her determination to keep HTC at the forefront of innovation and with her commitment to making the necessary investment to achieve this. The partnership allowed HTC to be **first to market** with the latest Microsoft updates.

In 2006 HTC launched the **first HTC-branded phones**. HTC then embraced Google's Android operating system, launching the world's first Android-based phone in 2009. In 2011 total revenues were NT$466 billion (US$14 billion) and the HTC brand entered the Interbrand Top 100 Best Global Brands list, the first Chinese brand to do so.

HTC's revenues began to suffer in late 2011 in the face of stiff competition from Apple's iPhone and Samsung's Galaxy. HTC has also faced patent challenges from Apple and Nokia. Wang remains confident. In recent years, the company has launched HTC-branded phones in China, India and Japan and **continues to innovate**. As she told Bloomberg news in June 2012, 'We have faced and overcome bigger challenges, and we will try even harder.'

In practice

- Create products that people have not yet imagined

- Expect failures

- Invest in research; be at the leading edge

- Form strategic partnerships; invest to stay in front

- As the competition catches up, try harder

CHINA VANKE
WANG Shi
1951–

WANG SHI HAS TAKEN an unlikely career path for a property developer whose company, China Vanke, is currently China's biggest property developer by sales. A soldier in the People's Liberation Army before becoming a railway engineer, Wang then took a job as a local government official in Guangdong Province and finally as a member of the Special Region Development Company for Shenzhen, China's first Special Economic Zone. He then started a business supplying chicken feed to Hong Kong and later began importing electronics goods, before making a prescient move into property development in 1988.

At that time, China's city-dwellers were provided with housing by the state, at a rent fixed at five per cent or less of people's salaries. In the 1990s, the government began to privatise housing by selling apartments to tenants, often at low prices. It was the beginning of a huge transfer of wealth from the state to individuals. Home ownership became a core aspiration of China's emerging middle class, and Wang's China Vanke was poised to become the biggest provider of housing in China – and in the world.

The ideas

The entrepreneurial bug bit Wang while he was at the Shenzhen Special Region Development Company. 'I felt depressed. My life was slow-paced,' Wang told *China Daily* newspaper in 2009. 'I wanted to try my hand at business and improve my life ... Shenzhen was like a bustling construction site in my eyes. I knew that's where I could **make the most of my talents** and start my enterprise.'

Shenzhen was still a small but rapidly growing city in a rural area; supplying live chickens to Hong Kong, 27 kilometres to the south, was a significant local business. Before the chickens ended up on the city's kitchen and restaurant tables, they needed corn to eat. Wang **set up a supply route** to take corn to Hong Kong and started his business.

He made good money until Hong Kong announced that it had found carcinogens in some chicken feed. Residents of Hong Kong stopped eating chicken and switched to pigeon. Then the typhoon season arrived and Wang's corn, sitting unwanted in freight wagons in Shenzhen, got wet and spoiled. Wang, heavily in debt, faced ruin. He made a **radical decision**, and started to buy up corn, persuading suppliers – whose business had dried up – to give him 100 days' credit. 'I never believed that people would quit eating chicken,' Wang said. 'If people in Hong Kong were to restart eating chicken, they would also need my corn.' As Wang's corn began to arrive in Shenzhen, Hong Kong announced that the earlier tests were wrong. Corn was not contaminated with carcinogens, and chicken was back on the menu. Wang made a killing.

Wang started to import electronic goods, then **moved into property** – a bold move in a country where most housing had been owned either collectively or by the state. 'I didn't know much about [property] management,' he told *Time* magazine in 2005, 'but I thought, Western companies already did it well, **so why not just copy that?**'

Wang reorganised his company in 1988 to form China Vanke, a shareholding real estate development company. The company was listed on the new Shenzhen Stock Exchange in 1991 – the second company to be listed, after the Shenzhen Development Bank. In 1993, Wang led the **first Shenzhen Stock Exchange takeover**, when Vanke acquired Shanghai property company Shenhu.

In recent years, Vanke has focused on building **small to medium sized houses for the mass market**, capitalising on its established brand and aiming to turn land into houses as quickly as possible, rather than holding onto land for possible speculative gains.

In 2013, Vanke made its first **foray into the U.S. market** with a joint venture for a $620 million development in San Francisco.

Wang was the first property developer in China to run a major **corporate advertising campaign**, establishing the Vanke as a known and trusted brand. 'We are becoming a dream that is shared by our clients, our staff, our industry and our society,' Wang told *Media* newspaper. 'To us, this is even more important than simply being the number one brand.'

In practice

- Start a business; explore your talents
- Spot likely new trends; get first-mover advantage
- Build a brand that people know and trust
- Make a contribution to society

91

S&A FOODS
Perween WARSI
1956–

Perween Warsi moved from India to North Wales, UK, with her husband, a doctor, in the mid-1970s. Although Indian and Pakistani restaurants and takeaways were a long-established part of British food culture, Warsi discovered that none of her favourite foods – and often not even the ingredients to make them ('my aubergines, my okra, my coriander, my chillies – I couldn't imagine life without green chillies') – were available in mainstream British shops. So she started to make samosas in her kitchen and persuaded local outlets to stock them. The samosas were an instant hit, and Warsi would soon parlay this initial success into a thriving ready-to-eat meal business. Today, S&A Foods operates six factories in the UK, supplying retailers and caterers not only with the Indian dishes Warsi missed from home, but with a wide selection of ethnic foods from around the world.

The ideas

Encouraged by the enthusiastic response to her homemade samosas, Warsi approached other outlets. Soon, she was employing five women to help her keep up with demand, and switched to **cooking at night** after a neighbour complained anonymously about the smell of cooking drifting from the family's apartment above her husband's surgery.

But Warsi's bigger ambition was to see her food on the shelves of the nation's supermarkets. 'I just wanted to **prove to the nation how tasty Indian food could be**, because I'm so proud of it,' she told *Derbyshire Life*. 'I have great food and somebody is selling not-so-good food. So surely people will buy mine?'

She made **'hundreds' of calls** to supermarkets until the Asda chain agreed to include her products in a blind tasting. Her foods came out tops. Warsi was ecstatic. 'Our products got the thumbs-up and it was the best day of my business life,' she told BBC News. 'It was absolutely fantastic – it was what I wanted so desperately and believed in.'

The early days, when the company was rapidly growing and operating out of a converted garage, were exhausting but rewarding, as Warsi **juggled 16-hour working days with the school run** and looking after the family. 'It was the most exciting time of my life. Seeing things happen, recruiting people, growing the business, launching new things ... it was amazing.'

Later, the company joined Hughes Food Group (HFG), providing the investment to allow S&A to move into a purpose-built factory and enter the ready-meals market. In 1990, HFG went into receivership. Warsi **asked to buy back her company**, but HFG refused. 'They were tough times,' Warsi told *Derbyshire Life*. 'When people come from large organisations and sit the other side of the table and say, "We're going to buy your company" ... that's heartbreaking. Here's the business you've built and nurtured and worked so hard for, and someone is saying, "I'm going to take your baby away."' In 1991, with support from the 3i venture capital group, Warsi led a management buyout and regained control of her company.

The company **diversified** into Thai, Malaysian and other food and pursues a policy of **relentless innovation**, releasing 300 products a year. 'It is everyone's responsibility to come up with new ideas,' Warsi said. 'It can be in design, packaging or processing.'

Warsi stays close to her staff, many of whom, like herself, have moved to Britain from other countries. She says that at times there have been up to **27 different languages spoken on her factory floor**.

Warsi launched a 'Call Perween' project, **encouraging staff to call her**; some of the calls are about personal matters; others are about new ideas or the company. She also launched a **'My Bright Idea'** campaign, awarding a £2,000 in a special Prize Day for the best idea of the year.

In practice

- If you have a better product, people will buy it

- Diversify

- Encourage everyone to think innovatively

- Invite comments and feedback

- Incentivise new ideas

IBM
Thomas J. WATSON
1874–1956

AFTER AN UNPROMISING START in various trades and businesses, Thomas J. Watson forged a career for himself as a salesman. While working as sales manager for the National Cash Register Company (NCR), he tried to galvanise his team by saying, 'We don't get paid to work with our feet. We get paid to work with our heads,' and wrote the word 'THINK' on an easel. He later had a small poster made up. The poster and the slogan were taken up by NCR, and were later used by Watson at the next company that he worked for, which Watson was to transform into the International Business Machines Company – IBM.

Watson, whose obituary in the *New York Times* referred to his reputation as 'the greatest salesman in the world,' focused throughout his career on delivering customer service and, as an inevitable corollary, on employing highly talented people. Once, when asked by a reporter if he had any hobbies, he replied, 'I collect salesmen.'

The ideas

In 1914, after leaving NCR, Watson joined the Computing Tabulating Recording Company (CTR) as general manager. The company's most technologically advanced product was punched-card data processing equipment. Watson concentrated on offering **customised solutions for larger businesses**.

He began to develop his distinctive style of management, insisting that executives be smartly dressed in dark suits and instilling a strong sense of **corporate pride and company spirit**. There were company sports teams and outings, a dedication to customer service and good incentives for sales success. In Watson's first four years, revenues doubled to £9 million. He expanded into Europe, Australia, Asia and South America. In 1924 he changed the company name.

With the onset of the Great Depression in the 1930s, Watson **maintained employment** and allowed inventory to build up in the conviction that, when the economy recovered, he would have a talented team in place and products waiting to fill demand. Despite the economic climate, he negotiated a $40,000 loan to enable the creation, in 1932, of a **research facility** at Endicott, New York.

The company's **labour-saving devices** found a ready market as companies contracted during the Depression. When the U.S. government introduced Social Insurance, requiring employees to make payments towards unemployment benefits and old age pensions – which entailed the collection of data about every employee's income and the calculation of benefits owed – Watson had the machines and the personnel needed to service the contract. IBM became the leading business machine company and one of the most generous employers in the U.S.

In 1937, IBM was approached by a Harvard university physicist, Howard Aiken, to build the world's first computer capable of carrying out **long calculations automatically**. Watson approved the astonishing investment of half a million dollars. The machine – over 50 feet long, eight feet high and weighing over five tons – was donated to Harvard University in 1944 and became known as the Harvard Mark 1. It paved the way for the company's first large-scale digital calculating machine and for the launch in 1952 of the IBM 701, which used vacuum tubes instead of electromagnetic switches, greatly reducing its size and making it the **first commercially viable computer** – though it was bought at first only by governments and research institutions.

Watson's policy had been not to sell but to **lease all of its machines**, and in 1952 it faced an antitrust suit from the government, which had calculated that IBM owned some 90 per cent of all of the business machines in the U.S. The company agreed to sell its machines rather than lease them, to supply parts and information to other companies wishing to service IBM machines and to license its patents.

Watson died in 1956, one month after giving control of IBM to his son, Tom Watson Jr. In 2011, IBM celebrated 100 years in business and, coincidentally, $100 billion in turnover. *Forbes* magazine asked IBM CEO Sam Palmisano which measure he thought Watson would have been most proud of. 'I say 100 years,' said Palmisano. 'Watson believed if you really created **value and not just technology** you could be around a very long time. That is more enduring than just getting big.'

In practice

- Focus on what adds most value

- Create an atmosphere of corporate pride and team spirit

- Maintaining employment and even inventory in downturns can create a competitive edge

- Invest in research

- Develop cutting-edge technologies, and commercial rewards will follow

GENERAL ELECTRIC
Jack WELCH
1935–

In 1960, JACK WELCH went straight from university to work for General Electric (GE). After just a year, however, he handed in his notice, planning to accept a new role at a smaller chemicals company. He had found the working environment in the giant multinational too bureaucratic, and felt that the 'standard' $1,000 pay rise that he had been given did not reflect his efforts and achievements.

His manager promised to create a working environment that would keep Welch free from red tape, allowing him to work in a small-company environment with the advantage of big-company resources.

Welch stayed with GE, and went on to become the company's youngest chairman and CEO in 1981. He ran the huge enterprise like a collection of small companies, capable of rapid change when needed and able to take advantage of new opportunities. Under his leadership, GE grew dramatically and consistently. At the time of his retirement in 2001, General Electric was the most valuable company in the world.

The ideas

When Welch took over as CEO in 1981, he embarked on a dramatic plan to **streamline** the giant conglomerate and drive earnings growth. GE would be either **number one or number two in any market** that it operated in, and would fix, sell or close any operation that did not make the grade.

Huge **lay-offs** of staff in Welch's early days earned him the nickname of 'Neutron Jack,' after the neutron bomb, which kills people but leaves buildings standing. 'I came into a company that had at least an extra 100,000, maybe 150,000 extra people,' Welch told CBS in 2009. 'It was the early '80s. We were making television sets in Syracuse, N.Y., and the Japanese were selling them at the mall cheaper than we were making them.'

When Welch's strategy of market dominance achieved its goal, giving GE divisions a clear dominance of precise markets, Welch moved the goalposts. He insisted that each market had to be defined so that **no division had more than a ten per cent share** of that market, hugely widening the competitive field.

GE began to move out of increasingly commoditised consumer appliances and towards services, such as **medical technologies, finance and television**.

Welch **promoted candour** in management, recognising the tendency, even in business, to avoid unpleasant truths. In keeping with his dislike of bureaucracy and 'standard' pay increases and bonuses, Welch **championed 'differentiation'** in all aspects of management. He insisted that his managers should identify the top-performing 20 per cent of their teams and give them exceptional rewards; the worst-performing ten per cent should be fired. 'Companies win when their managers make a clear and meaningful distinction between top- and bottom-performing businesses and people, when they **cultivate the strong and cull the weak**.'

Under Welch, wrote *BusinessWeek*, 'base salaries can rise by as much as 25 per cent in a year without a promotion. Cash bonuses can increase as much as 150 per cent in a year, to between 20 per cent and 70 per cent of base pay.' Welch also greatly expanded the granting of **stock options** to GE employees, but ensured that these were never routine and that, like all bonuses, they came with clear expectations as to future performance.

Welch introduced Motorola's **'Six Sigma' quality control programme** to GE – a demanding, statistically driven programme that aims to reduce defects to 3.4 per million products. The implementation of the programme – the largest corporate quality control programme ever undertaken, according to *BusinessWeek* – drove huge efficiencies, productivity gains and profits.

Welch's leadership style was **personal yet far-reaching**. Presentations by Welch to top management would be recorded on video, and used by managers to spread the word through the organisation. Welch would personally contact managers several layers down in the organisation to drive particular initiatives. He was also fond of **surprise visits**, including lunches arranged at short notice with middle managers. Employees, from direct reports to shop floor workers, would receive faxes of handwritten notes of thanks or praise, a copy of which would arrive by post soon afterwards.

Welch let his **managers act like entrepreneurs** driving their own companies, with the resources of GE behind them. '[We will] give them the benefits of a company the size of General Electric – financial, technological, and managerial – yet at the same time, provide them the freedom and flexibility that the owners of enterprises their size must have to win.'

In practice

'Jack's Rules' became a byword for the Welch management style. These represent some of his core leadership ideas:

- Control your destiny, or someone else will

- Face reality as it is, not as it was or as you wish it to be

- Be candid with everyone

- Lead, don't manage

- Change before you have to

- If you don't have a competitive advantage, don't compete

EBAY
Meg WHITMAN
1956–

THE ONLINE AUCTION SITE eBay was launched as AuctionWeb in 1995 in San Jose by Pierre Omidyar, a computer programmer who wanted to create a 'perfect market' where individuals could come together freely and trade anything they liked.

In 1997, the site's name was changed to eBay and won $6.7 million of venture capital. The financiers looked for a CEO to look after their investment, and their executive search agency contacted Meg Whitman, who was then working for the leading toy manufacturer Hasbro. She wasn't interested at first, but when she paid a visit to the operation in California, she began to see the potential. As she told *BusinessWeek*, 'eBay had two main things that really spoke to me. It enabled individuals to do things that they could not have done without the Web. The second thing was what Pierre said: "People have met their best friends on eBay."'

She recognised this as the way that communities of like-minded people tend to form around common interests. 'You tend to like people who like the same things you do,' she said. 'And so I saw it had the makings of a great brand.'

The ideas

After committing herself to eBay, Whitman saw her role as **focusing on the wants and needs** of the eBay community. 'Their passion for eBay (good and bad) was like nothing I'd ever seen in 20 years of business,' Whitman told the *New York Times* in 1999.

She set about **building the eBay brand**, hiring PepsiCo's head of marketing and launching a national advertising campaign. The company went public in 1998, raising $63 billion. Shares were offered at $18 but closed the first day's trading at over $47, valuing the company at nearly $1.9 billion and making Whitman a millionaire, thanks to her stock options. Whitman's advertising campaign began to drive more visitors to the site; by 1999 there were seven million members.

This success came at a cost: the volume of traffic caused the site to crash, sometimes for a whole day. Whitman helped to handle each crisis, working from a cubicle alongside her colleagues, handling customer complaints by phone and email and refunding millions of dollars worth of fees. She invested in a customer service operation that guaranteed a **response to customer enquiries within 24 hours**.

Her goal, she told *Salon.com* in 2001, was always to keep '**the small-town feel on a global scale.**'

Whitman opened the site to commercial sellers and made some highly focused **acquisitions of auction-related businesses**, including half.com, where used goods were sold at fixed prices, and, at the other end of the social scale, the fine art auctioneer Butterfield & Butterfield. The introduction of '**Buy It Now**' allowed users to buy without entering the bidding process.

Whitman began to **expand overseas**; when she left in eBay in 2008, the company was operating in 35 countries, and one of her regrets was her failure to break into the Japanese market.

During Whitman's ten years at eBay, sales grew from $4 million in 1998 to $8 billion in 2008 and eBay shares appreciated by 1,517 per cent. Whitman became a wealthy woman. The *Harvard Business Review* in January 2013 listed Whitman at number nine in the world ranking of best-performing CEOs.

In practice

- Create communities of like-minded people
- Keep the small-town feel on a global scale

- Focus on the needs and wants of the community; get involved

- Consider a low-key, consultative management approach

- Preserve the culture

YAHOO!
Jerry YANG
1968–

WHEN THE WORLD WIDE WEB was in its infancy, Jerry Yang and David Filo co-founded Yahoo! as a directory to make the web more user-friendly, listing the sites that were springing up on the web under relevant categories.

The two Stanford University post-grad students in electrical engineering resisted the idea of automating the process using 'spider'-based search software. 'No technology could beat human filtering,' Filo told *Fortune*, despite the fact that other search engines of the day – like Lycos, Infoseek and Excite – searched more web pages and delivered results faster than Yahoo.

By 1997, Yahoo was delivering more pages than all of the other three engines combined. 'Yahoo might never have won out,' *Fortune* argued, 'had it not been for Yang's obsession with what he saw as the fundamentals of his business: give users abundant reasons to visit your service, and promote the hell out of the brand.'

The ideas

Yang and Filo initially worked out of temporary offices in a converted trailer on the Stanford campus. Their website quickly drew traffic, and began to put a strain on the university's network. Stanford asked them to find a commercial host for their service; other internet start-ups began to take an interest.

Yang and Filo talked to venture capitalists and chose Sequoia Capital, whose partner David Moritz seemed to be on their wavelength. '[Moritz is] not a big believer that technology solves everything,' said Yang. 'But he does believe in the human element and in the art of what we were doing as well as the science.' Yang and Filo passed on responsibility for running the company to a CEO (Tim Koogle) and COO (Jeff Mallett). Japan's Softbank became Yahoo's largest shareholder, and entered a joint venture to launch Yahoo Japan.

Yahoo went public in 1996. Shares were offered at $24.50 and reached a high of $43 before settling at around $33, valuing the company at $848 million. Yang launched a **$5 million TV campaign** to raise awareness of the brand. The Netscape browser had originally granted an exclusive franchise to the Infoseek search engine, but in 1996 opened its site to other engines; Yahoo paid another $5 million to be one of five search engines featured on the site, and saw Infoseek's traffic fall by half.

By 1999, the company had **local operations in 15 countries** and five times as many visitors as AOL had subscribers. Revenues were approaching $600 million, allowing Yahoo to post a profit of $61.1 million in that year. Yahoo's share price plunged in 2000, after the bursting of the stock market bubble, but rallied as the company **remained profitable**, unlike so many other technology start-ups.

In 2000, the company switched to using Google's search engine, abandoning its original vision of categorisation by human beings. By 2004, it had developed its own **Yahoo Search**.

In 2005, Yang acquired a **minority share in Alibaba**, the Chinese ecommerce website, for $1 billion. In 2007, Yahoo turned to its founder to step into the role of CEO, but Yang – the man who never wanted to be CEO – failed to have the hoped-for impact on revenues and share price. He also turned down a 2008 **unsolicited bid from**

Microsoft to acquire Yahoo for $44.6 billion, equivalent to $31 per share in cash and Microsoft stock. In March 2013, Yahoo's stock was trading at over $20; at times after the Microsoft offer, shares dropped below $12.

A Forbes technology analyst, writing at the end of 2012, forecast that the increasing value of Yahoo's current stake in Alibaba, and the healthy state of the company's 35 per cent stake in Yahoo Japan, coupled with expected improvements to Yahoo's core business, meant that the company was currently undervalued and that the stock price in late 2013 night be closer to $40. Perhaps Yang was not so wrong to **resist his company's purchase by Microsoft**.

In practice

- Offer a useful service; add lots of extras; promote vigorously

- Recruit to your weaknesses

- Look for joint ventures with and investments in like-minded companies

- Be prepared to adapt the original vision

- Consider carefully whether an offer to buy is in the company's best long-term interest

SUNING GROUP
ZHANG Jindong
1963–

WHEN ZHANG JINDONG STARTED Suning Appliance in 1990, the goods that he was selling were luxury items. Since then, the huge growth of China's middle class has made these same products mass-market items.

Today, Suning faces stiff competition not only from other Chinese retailers, but also from established western retail giants such as Best Buy and Wal-Mart who have entered the China market. Zhang, however, is not especially troubled: 'Best Buy is just too Western!' he told the UK's *Telegraph* newspaper in 2009. 'They do not stock enough Chinese brands, and Chinese people do not want to buy foreign brands. Best Buy went and hired a lot of Shanghai staff, but went and westernised them. They only work eight hours a day!'

The ideas

Zhang studied Chinese literature at Nanjing Normal University, and then worked in a cloth factory. In 1990, he and his brother started a shop in Nanjing selling **air-conditioning units**.

While his brother later left retail for real estate, Zhang grew Suning into China's **largest electrical appliance retailer**, fuelled by the dramatic growth of China's increasingly middle-class urban population. Commenting on its 2009 interview with Zhang, the *Telegraph* noted that at the time, 30 million people – more than the population of Australia – were moving to China's cities each year, creating huge demand for home furnishings and electrical appliances.

Zhang's business received a useful boost recently when the Chinese government launched a stimulus package of cash subsidies for purchasers in rural areas of washing machines, refrigerators and computers, in a plan to **boost rural economies**.

When Zhang started out selling electrical appliances, the aspiring consumer wanted four items: a TV, a washing machine, a refrigerator and a music player. Now, middle-class consumers want everything. Zhang says that his company is geared up to become a **general merchandiser**. 'Suning from a management concept and technology point of view isn't simply an appliance company' he told *Forbes*, as he launched a new chain of Suning Expo Stores, selling everyday items.

Online, the **battle for China's ecommerce market** is already fierce, and will get fiercer still. The figure for internet users in China who use the internet to shop online is around 240 million, and a 2011 report by the Boston Consulting Group, quoted in *Forbes* magazine, forecasts that China's online retail market will surpass the U.S. market by 2015. Zhang plans to be a major player online and is beginning to position himself along the lines of Amazon or Wal-Mart. Online price wars are raging, but Zhang's pockets are deep.

According to *Forbes*, Suning has 1,700 stores nationwide in China, offering over a million items and generating $15 billion in annual sales. Zhang's overall stake in Suning Appliance is around 40 per cent, making his net worth in 2013 some $3.3 billion.

Zhang recently acquired electrical retailer Citicall in Hong Kong, and acquired a **foothold in Japan** by becoming the biggest shareholder in the LAOX home electronics store.

Zhang put in place a generous share distribution scheme for Suning employees: about **ten per cent of equity is owned by staff**, which has the potential to create 1,000 yuan millionaires in the next few years.

Zhang seems to be ready for future challenges. He had poked fun at Best Buy's staff for working 'only eight hours a day'; in 2005 he was reported by *China Daily* as saying, in a TV interview, 'My largest aspiration is to get **half a day off each month**.'

In practice

- Catch the wave; offer products that increasing numbers of people want

- Expand and diversify

- Sell online

- Grow internationally

- Share profits with colleagues

HAIER
ZHANG Ruimin
1949–

ZHANG RUIMIN WAS 17 when China's Cultural Revolution began in 1966. Like millions of other young people, he joined the Red Guards – a name given to all young people who took up Mao Zedong's call to sweep away China's 'Four Olds' (old customs, old culture, old habits, old ideas).

As China slipped towards anarchy, the Revolution was quietly ended and many ex-Red Guards were sent 'down to the countryside' to work on farms. Zhang was sent to work at a factory in Qingdao, where he worked his way up to deputy director, educating himself in business and management by reading and attending public courses, and was given a role in local government as deputy manager of the Household Appliance Division.

The factory, which was failing and heavily in debt, had got through three directors in one year; workers' pay was several months in arrears; employee turnover was extremely high; petty theft was rife; and products were poorly made and faulty. Zhang was parachuted in to try to rescue the operation, and his turnaround of the struggling refrigeration business is now the stuff of management textbooks.

The ideas

The factory, though state-supervised, was collectively owned. Given its losses, local Qingdao banks were unwilling to lend. Zhang **borrowed money from outside the city**. 'China's policy of reform and opening to the outside world meant that wealth was accumulating beyond the cities,' said Zhang. 'I was able to borrow money from the nearby production brigade.'

Zhang replaced the truck that brought workers to the factory with **a more comfortable bus**. People began to believe that the factory had a future. Next, Zhang began to **restore discipline**. The scale of the problem is highlighted by notices that Zhang needed to put up: 'Urinating or defecating in workshops is prohibited'; 'Stealing company property is prohibited.' Some workers caught stealing were deprived of factory membership and put on probation. Dismissal was prohibited by government, but the message was clear. Morale began to improve.

When a customer returned a faulty refrigerator and Zhang looked for a replacement, he found that one in five refrigerators in stock was faulty. He pulled 76 machines out of stock, gave employees sledgehammers and ordered them to **smash them up**. A refrigerator at the time was worth about two years' wages; many workers resisted. Zhang is recorded by China's *People's Daily* newspaper as saying, 'If we don't destroy these refrigerators today, what is to be shattered by the market in the future will be this enterprise!'

Zhang forged a partnership with leading German refrigeration manufacturer Liebherr. He was inspired by the company's approach to **quality control**. 'In Germany there was zero tolerance,' he told *Forbes* magazine in 2012. 'If one thing, even the smallest thing, was wrong, they wouldn't accept it.' Zhang took up the challenge. The company adopted the name Haier.

In 1991, Zhang championed investment in a new industrial park to secure **more capacity**. China entered a period of dramatic growth in 1993, and many competitors were late in starting their own expansionary plans. In 1999, Haier opened a plant in South Carolina, **challenging established U.S. companies** such as Whirlpool and GE.

Zhang committed Haier to innovation: the group spends three to five per cent of revenues on **research and development**, with research centres in China, Japan, Germany and the U.S. The company now manufactures not only freezers, refrigerators and washing machines but also wine coolers, cellphones and robots. Euromonitor recorded Haier as having a leading 7.8 per cent share of the global home appliance market in 2010. In 2011, group revenues were around $20 billion.

Zhang is now driving more radical change, reorganising the company into over **4,000 self-managed, customer-facing groups** that are rewarded according to their achievements. Groups are allowed to choose how they achieve their objectives; a manager's job is to ensure that the team have what they need in order to best serve the customer. 'Today, the biggest problem at Haier lies in the fact that its leaders are still embroiled in operational execution issues,' says Zhang. 'The enterprise will become great when it is able to operate by itself, with employees acting as their own leaders, understanding what to do to satisfy market and customer demand.'

In practice

- Make symbolic changes to prove that things are improving

- Restore discipline

- Focus on quality

- Form strategic partnerships

- Invest in capacity for future growth

- Encourage customer-facing groups to act as their own leaders

NINE DRAGONS PAPER
ZHANG Yin
1957–

As a young woman, Zhang Yin worked for a paper-products trading company in Shenzhen and saw an opportunity. China's growing volume of exports needed paperboard – a thick, light and relatively cheap paper-based product used for packaging – but one of the few commodities of which China is short is timber. This meant that there was a growing market for waste paper, from which paperboard could be recycled.

Zhang used $4,000 in savings to start her own company in Hong Kong. The company did well, but Zhang soon realised that she needed a bigger source of waste paper. She moved to the U.S., and set up a company that soon became the country's biggest exporter of waste paper, before returning to China to set up Nine Dragons Paper, which would become China's largest paperboard producer – making Zhang one of the richest self-made women in the world.

The ideas

Zhang was born Guangdong, on China's south coast. Her first job was as an accountant. In the early 1980s she moved to Shenzhen, China's first Special Economic Zone, and worked for a foreign-Chinese joint venture trading in paper products. What Zhang learned about the paper industry convinced her to **start up on her own**.

She moved to nearby Hong Kong, which was then still a British colony, and used her savings to start her own paper trading company. By 1990, she realised that she needed more waste paper. She moved to Los Angeles and set up a company to export waste paper to China. According to the *New York Times*, she and her husband drove around the garbage dumps of California in a Dodge minivan, setting up deals to **acquire waste paper** (which California had too much of) to ship to China.

In 1995, Zhang returned to China and raised a bank loan to set up **a paperboard production plant**, Nine Dragons Paper, in Dongguan, Guangdong Province.

The China operation soon dwarfed its U.S. sister company. The first paper machine went into production in 1998. In the early 2000s, two more machines were added, bringing production capacity to one million tonnes. In 2003, a new plant was opened at Taicang, in Jiangsu Province, on the Yangtze River delta. Today, Nine Dragons has the **biggest production capacity in the world** for manufacturing paperboard products from recovered paper and has diversified into the production of printing and writing papers.

In 2006, Zhang became the first woman to top the list of China's richest people, with her wealth estimated at $3.4 billion. Nine Dragon Papers is a family-owned business, but Zhang believes that **management should be free of interference from the owners**. 'We're not a company where the family boss manages every detail,' she told *Forbes*. 'I don't approve of this kind of system at all. I approve of how multinational companies are run. Although my company is small, I use this kind of management ideal.'

In practice

- Look for a gap in the market; start your own company
- Go where the market takes you
- Move up the value chain
- Achieve scale; diversify
- Adopt the management approach of major companies

WAHAHA
ZONG Qinghou
1945–

IN THE AFTERMATH OF Mao Zedong's disastrous Great Leap Forward, Zong Qinghou, along with millions of others, was sent to work on a farming commune to learn 'proletarian values.' In 1978, after 14 years, Zong finally returned to his birthplace of Hangzhou, and took up work as a salesman for a beverage maker that supplied a mini-grocery store owned by an elementary school.

In 1987, Zong and two partners took over the operation from the local government, having borrowed 140,000 yuan (about $22,000) from relatives, and started to sell drinks and ices to the school children.

Two years later, the enterprise built the Hangzhou Wahaha Nutritional Foods Factory and began to focus on nutritional drinks for children, sold through school shops. China's one-child policy had created a generation of doting parents and, with no direct competition for nutritional drinks aimed at children, Wahaha's flavoured, nutritionally enhanced milk drinks began to take off.

The ideas

The new enterprise's lack of management experience led to some **dangerous moments**. Wahaha took over a failing state-owned canned foods factory in Hangzhou, which increased overheads. In 1992, 236 million yuan was raised to launch Hangzhou Wahaha Food City Co Ltd and to build a factory. Poor project management and lack of cash flow led to a six-year delay in construction. Early diversification into alcoholic beverages and medicinal potions failed.

In 1994, with the help of **government grants** encouraging business to move from the economically active coastal areas to the interior,

Wahaha **took over three insolvent businesses** in central Sichuan, and set up a factory in the municipality of Chongqing, giving the company a base in western China and **reducing distribution costs**.

In 1996, Wahaha entered a **joint venture** with French food multinational Danone. Access to capital allowed investment in modern production equipment, greatly improving efficiency. The company launched the hugely successful Wahaha Pure Water and went on to develop a range of beverages including fruit and vegetable juices, sports drinks, Future Cola (Feichang Kele), vitamin-enhanced drinks and ready-to-drink teas. It also **diversified** into children's vitamins and clothing.

In 2011, according to Euromonitor International, Wahaha had a 7.2 per cent share of China's soft drinks market, behind Coca-Cola's 17.2 per cent and Tingyi's 13.2 per cent, but ahead of global drinks giant PepsiCo's 6.6 per cent.

Wahaha and Danone faced disagreements. After arbitration, Danone sold back its share of the JVs to Wahaha. Wahaha's great strength is recognised as its **nationwide distribution channels**, its strong presence in China's less-developed areas and its ability to vary its marketing strategies to **suit local market conditions**. In an interview with *China Business Review*, Wahaha's Foreign Liaison Office vice-director, Shan Qining, noted, 'Some products, such as our water, sell better in the city, and some products, like our cola, do better in the countryside. Consumers in all areas will choose Wahaha water, but consumers in large cities are unlikely to choose Future Cola ... [and] city grocery stores have very high entry fees.'

Wahaha has now exported its products around the world, even shipping Future Cola to the U.S. The company faces fierce global competition from major multinationals both at home and abroad but, of course, it has huge strengths in China where, as Zong says, the other companies 'don't know what [the] Chinese need.' Forbes listed Zong as **China's richest man** in 2010 and again in 2012. With reference to the reformer Deng Xiaoping, Zong says: 'People who get rich early should help the rest get rich.'

In practice

- Expect to make mistakes as you grow; survive these

- Widen your distribution base

- Enter partnerships to gain capital investment and expertise

- Adjust your offerings to suit local market conditions

- Use your local expertise to keep competition out

FACEBOOK
Mark ZUCKERBERG
1984–

MARK ZUCKERBERG IS A child of the computer age. His father, a dentist and an early user of digital radiography, taught his son to program in BASIC; the young Zuckerberg created a primitive instant-messaging program that allowed the family to send messages to computers round the house. When he was 11 years old, his parents hired a software developer to give him weekly lessons; the tutor described Zuckerberg to *New Yorker* magazine as 'a prodigy,' adding, 'sometimes it was tough to stay ahead of him.'

At Harvard, Zuckerberg came up with the idea for the social net-working site, Facebook. He saw Facebook as answering a basic human need to know about what other people were doing at that same moment, as opposed to search engines, which could only find historic information that had already been made available. As he told *The New Yorker*, 'Most of the things we care about are in our heads ... and that's not out there to be indexed, right?'

The idea

Before launching Facebook, Zuckerberg first built a program that let students see photographs of other Harvard students and vote on their attractiveness. The system was popular enough to crash the campus online network.

Zuckerberg was then approached by three senior students to help with a more traditional collection of student profiles, called Harvard Connection. Zuckerberg started work on the project, but left to create his own version, which he and four Harvard friends launched in February 2004 as thefacebook.com. The Harvard Connection team later accused Facebook of stealing their idea. Zuckerberg maintained that the two sites were very different. The case was settled out of court.

Facebook, which allowed users to create their own profile page, upload photographs and communicate with other users, was a big hit. Zuckerberg and his friends **dropped out of Harvard to work on Facebook full time**. Peter Thiel, co-founder of the online payment system, PayPal, invested $500,000 in the new company. The site was **offered to other universities** and colleges; by the end of the site's first year it had **one million users**.

In 2005, the company received a further £13.7 million of **venture capital support**. The following year, the search engine Yahoo offered to buy Facebook for $1 billion. Zuckerberg refused the offer. As the CEO of Yahoo, Terry Semel, told *New Yorker* magazine, 'I'd never met anyone who would **walk away from a billion dollars**. But [Zuckerberg] said, "It's not about the price. This is my baby, and I want to keep running it, I want to keep growing it." I couldn't believe it.'

Facebook's popularity continued to grow, as it was offered to more universities and eventually to high schools, and then to anyone over the age of 13. Companies began to show increasing interest in **advertising** to the site's young users. In 2007, Facebook announced that it would become a 'platform,' and that other designers were **welcome to build applications** that would run on the site.

The company maintained a slightly anarchic culture, its motto being 'move fast and break things.' Changes to the site are tested live on real users; pages are **tested constantly** to see which aspects are most popular. Every engineer is given equal access to the code, and all changes are uploaded to the site daily. Sometimes the site crashes. Sometimes new products are released by accident. '**We make more mistakes** than other companies do,' Zuckerberg told *Businessweek* magazine. 'You can't have everything, so you just have to choose what your values are and where you want to be ... for us, this is the right way to go.'

In May 2012, Facebook launched on Nasdaq Exchange, raising $16 billion and giving the company a peak valuation of $104 billion, though share prices fell sharply after the launch amid accusations that the share price had been overhyped.

In 2012, Facebook reached **one billion users**. It sees its goal as accumulating data on everything that its users consume and do, making it possible to build a robust model of other things that they are likely to enjoy. As a leading Facebook engineer told *BusinessWeek*, 'We are trying to map out the graph of everything in the world, and how it relates to each other.'

In practice

- Develop a product that taps into people's natural behaviour

- Drop everything to pursue your vision

- If it really is your baby, it will not be for sale

- Find like-minded people

- Invite others to develop ideas on your platform

- 'Move fast and break things'

Sources and Further Reading

Dhirubhai AMBANI

Dhirubhai Ambani and Reliance, IBS Center for Management Research http://bit.ly/11DxnJf

'Thousands bid farewell to Dhirubhai Ambani', *Times of India*, July 7, 2002 http://bit.ly/XILMDA

Hamish McDonald, 'Remembering the Prince of Polyester,' Time, July 15, 2002 http://ti.me/17606IV

Bernard ARNAULT

Carol Matlack, 'Handbags at the Barricades,' *Businessweek*, March 28, 2011, Issue 4222 http://bit.ly/13pRRJu

Martha Duffy, 'The pope of fashion', *Time*, April 21, 1997 http://ti.me/10kXQP6

'Bernard Arnault,' *Reference for Business Biography* http://bit.ly/115DsfV

'LVMH Moët Hennessy Louis Vuitton SA History', *Funding Universe* http://bit.ly/11loUZS

Mary Kay ASH

Enid Nemy, 'Mary Kay Ash, Who Built a Cosmetics Empire and Adored Pink, Is Dead at 83', *New York Times*, November 23, 2001 http://nyti.ms/17JdIuR

'Mary Kay Ash', American National Business Hall of Fame, article originally published in T*he Journal of Business Leadership* Volume 1, Number 1, Spring 1988 http://bit.ly/Z19MUk

Vinita BALI

Naazneen Karmali, 'Tough Cookie', *Forbes Asia*, Feb 2012, Vol. 8, Issue 2 http://onforb.es/11E3b01

Rahul Sachitanand, 'Britannia's new recipe', *Business Today*, July 12, 2009 http://bit.ly/ZuLJMe

Srinivas K. Reddy, 'MIR talks to Vinita Bali, Managing Director and CEO of Britannia Industries,' GfK *Marketing Intelligence Review*, February 7, 2010, Vol. 2, No. 2 http://bit.ly/ZuL0iX

Jeff BEZOS

Adam Lashinsky, Doris Burke, J.P. Mangalindan, 'Jeff Bezos: The Ultimate Disrupter', *Fortune*, December 3, 2012, Vol. 166, Issue 9 http://bit.ly/15pfiTv

George Anders, 'Jeff Bezos Gets It', *Forbes Asia*, May 2012, Vol. 8, Issue 6 http://bit.ly/14zoZzb

Richard L. Brandt, 'Birth of a Salesman', *Wall Street Journal*, October 15, 2011 http://on.wsj.com/11lymg7

Sara BLAKELY

Stacy Perman, 'How Failure Molded Spanx's Founder'. *BusinessWeek*, November 21, 2007 http://buswk.co/ZAnmJl

Kai Ryssdal, 'Interview: How Spanx became a billion-dollar undergarment empire', *Marketplace*, March 14, 2012 http://bit.ly/ZAnoBj

William Edward BOEING

Robert A. Searles, 'The Original Bill from Seattle', *Business & Commercial Aviation*, January 2002, Vol. 90, Issue 1 http://bit.ly/17JkT6j

Boeing website: History http://bit.ly/XTJ0NV

Richard BRANSON

Richard Branson, *Losing My Virginity*, Crown Business, 2011

Warren BUFFET

Carol J Loomis, 'The Value Machine', *Fortune*, February 19, 2001, Vol. 143, Issue 4 http://bit.ly/13kYw3I

Paul J. Lim, 'Six keys to investing Buffett style', *U.S. News & World Report*, August 6, 2007, Vol. 143, Issue 4 http://bit.ly/XIZ42W

Warren Buffet, Chairman's letter, March 2013 http://bit.ly/15jc2ZC

Andrew CARNEGIE

Andrew Carnegie, *The Autobiography of Andrew Carnegie*, CreateSpace Independent Publishing Platform, 2012

Wyn Derbyshire, *Six Tycoons*, Spiramus Press, 2009

Dhanin CHEARAVANONT

Robert Horn, 'Chearavanont', *Time*, April 19, 2004 http://ti.me/YzigNG

Andrew Tanzer, 'The birdman of Bangkok, *Forbes* magazine, April 13, 1992, Vol. 149, Issue 8

Brian Mertens, 'From Farm To Fork', *Forbes Asia*, December 2011, Vol. 7, Issue 14 http://onforb.es/14BmI6K

Eva CHEN

Chaniga Vorasarun, 'Branding Exercise', *Forbes Asia*, December 10, 2007, Vol. 3, Issue 21 http://onforb.es/13uneCB

Andy Greenberg, 'Trend Micro's Eva Chen', *Forbes* magazine, October 29, 2009 http://onforb.es/177JdxD

Eva Chen interview with Amy Zipkin, 'Trained to find a way', *New York Times*, December 13, 2008 http://nyti.ms/15qZvnd

Kim Girard, 'Sometimes Worms Just Need a Time-Out', *Business 2.0*, May 2004, Vol. 5, Issue 4 http://cnnmon.ie/11qaEh9

CHUNG Ju-Yung

Richard M. Steers, *Made in Korea: Chung Ju Yung and the Rise of Hyundai*, Routledge 1999

Mark Clifford, *Troubled Tiger: Businessmen, Bureaucrats and Generals in South Korea*, M.E. Sharpe, 1997

Michael Schuman, 'The Miracle Workers', *Time* magazine, August 15, 2005 http://ti.me/103HHWZ

Chung Ju-yung, Obituary, *The Telegraph* http://bit.ly/15r3cJu

Charles A. COFFIN

'Charles Albert Coffin', Obituary, *Time* Magazine, July 26, 1926 http://ti.me/15r5EzN

Jed Graham, 'The Man Who Electrified GE', *Investors Business Daily*, January 21, 2011 http://bit.ly/17KUwgw

Jim Collins, 'The Ten Greatest CEOs of All Time', *Fortune* magazine, July 21, 2003, http://cnnmon.ie/XUQNev

Terence CONRAN

Jonathan Glancey, 'Old Habitats Die Hard', *The Guardian*, December 2001 http://bit.ly/6dR4xR

Liz Nickson, 'The Conrans: A Genuine Dynasty', *Time*, July 20, 1987 http://ti.me/17dD2WQ

John A. Byrne, 'The Power of Great Design', *Fast Company*, June 2005 http://bit.ly/115B4HG

Terence Conran, The Design Museum http://bit.ly/zsjClf

'Terence Conran, 50 Years in Design' http://bit.ly/17dDnJc

Michael DELL

Andrew E. Serwer, 'Michael Dell Turns The PC World Inside Out, *Fortune*, September 8, 1997 http://cnnmon.ie/YpN5UV

'Michael Saul Dell', Gale Encyclopaedia of Biography http://bit.ly/XClPFD

Christopher Helman, 'The Second Coming', *Forbes*, October 12, 2007, Vol. 180, Issue 12 http://onforb.es/115N4sJ

'Dell Direct' Stanford University Graduate School of Business Case Study EC-17, November 2000 http://bit.ly/104JHW2

Walt DISNEY

Brian Dakks, 'Walt Disney: More Than Toons, Theme Parks', CBS News, February 11, 2009 http://cbsn.ws/XN8RqM

Mark Langer. 'Walt Disney', American National Biography Online, February 2000 http://bit.ly/YpQEKR

Neal Gabler, *Walt Disney; Triumph of the American Imagination,* Random House USA, 2007

DONG Mingzhu

Jane Lanhee Lee Naville, 'Cooling Off China', *Forbes A-sia*, May 10, 2009, Vol. 5, Issue 15 http://onforb.es/XUU79p

Didi Kirsten Tatlow, 'Setting the pace with toughness', *New York Times*, January 26, 2011 http://nyti.ms/15raXiy

Peter Foster, 'Gree Electric's Dong Mingzhu: why China's leading businesswoman doesn't do holidays', *The Telegraph*, January 27, 2013 http://bit.ly/15rb5P7

Robert Lawrence Kuhn, 'Guangdong Visions: Forging China's Future', *BusinessWeek*, August 5, 2009 http://buswk.co/117cCny

James DYSON

'James Dyson, Business Whirlwind,' BBC Business http://bbc.in/ZBS7y3

Burt Helm, 'James Dyson,' *Inc*, March 2012, Vol. 34, Issue 2 http://bit.ly/11kOdNa

Hannah Clark 'James Dyson Cleans Up,' *Forbes*, August 1, 2006http://onforb.es/11nSdLv

Thomas EDISON

Randall E. Stross, *The Wizard of Menlo Park*, Broadway, 2008

Frank L. Dyer and Thomas C. Martin, 'Edison, His Life and Inventions', Project Gutenberg, January 21, 2006 [EBook #820] http://bit.ly/ZDYNuF

Henry FORD

Samuel Crowther, 'Henry Ford, 'Why I favor five days' work with six days pay,' *World's Work*, October 1926, pp. 613–616 http://bit.ly/11ouomS

Jack Nerad, 'Ford Model A', DrivingToday.com http://bit.ly/10nA1Gc

Wyn Derbyshire, *Six Tycoons*, Spiramus Press, London, 2011

Bill GATES

James Wallace and Jim Erickson, *Hard Drive: Bill Gates and the Making of the Microsoft Empire*, John Wiley & Sons Inc, 1992

Julie Bick, 'The Microsoft Millionaires Come of Age', *New York Times*, May 29, 2005 http://nyti.ms/ZWinlw

Louis GERSTNER

Louis Gerstner, *Who Says Elephants Can't Dance*, HarperBusiness, 2003

Jonathan Gifford, 'Louis Gerstner's vision for IBM: The customer is always right' http://bit.ly/14Cr5hY

Carlos GHOSN

Diane Brady, 'Carlos Ghosn on Preserving the Renault-Nissan Alliance', *BusinessWeek*, December 8, 2011 http://buswk.co/10nSUJp

Scott Stoddard, 'Ghosn Steers Nissan Straight', *Investors Business Daily*, December 5, 2008 http://bit.ly/15nY6xj

Risaburo Nezu, 'Carlos Ghosn: cost controller or keiretsu killer?', *OECD Observer*, April 2000 http://bit.ly/11LTyNf

David Magee, *Turnaround: How Carlos Ghosn rescued Nissan*, Harper Business 2002

Carlos Ghosn, 'Partnerships and Alliances' http://bit.ly/11LTFIB

King C. GILLETTE

Paul Lukas, 'Gillette', *Fortune Small Business*, April 2003, Vol. 13, Issue 3 http://cnnmon.ie/12ulvt3

Alan R. Elliott, 'Gillette, the king of razors', *Investors Business Daily*, October 19, 2010 http://bit.ly/ZDQ7oZ

Russell Adams, *King C. Gillette: The Man and His Wonderful Shaving Device*, Little, Brown & Company, 1978

Bill GORE

Alan Deutschman, 'The Fabric of Creativity', *Fast Company*, December 1, 2004 http://bit.ly/12uMnud

Gary Hamel,' Innovation Democracy: W.L. Gore's Original Management Model', *Management Innovation eXchange*, September 23, 2010 http://bit.ly/11qthTK

Katharine GRAHAM

Marilyn Berger, 'Katharine Graham of Washington Post Dies at 84', *New York Times* July 18, 2001 http://nyti.ms/117uwoX

J.Y. Smith and Noel Epstein, 'Katharine Graham Dies at 84', *The Washington Post*, July 18, 2001 http://bit.ly/15gbV1f

Katherine Graham, *Personal History*, Phoenix, 2002

Philip GREEN

Chris Blackhurst, 'Leaders: Philip Green', *European Business Forum*, Spring 2006, Issue 24 http://bit.ly/10pqvTb

Jennifer Reingold, 'The British (retail) invasion', *Fortune*, July 7, 2008, Vol. 158, Issue 1 http://cnnmon.ie/15u6ZWu

Andrew GROVE

Richard S. Tedlow & David Ruben,' The Dangers of Wishful Thinking', *The American*, January/February 2008 http://bit.ly/15rioGI

'Paranoid survivor', *The Economist*, Technology Quarterly: Q3 2009, September 3, 2009 http://econ.st/Z98LJR

Richard S. Tedlow, 'The education of Andy Grove', Fortune, December 12, 2005 http://cnnmon.ie/11qHT5z

Joshua Cooper Ramo, Andrew Grove: a survivor's tale', *Time*, December 29, 1997 http://ti.me/11vqHdE

Special report: Strategy classics', Business Strategy Review, Autumn 2008, Vol. 19 Issue 3http://bit.ly/105K6QQ

Romi HAAN

Andrew Salmon, 'Korea's Rebel With a Steam Mop', *Forbes Asia Magazine*, January 16, 2012 http://onforb.es/ZzUmVy

Thomas Haire, 'DRMA Marketer of the Year Spotlight: HAAN Steams Into the Spotlight', *Response* magazine, March 4, 2010 http://bit.ly/ZbPTJe

Alice Bumgarner, 'Interview with Romi Haan', *IdeaConnection*, July 2, 2012 http://bit.ly/XWVZ1I

John HARVEY-JONES

John Harvey Jones, *Making it Happen: Reflections on leadership*, Profile Books 2005

Jonathan Gifford, 'The Triumph of Common Sense: John Harvey-Jones and ICI' http://bit.ly/XWW5Gq

Bill HEWLETT and David PACKARD

David Packard, *The HP Way: How Bill Hewlett and I built Our Company*, Harper Business, 2006

Soichiro HONDA

Soichiro Honda, *Bloomsbury Business Library*, Business Thinkers & Management Giants, 2007 http://bit.ly/YXIxJ9

David E. Sanger, 'Soichiro Honda, Auto Innovator, Is Dead at 84', *New York Times*, August 6, 1991 http://nyti.ms/11aOOzy

Soichiro Honda, Gale Encyclopedia of Biography http://bit.ly/16YtKjj

Tony HSIEH

'Q&A with Tony Hsieh '95', Harvard School of Engineering and Applied Sciences http://hvrd.me/17auX7m

Tony Hsieh, 'How I Did It: Zappos's CEO on Going to Extremes for Customers' *Harvard Business Review*, July 2010 http://bit.ly/170feMo

Tony Hsieh, 'How I did it', *Inc. com*, September 1, 2006 http://bit.ly/106aQ3P

'10 Steps to Zappos success' *Inc.com* http://bit.ly/11rmpFB

Kai Ryssdal, 'Zappos CEO on corporate culture and "Happiness"', *Marketplace*, August 20, 2010 http://bit.ly/11rmt8c

Lee IACOCCA

Peter Nulty and Patty de Llosa, 'Lee Anthony Iacocca', *Fortune*, May 4, 1993, Vol 127, Issue 7 http://bit.ly/15ggWGU

L.Reibstein, F. Washington, 'Lee's last stand' Newsweek, June 1, 1992, Vol 119, Issue 1 http://bit.ly/ZWqLlh

'Lee Iacocca',Bloomsbury Business Library Business Thinkers and Management Giants, 2007

William F. Crittenden, Kathleen Kelly, 'Leaders in Selling and Sales Management: Lee Iacocca', *Journal of Personal Selling & Sales Management*, Vol xi, Number 3 (Summer 1991)

'Chrysler and the 1979 Bailout', Investopedia, April 24, 2009 http://bit.ly/ZsVyqQ

Mohamed 'Mo' IBRAHIM

Guy Dennis, 'Out of Africa', *The Telegraph*, January 8, 2006 http://bit.ly/17aF245

Geraldine Bedell, 'The man giving Africa a brighter future,' *The Observer*, February 1, 2009 http://bit.ly/10qaoVe

Anver Versi, 'Dr Mo Ibrahim Doing meaningful things is my motivation', *African Business*, May 2006, Issue 320 http://bit.ly/11T3nsT

Steve JOBS

Jeffrey S. Young, William L. Simon, *iCon: The Greatest Second Act*

in the History of Business, Wiley, 2006

Best Performing CEO's, Harvard Business Review, January 2010 http://bit.ly/117DMcG

Herb KELLEHER

Jane Whitney Gibson & Charles W. Blackwell, 'Flying High with Herb Kelleher: A Profile in Charismatic Leadership', *Journal of Leadership Studies*, June 22, 1999 http://bit.ly/107flps

Alynda Wheat, 'The Chairman of the Board Looks Back', *Fortune*, May 28, 2001, Vol. 143, Issue 11 http://cnnmon.ie/XY6BNm

Vinod KHOSLA

Vinod Khosla, Entrepreneurial Thought Leaders Lecture, Stanford University, April 24, 2002 http://stanford.io/14GCD3w

Amar V. Bhide, 'Vinod Khosla and Sun Microsystems (A), Harvard Business School, September 28, 1989 http://bit.ly/12xtbMp

Gerard KLEISTERLEE

Interview with Gerard Kleisterlee, *The Focus*, Egon Zehnder International, http://bit.ly/XYaMsK

Ian Wylie, 'Can Philips Learn to Walk The Talk?' *Fast Company*, December 31, 2002 http://bit.ly/13oX14D

Adam Smith, 'The Complex Task of Simplicity', *Time International* (Atlantic Edition), March 3, 2008, Vol. 171, Issue 9 http://ti.me/17bM600

Interview with Gerard Kleisterlee, *European Business Forum*, Spring 2007, Issue 28, p60–63

Philip KNIGHT

Daniel Roth, 'Can Nike Still Do It Without Phil Knight?', *Fortune*, April 4, 2005, Vol. 151, Issue 7 http://cnnmon.ie/ZlRnjB

'Philip H. Knight', Entrepreneur. com, October 9, 2008 http://bit.ly/116rAMg

Geraldine E. Willigan, 'High-Performance Marketing: An Interview with Nike's Phil Knight', *Harvard Business Review*, July/August 1992, Vol. 70, Issue 4 http://bit.ly/YLgq0P

KOO In-hwoi

History of Goldstar CCO Ltd, FundingUniverse.com http://bit.ly/17Q201J

KOO Bon-moo

'The Koo Dynasty: Children of a Chaebol', *Euroasia Industry*, March 2, 2012 http://bit.ly/107yBs6

Kim Yoo-chul, 'LG shrugs off doubt, comes back with vengeance', *Korea Times*, March 21, 2012 http://bit.ly/17bZ6mx

Cho Mu-hyun,' LG boss calls for drastic change', *Korea Times*, September 26, 2012, http://bit.ly/107yFlr

Justin Doebele, 'Ends and Means, *Forbes*, February 17, 2003, Vol. 171, Issue 4 http://onforb.es/11cgbZV

Ray KROC

Daniel Gross, 'Ray Kroc, McDonald's and the Fast Food Industry', *Forbes Greatest Business Stories Of All Time*, Wiley, 1966 http://bit.ly/14qC91A

Jacques Pepin, ' Burger Meister Ray Kroc,' *Time*, December 7, 1998 http://ti.me/YXWKWF

'Ray Kroc Burger Baron', Entrepreneur.com, October 9, 2008 http://bit.ly/ZwuUwd

A.G. LAFLEY

Gregory Jones, 'How A.G. Lafley used innovation to increase Procter & Gamble's billion-dollar brands', *Smart Business*, September 2011, Vol. 21 Issue 4 http://bit.ly/Zdvnsy

Noel Tichy, 'Lafley's Legacy: From Crisis to Consumer-Driven, *BusinessWeek* Online, November 6, 2009 http://buswk.co/107B99E

Daniel Eisenberg, 'A Healthy Gamble', *Time* Magazine, September 16, 2002 http://buswk.co/107B99E

Estée LAUDER

Richard Severo, 'Estée Lauder, Pursuer of beauty and cosmetics titan, dies at 97,' *New York Times*, April 26 2004 http://nyti.ms/13Hk4eS

'Estee Lauder', *The Telegraph*, April 27 2004 http://bit.ly/12xT6DF

Grace Mirabella, 'Beauty Queen: Estee Lauder', *Time* magazine, December 7, 1998 http://ti.me/11tMKTv

LEE Byung-chull

Chang Jin-Ho, 'Samsung founding chairman Lee Byung-Chull's place in Korean business Management, *SERI Quarterly*, April 2010, pp 58–69 http://bit.ly/17UN9Dj

Andrei Lankov, 'Lee Byung-chull', *Korea Times*, October 12 2011 http://bit.ly/14MILZq

Lee Kun-hee, Buisness philosophy of Lee Byung-chull, *Korea Times*, February 11, 2010 http://bit.ly/12aYwDs

Robin LI

David Barboza, 'The Rise of Baidu (That's Chinese for Google)', *New York Times*, September 17, 2006 http://nyti.ms/XNwwHz

Brad Stone, Bruce Einhorn, 'How Baidu Won China', *BusinessWeek*, November 15, 2010, Issue 4204 http://buswk.co/16YDyKa

LI Ka-shing

Russell Flannery, 'Li Ka-shing's Midas Touch', *Forbes*, July 3, 2012 http://onforb.es/12FvqND

Kate Linebaugh, Jane Spencer, 'The Revolution of Chairman Li: China's Richest Man Leads Others to Give, Bucking Nation's Taboos', *Wall Street Journal*, Wealth Report, November 2, 2007 http://on.wsj.com/12bf921

Reference for Business, 'LI Ka-shing' http://bit.ly/10wLfIz

LIU Chuanzhi

'Liu Chuanzhi', *Reference for Business* http://bit.ly/12FCIRJ

Interview with Liu Chuanzhi, *McKinsey Quarterly* http://bit.ly/11AYHXw

'Liu Chuanzhi on Rebuilding the Lenovo Brand', Knowledge@ Wharton, January 5, 2011 http://bit.ly/XU4NTt

'Legend in the making', *The Economist*, September 13, 2001 http://econ.st/11zdYcA

LIU Yonghao

'Asia's Leaders – The Next Generation', *Asiamoney*, October 1999, Vol. 10, Issue 8

Russell Flannery, 'Not Just Chicken Feed', *Forbes Asia*, November 14, 2005, Vol. 1, Issue 7 http://bit.ly/17gnNhL

'The excellent chicken-feed of Liu Yonghao', *The Economist* (U.S.), July 6, 1996 http://bit.ly/12FNE1L

Olivia LUM

Shivaranjani Subramaniam, 'Olivia Lum', *Singapore Infopedia* http://bit.ly/ZMGfJL

Justin Doebele, 'Water queen', *Forbes Asia*, September 19, 2005, Vol. 1, Issue 2 http://bit.ly/17Sk2xs

MA Huateng

Bruce Einhorn and Brad Stone,' Tencent: March of the Penguins', *Businessweek*, August 4, 2011 http://buswk.co/ZIZwV2

'China: Tencent Holdings', BusinessWeek.com, November 13, 2005 http://buswk.co/Zt7IW4

Sarah Lacey, 'What Valley Companies Should Know about Tencent', techcrunch.com, June 20, 2010http://tcrn.ch/14qGVMk

'Ma Huateng, Co-Founder of the QQ Empire', shangbao.net http://bit.ly/117Qzvl

Yang Yang, 'Exclusive interview with the CEO of Tencent', *Corporation*, November 6, 2010, Issue 493, page 25 http://bit.ly/YLxiEl

Jack MA

Gady Epstein, 'The Face of China Inc.', *Forbes*, November 4, 2011, Vol. 187, Issue 6 http://onforb.es/11DZG9q

Bruce Einhorn, Frederik Balfour, 'Jack Ma is the Loneliest Billionaire in China', *Businessweek*, June 18, 2012 http://buswk.co/17iuDTY

Rebecca Fannin interview, 'How I did it: Jack Ma, Alibaba.com', *Inc.com*, January 1, 2008 http://bit.ly/15HeDNw

Helen H. Wang, 'How eBay failed in China', *Forbes* http://onforb.es/13uRycH

'Total Taobao Sales Exceeded 1 Trillion Yuan in 2012' http://bit.ly/15HeObs

John MACKEY

Justin Fox, "What Is It That Only I Can Do?", *Harvard Business Review*, Jan/Feb 2011, Vol. 89, Issue 1/2 http://bit.ly/17TdKh9

Nick Paumgarten, 'Does Whole Foods' C.E.O. know what's best for you?', *New Yorker*, January 4, 2010 http://nyr.kr/10dyuLF

Mark Hamstra, 'John Mackey, *Supermarket News*, July 12, 2009, Vol. 57, Issue 49

Danielle Sacks, 'The miracle worker', *Fast Company*, December 2009/ January 2010, Issue 141 http://bit.ly/15HljLj

John Mackey, 'Conscious Capitalism: Creating a New Paradigm for Business,' wholeplanetfoundation.org http://bit.ly/11CzMnC

Anand MAHINDRA

Kushan Mitra, 'Top Gun: How Anand Mahindra built a $12.5 billon empire ground up,' *Business Today*, October 2, 2011, http://bit.ly/11CzMnC

Anuradha Raghunathan, 'Putt-Putt Tractors, Revved-Up Goals', *Forbes Asia*, April 24, 2006, Vol. 2, Issue 7 http://onforb.es/17TluzC

Annie Turnbo MALONE

'Annie Turnbo Malone', Gale Encyclopaedia of Biography http://bit.ly/17XIEsE

'Annie Turnbull Malone', Blackpast.org http://bit.ly/12IronK

'Madame C. J. Walker', Biography.com http://bit.ly/13v1W40

Michael MARKS

Gareth Shaw, 'Michael Marks, *Oxford National Dictionary of Biography*, OUP, 2004 http://bit.ly/YRraGq

Marks & Spencer corporate website http://bit.ly/12Izyg6

Konosuke MATSUSHITA

'Business Abroad: Following Henry Ford', *Time*, February 23, 1962 http://ti.me/YZuBzu

'The Founder', Panasonic, http://panasonic.net/history/founder/

'A message from the founder, PHP Institute http://bit.ly/15ooUhh

Kiran MAZUMDAR-SHAW

Devi Shetty, Raghunath Mashelkar, 'Of a different DNA,' *Business Today*, January 9, 2011, Vol. 20 Issue 18, p82-83 http://bit.ly/11I42Is

Becky Anderson, '$800 million bitotech business founded in a garage', CNN, November 15, 2012 http://bit.ly/10AeKt7

William MCKNIGHT

'William McKight', Funding Universe http://bit.ly/15HDosK

Paul Lukas, '3M Mining Company Based on a Mistake, *Fortune Small Business*, April 1, 2003 http://cnnmon.ie/11QuaU8

'A Century of Innovation: The 3M Story' http://bit.ly/11I5Ydy

George W. MERCK

'What The Doctor Ordered' *Time*, August 18, 1952 http://ti.me/ZIF3jP

Scott S. Smith, 'George Merck Delivered Healthy Medical Growth', *Investors' Business Daily*, March 21, 2012 http://bit.ly/17j0Ev4

Lakshmi MITTAL

Nelson D Schwarz, 'Emperor of Steel', *Fortune*, July 24, 2006, Vol. 154, Issue 2, p100–110 http://cnnmon.ie/11DmPdf

'The Carnegie from Calcutta, *The Economist*, January 9, 1998 http://econ.st/13vvw9z

Lakshmi Mittal, *Reference for Business* http://bit.ly/15MXHVi

Sunil Bharti MITTAL

Clay Chandler, 'Wireless Wonder: India's Sunil Mittal', *Fortune*, January 17, 2007 http://cnnmon.ie/Yx6ALx

Vinod Nair, 'Sunil Mittal Speaking: I Started with a Dream', *Times of India*, December 22, 2002http://bit.ly/13nK5z0

Michael Schuman, 'Speed Dialling', *Time*, November 25, 2002,http://ti.me/14ysHt4

Akio MORITA

Akio Morita, *Made in Japan*, Harper Collins, 1994

Kenichi Ohmae, 'Akio Morita: Guru of gadgets', *Time*, December 7, 1998 http://ti.me/Y5gOYp

Andrew Polloack, 'Akio Morita, co-founder of Sony and Japanese business leader, dies at 78', *New York Times*, October 4, 1999 http://nyti.ms/YSo19i

Alan MULALLY

Diane Brady interview, 'Alan Mulally on Ford's Amassing Debt in the Downturn', *BusinessWeek*, September 20, 2012 http://buswk.co/14QrWvr

Charlie Rose talks to Alan Mulally, *BusinessWeek*, August 1, 2011, Issue 4240 http://buswk.co/ZIIN59

Carmine Gallo, 'Alan Mulally, Optimism, and the Power of Vision' *Forbes*, April 25, 2012 http://onforb.es/ZIINC3

Paul A. Eisenstein, 'With 2nd Debt Upgrade Ford Regains Control of Blue Oval Logo', *The Detroit Bureau*, May 23, 2012 http://bit.ly/17XOVDB

Prasad Kaipa and Mark Kriger, 'Empowerment, Vision, and Positive Leadership: An Interview With Alan Mulally', *Journal of Management Inquiry*, June 2010, Vol. 19, Issue 2 http://bit.ly/11EXBKr

Anne MULCAHY

Ellen McGirt, 'Fresh Copy', *Fast Company*, December 2011 / January 2012, Issue 161
http://bit.ly/14865z5

Betsy Morris, 'The Accidental CEO', Fortune, June 23, 2003
http://cnnmon.ie/15I22JJ

Report on Society for Human Resource Management Strategy Conference, 2010: Nancy M Davis, 'When an HR Leader Takes Charge', *HR Magazine*, December 2010, Vol. 55, Issue 12
http://bit.ly/11F00EM

Rupert MURDOCH

Ronald Grover and Tom Lowry, 'Rupert's World, *BusinessWeek*, January 19, 2004
http://buswk.co/YUcoyP

Richard Zoglin, 'Murdoch's Biggest Score', *Time*, June 6, 1994
http://ti.me/17WIQpm

Andrew Walker, 'Rupert Murdoch: Bigger than Kane', BBC News, July 31, 2002 http://bbc.in/10eTKRi

David Conn, 'How football has kept the Murdoch empire afloat', *The Guardian*, June 15, 2002
http://bit.ly/14bobQy

N.R. Narayana MURTHY

Narayana Murthy, speech to New York University Stern School of Business, Rediff India Abroad
http://bit.ly/14bwcVD

Naazneen Karmali, interview with N.R. Narayana Murthy for India Seminar 1999 http://bit.ly/13wRysr

Chris Wright, 'India's modest chief mentor,' *Asiamoney*,

October 2006, Vol. 17, Issue 9
http://bit.ly/12K2CUr

NING Gaoning

Ning Gaoning, 'The first and foremost responsibility of an entrepreneur is to build an innovative enterprise', March 19, 2012 http://bit.ly/ZKi55B

Jane Cai, 'State's cowboy keeps profits rolling', *South China Morning Post*, November 19, 2012
http://bit.ly/12K5LDv

Indra NOOYI

'Pepsi: Repairing a poisoned reputation in India', *BusinessWeek*, June 11, 2007 http://buswk.co/13xOvAp

'Performance with Purpose: Indra Nooyi letter to stakeholders
http://bit.ly/14ei3a9

Indra Nooyi: Keynote interview, BlogHer, San Diego, August 5/6, 2011, http://bit.ly/10fOA7E

Pepsico 'Direct Seeding' press release http://bit.ly/11nMWmQ

Archie NORMAN

Richard Thompson, 'Supermarket Calculator', *Independent*, July 12, 1992 http://ind.pn/Y01TN4

Helia Ebrahimi, 'Archie Norman: the ex-Asda boss who saves businesses on the shelf', *The Telegraph*, July 3, 2009
http://bit.ly/17YfQfN

'Get your people on board: Archie Norman on turnaround success and the importance of staff happiness', *Growing Business*,
http://bit.ly/10fStta

Carol Kennedy, 'Determined of

Tunbridge Wells', *Director*,
November 1999, Vol. 53, Issue 4

Jorma OLLILA

'A Finnish fable', *The Economist*
(U.S.), October 14, 2000
http://econ.st/13xVhWL

Richard C. Morais, 'Damn
the torpedoes', *Forbes*, May
14, 2001, Vol. 167, Issue 11
http://onforb.es/11HLjkk

John S. McClenahen, 'Jorma Ollila,
CEO of the Year', *Industry Week*,
November 20, 2000, Vol. 249,
Issue 19 http://bit.ly/17ZRxRj

Lucy Williamson, 'Samsung
overtake Nokia in mobile phone
shipments', BBC Business, April
27, 2012 http://bbc.in/11VLg32

Larry PAGE

Origin of 'Google' name
http://bit.ly/101Wwcr

Brad Stone, 'The Education of
Larry Page', *BusinessWeek*,
April 9, 2012, Issue 4274
http://buswk.co/YxonCc

Miguel Helft, 'Larry Page Looks
Ahead', *Fortune*, January 14, 2013,
Vol. 167, Issue 1 http://bit.ly/12pEiXQ

John Battelle, 'The Birth of Google',
Wired magazine, August 2005,
Issue 13.08 http://bit.ly/15ieVtz

Azim PREMJI

Diane Brady, 'Hard Choices: Wipro's
Azim Premji', *Businessweek*,
September 20, 2010, Issue 4196
http://buswk.co/ZnJOER

Subrata N. Chakravarty, 'What's
cooking at Wipro?', *Forbes*,
December 14, 1998, Vol. 162,
Issue 13 http://onforb.es/17kVZZC

Andrew Cave, 'Azim Premji believes
education is key to India's
economic future', *The Telegraph*,
August 28, 2010 http://bit.ly/12oCCN9

'IBM Withdraws from India', *Time*
Magazine November 28, 1977
http://ti.me/11nVs5o

Gina RINEHART

David Leser, 'Gina Rinehart,
Australian tycoon', *Newsweek*,
February 10, 2012, Vol. 159, Issue
8 http://bit.ly/11HWoCO

Pamela G. Hollie, 'The richest
man in Australia, *New York
Times*, December 12, 1982
http://bit.ly/1800gmH

Tim Treadgold, Miner's Daughter,
Forbes, March 28, 2011, Vol. 187,
Issue 5 http://onforb.es/ZwN8TS

John D. ROCKEFELLER

Ron Chernow, *Titan: The Life of John
D. Rockefeller*, Vintage, 2004

Anita RODDICK

Jumana Farouky, 'Anita Roddick,
the Queen of Green', *Time
Business and Money*, September 11,
2007 http://ti.me/17YHSHQ

Veronica Horwell, 'Anita Roddick',
The Guardian, September 11,
2007 http://bit.ly/10DFicZ

'Anita Roddick: Cosmetics with a
conscience', *Entrepreneur,* October
10, 2008 http://bit.ly/17I7qR1

Laurence Marks, 'Chattering
evangelist', *The Independent*,
August 28, 1994 http://ind.pn/15St4OT

Jon Entine, 'Body flop', *Toronto
Globe and Mail*, Report on
Business Magazine, May 31, 2002
http://bit.ly/17I7pwy

Howard SCHULTZ

James Detar, 'Schultz, Star Of Starbucks', *Investor's Business Daily*, August 13, 2012 http://bit.ly/13yaPtJ

Bill Saporito, 'Starbucks' Big Mug', *Time* Magazine, July 2, 2012, Vol. 180, Issue 1 http://ti.me/10DIUvy

'Starbucks' Howard Schultz on how he became coffee king', *The Mirror*, August 5, 2010 http://bit.ly/11Gg4HM

Jon Certner, 'For Infusing a Steady Stream of New Ideas to Revive its Business' *Fast Company*, March 2012, Issue 163 http://bit.ly/11WkfMI

Alfred P. SLOAN

Obituary, 'Alfred P. Sloan Jr. dead at 90; G.M. leader and philanthropist' *New York Times*, February 18, 1966 http://nyti.ms/11WvjcT

Scott S. Smith, 'Alfred Sloan shifted GM into The No. 1 car firm', *Investors Business Daily*, January 31, 2013 http://bit.ly/11ogG31

Alfred P. Sloan, *My Years with General Motors*, Sidgwick & Jackson Ltd, 1986

Darwin SMITH

Clay Latimer, 'The Diaper-Dandy CEO', *Investors Business Daily*, February 14, 2012 http://bit.ly/13ygjV9

Jim Collins, 'Level 5 Leadership: The Triumph of Humility and Fierce Resolve', *Harvard Business Review*, July/August 2005 http://bit.ly/12LnpHg

David Barboza, Obituary: 'Darwin E. Smith, 69, Executive Who Remade a Paper Company', *New York Times*, December 28, 1995 http://nyti.ms/ZRLB5j

Fred SMITH

Brian Dumaine, 'How I Delivered the Goods', *Fortune Small Business*, October 2002, Vol. 12, Issue 8 http://cnnmon.ie/10ghLr3

'Fred Smith', *Reference for Business, Encyclopaedia of Business*, 2nd edition http://bit.ly/15KNPvF

Meg Greene, 'Fred Smith 1944–', *International Directory of Business Biographies* http://bit.ly/11okuBn

Matthew Boyle, Chester, Cai, 'Why FedEx Is Flying High', *Fortune*, January 11, 2004, Vol. 150, Issue 9 http://cnnmon.ie/11lbOGr

Fred Smith, 'Market Leadership', *Leadership Excellence*, March 2006, Vol. 23 Issue 3

Martin SORRELL

Nelson D. Schwartz, Joan Levinstein, Susan M. Kaufman, 'Bigger and bigger', *Fortune*, November 29, 2004, Vol. 150, Issue 11 http://bit.ly/11omuJW

Todd Benjamin, 'Martin Sorrell: Persistence and determination,' CNN international, December 16, 2005 http://bit.ly/14fLMj1

Mark Tungate, *Adland: A Global History of Advertising*, Kogan Page, 2007

Jamsetji Nusserwanji TATA

F. H. Brown, rev. B. R. Tomlinson, 'Tata, Jamshed Nasarwanji (1839–1904), entrepreneur and industrialist in India', *Oxford National Dictionary of Biography* http://bit.ly/17Z9qgm

N Sivakmar, 'The Business Ethics
of Jamsetji Nusserwanji Tata',
Journal of Business Ethics, 2008,
83:353–361 http://bit.ly/11oo7al

Justin Huggler, 'From Parsi Priests
to Profits: Say Hello to Tata', *The
Independent*, February 1, 2007
http://ind.pn/13ynOGO

Ratan TATA

Meenakshi Radhakrishnan-Swami
et al, 'The Tata's Without Ratan',
Outlook Business magazine,
October 16, 2010 http://bit.ly/15T87mw

Emma De Vita, 'Fast Track India',
Management Today, August 2009,
pp 34–37

Nupur Acharya and Sudeep Jain,
'Ratan Tata: The Journey', *Wall
Street Journal*, December 28,
2012 http://on.wsj.com/Zxkan2

Kiichiro TOYODA

Kazuo Wada, University of
Tokyo, 'Kiichiro Toyoda and
the Birth of the Japanese
Automobile Industry', July
2004, CIRJE Discussion Papers
http://bit.ly/180k5Kw

Scott S. Smith, 'He Steered Toyota
Motor Toward The Fast Lane,
Investors Business Daily, November
4, 2012 http://bit.ly/11ot9DS

Cornelius VANDERBILT

'Commodore Vanderbilt's life,'
New York Times, January 5, 1877
http://bit.ly/YODR4t

Sam WALTON

Sam Walton & John Huey, *Sam
Walton: Made in America*, Bantam
1993

Cher WANG

'Taiwan's Priestess Of The PDA',
BusinessWeek.com, July 10, 2005
http://buswk.co/ZRXWGW

Laura M. Holson,'With
Smartphones, Cher Wang
Made Her Own Fortune', *New
York Times*, October 26, 2008
http://nyti.ms/ZRXXL1

Heng Shao, 'Fall From Grace For
HTC', Forbes.com, August 29,
2012 http://onforb.es/ZLByTq

'AsiaD: Cher Wang full session'
http://on.wsj.com/ZQzgPQ

Tim Culpan, 'HTC says strategy is
correct, better results in second
half', Bloomberg.com, June 12,
2012 http://bloom.bg/11lnfxZ

WANG Shi

'China Vanke 2011 Profit Rises 32%
on Mass-Market Home Sales,'
Bloomberg News, March 13, 2012
http://bloom.bg/Y1fbJ3

Peter Simpson, 'Vanke', *Media:
Asia's Media & Marketing
Newspaper*, December 17, 2004
http://bit.ly/YY2f40

'Shi Wang Executive Profile'
investing.businessweek.com
http://buswk.co/ZStpZq

'Wang Shi: Life is an adventure',
China Daily, January 9, 2009
http://bit.ly/ZM1GxG

Geoffrey Lean, 'Meet Wang Shi, a
builder with energy to spare', *The
Telegraph*, December 11, 2009
http://bit.ly/180TSvr

Perween WARSI

'UK curry queen has empire in her
sights', BBC News, September 19,
2002 http://bbc.in/ZLCl1s

'The spice of success: Perween Warsi', *Derbyshire Life*, August 22, 2012 http://bit.ly/12LF40X

Michelle Rosenberg, 'Truly inspired woman: Perween Warsi', *Growing Business*, February 1, 2008 http://bit.ly/11oySJO

Thomas J. WATSON

'Thomas J. Watson Sr. Is Dead; I.B.M. Board Chairman Was 82', *New York Times*, June 20, 1956 http://nyti.ms/15irDbH

James Detar, 'Watson Kept IBM Humming', *Investor's Business Daily*, March 18, 2009 http://bit.ly/15irEwt

'Thomas J. Watson', *Notable Names Database* http://bit.ly/11m1uIH

Rich Karlgaard, 'IBM at 100', *Forbes* magazine, June 27, 2011 http://onforb.es/11hk6WX

David Stebenne, 'Thomas J. Watson and the Business-Government Relationship, 1933–1956', *Enterprise & Society*, Volume 6, Number 1, March 2005 http://bit.ly/Z635zq

Belden, Thomas, Belden, Marva, *The Lengthening Shadow: The Life of Thomas J. Watson*, Little, Brown & Company, 1962

Jack WELCH

John A Byrne. How Jack Welch Runs GE, *Businessweek*, June 8, 1998 http://buswk.co/13z2ztq

Rebecca Leung, 'Jack Welch, "I fell in love"', CBS, February 11, 2009 http://cbsn.ws/12MfOYM

Jack Welch, 'On Differentiation: Or, making winners out of everyone' http://bit.ly/ZoIkz7

Jack Welch with John A. Byrne, *Jack: What I've learned leading a great company and great people*, Warner Books Inc, 2001

Meg WHITMAN

Chris Taylor, 'Meg Whitman: Host of eBay's Passionate Party', *Time*, April 26, 2004 http://ti.me/ZRqfGe

Q&A: A talk with Meg Whitman, *BusinessWeek* online, March 18, 2001 http://buswk.co/14j3IJL

Laura M. Holson, 'Defining the On-Line Chief; eBay's Meg Whitman Explores Management, Web Style', *New York Times*, May 10, 1999 http://nyti.ms/ZpOf8B

Loren Fox, 'Meg Whitman', *Salon.com*, November 27, 2001 http://bit.ly/17mj66g

Michael V. Copeland, 'Meg vs. Carly: The CEO Chronicles', *Fortune International (Europe)*, July 26, 2010, Vol. 162, Issue 2 http://bit.ly/17mjbXw

Jerry YANG

Randall E. Stross, 'How Yahoo! Won the Search Wars', *Fortune*, March 2, 1998, Vol. 137, Issue 4 http://cnnmon.ie/ZA8Z8j

Brent Schlender, 'How a Virtuoso Plays the Web', *Fortune*, March 6, 2000, Vol. 141, Issue 5 http://cnnmon.ie/13kKY8p

Eric Jackson, 'Yahoo's remaining stake in Alibaba could be worth its current market cap by net year', *Forbes* Investing, November 14, 2012 http://onforb.es/13puCiB

ZHANG Jindong

Malcolm Moore, 'Suning appliance king Zhang Jindong set to plug into foreign markets', *The Telegraph*, August 25, 2009
http://bit.ly/182oERG

Russell Flannery, 'Clicking With New Customers', *Forbes Asia*, October 11, 2012
http://onforb.es/11Kb08X

Jiang Zhuqing, 'Private enterprises expanding quickly', *China Daily*, February 4, 2005 http://bit.ly/12NnTg2

'Preparing for China's urban billion', McKinsey Global Institute, February 2009
http://bit.ly/10G7DPL

ZHANG Ruimin

Zhang Ruimin, 'Raising Haier', *Harvard Business Review*, February 2007, Vol. 85, Issue 2
http://bit.ly/14WaMwu

Ronj Gluckman, 'Every Customer Is Always Right', *Forbes* magazine, May 21, 2012, Vol. 189 Issue 9
http://onforb.es/12NkItY

Zhang Ruimin, 'Voices From China, The Chief Executive' Forbes.com, September 28, 2009
http://onforb.es/182ilrT

Geoff Colvin, 'The Next Management Icon: Would You Believe He's From China?', *Fortune* magazine, July 25, 2011, Vol. 164, Issue 2
http://cnnmon.ie/Y9IbR7

ZHANG Yin

Russell Flannery, 'China's Richest Dragon Lady', *Forbes* magazine, November 13, 2006
http://onforb.es/ZS7ceX

David Barboza, 'Blazing a Paper Trail in China', *New York Times*, January 16, 2007, http://nyti.ms/ZpIlx3

'Woman Tops China's New Rich List, BBC News, October 11 2006
http://bbc.in/12upV3x

ZONG Qinghou

'The Chinese beverage company's expansion is no laughing matter', Paula M. Miller, *China Business Review* http://bit.ly/15MO5KO

'Meet Zong Qinghou, China's wealthiest man', *Bloomberg News*, November 10, 2012
http://ind.pn/14WIWkT

Michael Wei, 'China's richest man wants to go shopping', *BusinessWeek*, March 17, 2011
http://buswk.co/12NtEu8

Mark ZUCKERBERG

Ashlee Vance, 'The Making of 1 Billion', *BusinessWeek*, October 8, 2012, Issue 4299
http://buswk.co/12NCqs2

Jose Antonio Varga, 'Letter From Palo Alto, the Face of Facebook', *The New Yorker*, September 20, 2010 http://nyr.kr/Y9Y5vl

About the Author

JONATHAN GIFFORD is a businessman, historian and author, whose writing focuses particularly on the human aspects of leadership and management. After reading philosophy at the University of Kent at Canterbury, he worked for a number of major media organisations, beginning his career at the *Guardian* newspaper in the 1970s. He went on to work for the *Sunday Express*, the *Mail on Sunday*, and later for BBC Magazines, where he launched the award-winning *BBC History Magazine* in 2000.

Gifford is the author of *History Lessons: What business & management can learn from the great leaders of history* (2009); *100 Great Leadership Lessons* (2010); and *Blindsided: How business and society are shaped by our irrational and unpredictable behaviour* (2012). His next book, *100 More Great Leadership Ideas*, will be published by Marshall Cavendish in summer 2013.

A partner in the marketing consultancy Bluequest Media, Gifford also lectures in business leadership and marketing for the European Communications School in London. He lives in Oxfordshire with his wife and children.

www.jonathangifford.com